On the Brink of Change ...

Noel Tyl in "The Necessity of Crisis" ...
The client's crisis of growth becomes the astrologer's challenge. Measurement becomes diagnosis.

Christian Borup in "The Psychological Implications of the Birth-crisis" ...
The birth chart is the starting point. The first major transition crisis in everybody's life. The confrontation with the world—with life. This "horary" is your first "hello" to the world, and it tells the story of the expectations you have of life.

Gloria Star in "Family Crises in the Early Years" ...
When analyzing the chart of an adult for early family crisis, we have keys to unlocking the pain, confusion, or doubt of the inner child.

Diana Stone in "Root Causes of Mental Crises" ...
Nearly all my clients undergoing rebirth get in touch with a certain ecstatic sense of purposefulness even in the darkest of times.

Robert Hand in "Saturn, Action, and Career Crises" ...
Most people, even quite intelligent and conscious people, spend their lives moving along their paths not understanding what they are doing and where they are going.

Timothy Lee Bost in "Person-Centered Financial Astrology" ...
Although there are many potential triggers for financial crisis, every individual who is confronted with time of financial stress ultimately has to deal with questions of self worth.

Joan Negus in "Averting the Relationship Crisis" ...
You might ultimately decide to terminate the relationship, but if you do this without investigation, you could then make the *same* mistakes in relationship after relationship.

Tim Lyons in "Astrology's Midlife Crisis" ...
The midlife crisis transits ask us to be responsible for something beyond ourselves by being more conscious of the chaos within, the demand for change.

To Write to the Authors

If you wish to contact the authors or would like more information about this book, please write to the authors in care of Llewellyn Worldwide, and we will forward your request. Both the authors and publisher appreciate hearing from you and learning of your enjoyment of this book and how it has helped you. Llewellyn Worldwide cannot guarantee that every letter written to the authors can be answered, but all will be forwarded. Please write to:

Llewellyn's New Worlds of Mind and Spirit
P.O. Box 64383-390, St. Paul, MN 55164-0383, U.S.A.
Please enclose a self-addressed, stamped envelope for reply, or $1.00 to cover costs. If outside U.S.A., enclose international postal reply coupon.

Free Catalog from Llewellyn

For more than ninety years Llewellyn has brought its readers knowledge in the fields of metaphysics and human potential. Learn about the newest books in spiritual guidance, natural healing, astrology, occult philosophy and more. Enjoy book reviews, new age articles, a calendar of events, plus current advertised products and services. To get your free copy of *Llewellyn's New Worlds*, send your name and address to:

Llewellyn's New Worlds of Mind and Spirit
P.O. Box 64383-390, St. Paul, MN 55164-0383, U.S.A.

Llewellyn's New World Astrology Series
Book 11

How to Manage the Astrology of Crisis

Resolution through Astrology

edited by
Noel Tyl

1993
Llewellyn Publications
St. Paul, Minnesota, 55164-0383, U.S.A.

FIRST EDITION, 1993

Cover Painting by Gabriele Berndt

Library of Congress Cataloging-in-Publication Data
How to manage the astrology of crisis : resolution through astrology /
   edited by Noel Tyl.
      p.   cm. — (Llewellyn's new world astrology series)
    Includes bibliographical references.
    ISBN 0-87542-390-6
    1. Astrology and psychology. 2. Life change events—Miscellanea.
   3. Counseling—Miscellanea. 4. Horary astrology. I. Tyl, Noel, 1936–.
   II. Series.
   BF1729.P8H68   1993   92-39191
   133.5—dc20   CIP

Llewellyn Publications
A Division of Llewellyn Worldwide, Ltd.
St. Paul, Minnesota 55164-0383, U.S.A.

THE NEW WORLD ASTROLOGY SERIES

This series is designed to give all people who are interested and involved in astrology the latest information on a variety of subjects. Llewellyn has given much thought to the prevailing trends and to the topics that would be most important to our readers.

Future books will include such topics as dimensions of consciousness, astrology and past lives, and many other subjects of interest to a wide range of people. This project has evolved because of the lack of information on these subjects and because we wanted to offer our readers the viewpoints of the best experts in each field in one volume.

We anticipate publishing approximately four books per year on varying topics and updating previous editions when new material becomes available. We know this series will fill a gap in your astrological library. Our editor looks for only the best writers and article topics when planning the new books, and we appreciate any feedback from our readers on subjects you would like to see covered.

Llewellyn's New World Astrology Series will be a welcome addition to the novice, student, and professional alike. It will provide introductory as well as advanced information on all the topics listed above—and more.

Enjoy, and feel free to write to Llewellyn with your suggestions or comments.

Other Books in this Series

Forthcoming

Contents

Noel Tyl

For over 20 years, Noel Tyl has been one of the most prominent astrologers in the Western world. His 17 textbooks, built around the 12-volume *Principles and Practice of Astrology*, were extraordinaily popular throughout the 1970s, teaching astrology with a new and practical sensitivity to modern psychotherapeutic methodology. At the same time, Noel presented lectures and seminars throughout the United States, appearing in practically every metropolitan area and on well over 100 radio and television shows. He also founded and edited *Astrology Now* magazine.

His book *Holistic Astrology: The Analysis of Inner and Outer Environments*, distributed by Llewellyn Publications, has been translated into German and Italian. He is one of astrology's most sought-after lecturers throughout the United States, and his international lectures are very popular throughout Denmark, Norway, Germany, and Switzerland, where for the first three World Congresses of Astrology he was a keynote speaker.

Most recently, Noel wrote *Prediction in Astrology* (Llewellyn Publications), a master volume of technique and practice, and he edited Books 9 and 10 of the Llewellyn New World Astrology Series, *How to Use Vocational Astrology*, and *How to Personalize the Outer Planets*. Noel is a graduate of Harvard University in psychology, and lives in Alexandria, Virginia.

Introduction

The Necessity of Crisis— A Modality for Astrological Counseling

Noel Tyl

Western cultures, western societies teach us to do all we can to avoid tension. The "American way," the "Western way," is a way of leisure. Our advertisements urge us to live the good life. Our cinema beatifies love, comfort, success, the triumph of good over evil. Our labor unions push for greater benefits for workers, for shorter work weeks. The "leisure time" industry is enormous. And, most recently, a physical fitness energy has arisen to restore strength to lazy-limp backs and couch-corpulent stomachs!

In an anxious outburst recently, a client of mine declaimed, "I can stand *anything* but pain!" "What else *is* there to stand?" we could ask in turn. The point is that all of us are swept up within a pleasure-orientated way of life that supposedly establishes status, attracts love, and provides a foundation for an even better life for our children.

To live the good life is a powerful goal, and difficulties enroute to that socially inculcated goal represent problems that have to be solved and pains that have to be avoided. Difficulty, problems, pain—these states are part of the process we go through to get to where we are told we should be.

Difficulty, problems, pain are the components of crisis—the confrontation with growth. Our language calls it "growing pains!" To one degree or another, dealing with that which is critical, dealing with crisis, with acute developmental tension, is what

1

strengthens our identity, tells us more about who we are in life, exercises our resources, and keeps us alert to the values of life.

The celebrated American psychoanalyst Rollo May has written copiously about anxiety. He says, "The *positive* aspects of selfhood develop as the individual confronts, moves through, and overcomes anxiety-creating experiences."

Soren Kirkegaard said it too, "The more consciousness, the *more self*" and "The more original a human being is, the deeper is his anxiety."

Throughout many theorists' study about the process of individuation and the confrontation with difficulty it is very easy to see that *anxiety is fundamental*—Dr. May has said "essential"—*to the human condition*. The psychologist Otto Rank viewed anxiety in terms of *"individuation through necessary separation."* Each separation we endure in life—starting with the birth separation— increases the opportunity for individual autonomy. In this light, we can say with validity that our needs for our parents are twofold: for nurturance and eventually for contrast. We can understand that losing a job gives us the opportunity to do something different or better. We can appreciate that partners in marriage can affect separation simply because they have outgrown each other, i.e., that one's individuation has outdistanced the other.

The psychologist Harry Stack Sullivan maintained that personality developed out of the need to define which behaviors will gain support and reward and which behaviors will not. This stressful process naturally begins in the early home to please the parents and keep the peace and extends later on to all the other echelons of social interaction. Sullivan had the idea that "the self is formed to protect us from anxiety."

The theologian Paul Tillich, in his famous book *Courage to Be*, cited anxieties about death, meaninglessness, and guilt as the great concerns of our times.

Now, as we begin to bring these thoughts specifically into our world of astrology, we should note that anxiety about death does not necessarily mean life termination. In the horoscope, the 4th House is abbreviated "the end of the matter," but it is also the House of new beginnings. In our process of development, we constantly experience ends and new beginnings. There are deaths of many different kinds within our experience of crisis. There are many separations.

Anxieties about meaninglessness rest upon the concept of worth, in terms of money and/or love, which involves the Succedent Grand Cross of Houses. Meaningless is closely related to the anxiety of disapproval. Support and reward are desperately needed for life to have meaning and stability.

To me, guilt—Tillich's third great concern—is the feeling that we have not done our best to help others fulfill *their* needs. So much of our experience of crisis *is* within relationships, where ego meets ego, where I meets Thou, where complex needs meet need complexes, where cooperation and dependency are essential for fulfillment. Guilt can not exist without relationship to something, to some person, belief, or value. Very often, to alleviate the pain of guilt, we sacrifice some selfhood through reparation, we give away part of ourself, we adjust our stand, in order "to make good" in the situation.

Other thoughts from Kierkegaard are provocative indeed: "Anxiety is always to be understood as oriented toward *freedom*." In other words, "the good *is* freedom." He observed time and again that the more possibilities an individual has—and this can read as "creativity"—the more potential anxiety he has at the same time. The sense of possibility means "I can," and the resource of creativity means "I know how to." In this sense, it's valid to surmise that no one encounters a problem in life that he or she can not solve.

In summation of these points, we can agree with Dr. May and many other thinkers that anxiety *is* natural to the human condition, that it actually fuels the system, that it defines the process of becoming, that it tells us who we are, relieves boredom, challenges creativity, establishes meaning, and effects growth. These views are extremely important to our effectiveness as astrological counselors, as we shall see a little later.

The Astrology

It is impossible for an astrologer to study the concept of crisis, the dynamics of anxiety and fear, the dichotomization of pleasure and pain and not have an acute consciousness of the Saturn principle. The tensions that keep us alive—even the tension that keeps us standing upright and productive at ninety degrees to the surface of the earth—all have to do with the internalization of discipline, structure, and the how-to's of living with others within a society. Just as our muscles, organs, and flesh are held together in the tension of the human form by the Saturnine skeleton so are our identities cultivated and kept in line by the structured expectations of the world we live in. Everything we are is organized and held together in a structure of discipline exercised throughout periods of time.

Specifically within the horoscope, we know the powerful insights afforded by the symbol of Saturn retrograde. My research of this factor for twenty years reveals unequivocally that a lifelong anxiety structure is established with regard to a sense of inferiority, of not being loved, taken on in the early home through the absence, passivity, or tyranny of the father.

We know unequivocally that Saturn in the 11th House signals a tremendous need for love since structured controls will manifest somehow in the affairs of that House, receiving love, which is the love-giving 5th House from the 7th House, the House of others.

We know securely that Saturn aspects in the fourth harmonic (conjunction, semi-square, square, sesquiquadrate, and opposition) with the Sun, Moon, Mercury, and Venus especially manifest emotional anxiety and specific fears, almost always in connection with parental expectations during early growth, which are then worked out in frustrations within relationships and passed on by example and through interaction with one's own children.

It is well known that in families in which parents have a good deal of anxiety there will be greater anxiety among the children of those families. Life will play out through many crises, and this atmosphere will be passed on through interaction with the children and the modeling of male-female relationship on the home scene. The children get caught in the parents' traffic pattern.

So often, when the ruler of the 11th House is in a demanding aspect with Saturn, for example, or if Saturn is in the 11th and under strong developmental tension, the anxiety within personality development has much to do with *being loveable*, being able to attract love. Immediately through rulerships and aspect patterns, we see the ramifications of such anxiety related to the parental axis, to relationships in the 7th, to self-worth concerns in the 2nd, to the ability to give love to others in the 5th, etc. Love is the keenest reward in our development.

Somehow these anxieties and the specific fears that emerge from the anxieties are *necessary*. They are present within our mandala of the birth moment. Astrologers can interpret them and deduce character traits, anticipate behavior, and, indeed, foresee times of crisis within the thrust for selfhood and in interaction with the environment. The creative principle—our God—reveals so much to us through our astrology. Life can not be a punishment, can not be pain. We do acknowledge divine purpose within the miracle of life. There must be growth out of what we do call pain in the confrontation with crisis.

To dramatize this concept, how should we regard the crucifixion of Jesus? This miraculous man was sent to our world as an example: even the very Son of God would have to undergo crisis to make the point of His life. The Resurrection tells us that, even through the worst crisis, death, there *is* new life. We see the inexorable continuance of living time through crisis, through separation and death, away from meaninglessness, into further growth and significance. We reveal this in our language when we say, "This too shall pass," "Time heals all wounds," "Your time is coming!" And when we say, "Time and tide wait for no man!" we are being urged to get moving, to get with it, to catch up, to get on with life. Again, Saturn is the all-pervasive symbol of time, test, and teaching.

When we begin to understand the necessity for what we see in our horoscopes, we become more comfortable with our lot. The sense of necessity implies purpose: I must get through this painful situation, this terrible period of time, in order to get on with IT. Finding the IT has, of course, inspired every religion on earth and all the special studies in spiritual matters that come ever closer to our studies in astrology.

When we study horoscopes of the famous, we regularly see patterns of high developmental tension. When we learn about their lives, we learn about dramatic hardships, poignant struggles, great tensions. These pains even seem somehow to be in proportion to the fame. We say often, "He's a self-made man" or "Gosh, she went through a lot to get where she is." Developmental tension, anxiety, and fear spur development and fulfillment. The famous become famous by overcoming adversity. We all become who we are by managing crisis. Our adjustment throughout the life-effort constantly restructures our behaviors to fulfill our needs more efficiently in relation to the expectations of our environment.

It is hope that leads the way. Hope arouses courage. It has been said that so much talent is lost to the world for want of a little courage, that timidity works against making the first effort and guarantees obscurity. The symbol for hope is Jupiter, the inversion of the Saturn symbol, the symbol of our needs for reward, our philosophical grasp of our purpose, our gusto to get on with it.

In Fire signs, Jupiter suggests hope for reward in terms of gaining recognition. In Water signs, this hope is in terms of gaining emotional security; in Air signs, the rewards of appreciation; in Earth signs, the rewards of establishing personal value.

When Jupiter opposes Saturn in the horoscope, hope is in full awareness of fear. The personally orientated hope network of thoughts and plans and needs seems to go against what society is demanding or enforcing—while choice tends to be muddled, and judgment vacillates. All faculties are working that much harder toward consensus and growth.

When Jupiter and Saturn are in conjunction, hope and fear are highly focused. Hope for growth balances fear of challenge. Instinctively, we know that hardships are justified if growth is achieved. The conjunction symbolizes a sense of natural law and order.

When we search for ways to face up to crisis, our mind takes over. It registers anxiety and the need to plan, to think through, and to cope. In this realm, anxiety generates growth through mental awareness and resourcefulness. And our mind also begins to specify fears. For example, with Mercury in Pisces and under high developmental tension by aspect, the fear can be articulated as the fear of being taken advantage of; in Aries, the fear of being ignored, perhaps stimulating the nervous thrust of overstating one's position, to protect by attack.

For Mercury in Leo and Sagittarius, passion and temper can become modes of expression, all about being overlooked. In the Air signs, we see the fears of being unappreciated, and in the Earth signs, the fears of losing value.

These fears, like our hopes for reward, reflect how the mind needs to work, to develop *through* anxiety *toward* self-development.

As we, and our clients, necessarily face up to the anxiety in crisis after crisis, as we become who we are, we use all the defensive resources we have. Astrologically, these too are indicated in the horoscope. Just as anxiety is essential for life itself, so defensiveness is essential for security during that life development. It is the *degree* of defensiveness that is extremely important to the grace with which we grow in the face of crisis.

For example, defensiveness can become so strong and isolating that insecurities can not be attended to for the lack of relationship and the essential resource-exchange with other people. This is the well-known profile of defensive withdrawal.

Defensiveness can become patterned into habit and represent a waste of energies, energies diverted from development. This is especially noticeable in adult life when early life problems no longer exist or have been put into proper perspective. The patterns of behavior may still be routinized as defensive habit.

Defensiveness can be weakened through over-dependence on someone else, through what we now call "co-dependency," becoming part of someone else's problems or taking those problems on, essentially to avoid one's own. This is the profile of defensive self-sacrifice.

Perhaps the most natural defense mechanism is fantasy, when the mind conjures up an improved self-image, projects an intense idealization out onto the world, specifies what could be and what will be, and transcends the anxieties of the real moment. We see this through relationships between Mercury and Neptune, of course, and through Mercury and Venus, often including the Sun. When Jupiter is involved, we usually see the introduction of religious rationale as well within the idealization process.

Other defense mechanisms are dramatically presented through Grand Trines in the horoscope, linking three or more planets into closed circuits of self-sufficiency: in Earth, practical self-sufficiency, "I can do it myself, thank you"; in Water, emotional self-sufficiency, "I don't want to be hurt any more, so stay away"; in Air, intellectual self-sufficiency, "I'm better than you think I am, I assure you"; and in Fire, motivational self-sufficiency: "You can't tell me anything I don't know; I know where I'm going and I don't need your energies to get there!"

When these Grand Trine constructs do not contain the Sun or the Moon, we often find two persons in one: one person following the defensive structure of the Grand Trine, which works against relationship, obviously; and the other self following the life stream begun in synthesis of the Sun and Moon symbologies.

In times of crisis, we and our clients fear recognizing failure, failure to live up to some construct of parental expectations, idealization projection, or the prescriptions of our important, immediate environment, our relationship or our work situation. But the crisis has to be. The arousal of anxiety has to be. The awakening of hope and the invigoration of coping mechanisms has to be.

What comes to the rescue so often is change, bold change: of a relationship or work situation, of geography, even citizenship! We move, we relocate. We become intensified as an individual, most often disrupting a relationship; we break the bonds of environmentally enforced controls; and we take new steps to get with the IT we talked about earlier. This is the crisis of Uranus, usually in Solar Arc and/or transit relationship to the angles of our horoscope. As well, it is the changing of gears that we see in the quadrature transits or powerful arcs of Saturn.

Again, these mechanics of self-extrication, these behavioral profiles of reaction within stress in the swirl of crisis *are predictable*. Since they are predictable, since they are there within the horoscope, *they are necessary*. They must be evaluated objectively and they must be assimilated into the growth process. In this way, anxiety can inspire resourcefulness, pain can give way to hope, and fear can structure strategy.

The Astrologer in the Midst of Crisis

Under stress, within change, within the process of becoming— with the same pressures that a plant has, pushing against its soil, braving the bending winds, the wet and the cold to reach the Sun—we and our clients tend first to limit our world, to negate possibilities. This is the flight mechanism designed to protect us from anxiety. It's a first reaction.

For example, we hear all the time, "I don't want to know" about something potentially painful. "If my spouse were having an affair, I wouldn't want to know." Or, "I'm not going to have that medical test, because I don't want to know the verdict." In other words, I wouldn't be able to stand the pain if it were bad news, and it's part of the human condition always to anticipate the worst [and this attitude undoubtedly stems from the primal fear of our inevitable death]. In this all-too-normal perspective, the possibility of doing something about the overall crisis is clumsily and dramatically curtailed. In a relationship crisis, we know that only if there is communication is there the potential for solution, and yet the couple involved is not communicating one with the other.

Under crisis, we and our clients must *enlarge* our scope of activity to stimulate enhancement of selfhood. We need freedoms, respect for necessary controls, enlarged self-awareness, a sense of responsibility, and a reinforced dignity. To quote Kierkegaard once again in his existential wisdom, "To venture causes anxiety, but not to venture is to lose oneself."

When a client comes to an astrologer, all of this—the anxieties and fears developed throughout a lifetime, the hopes, the defenses, the pushing and clutching to reach the Sun—all of this is within the horoscope, lived in the life, and now presented to the astrologer. The client's crisis of growth becomes the astrologer's challenge. Measurement becomes diagnosis.

Not at all too soon, the professional astrologer learns that any genius he or she presumes to have as an analyst is based upon knowing *what is important* in a horoscope. There is little time or even significance for a "grocery list" of observations. The art of astrological analysis rests on synthesis, on organization of the keystones of the client's development through time, recognizing need fulfillment and formative tensions, and framing the probability of future projections.

All too soon, the professional astrologer finds out how difficult it is to talk about things that are distressing for the client to hear, to review, to relive, or to anticipate. Most people want to keep things the same as they are, even in difficult times, because what is or what has been going on for a long time *is predictable*. They can manage, but change would be frightening because of its new demands upon personal resources, its challenge for growth to one more level or into one more direction in the process of becoming.

Special teachings on the periphery of astrology even suggest that there are no mistakes in life, no disorientation, no hard times; that everything is always the way it should be. This simply is a blunt-edged and blind effort to salvage ego in time of stress or in memory of difficulty. We shall see in a moment that there are many better ways than that to reinforce the client's dignity.

People do make mistakes in the management of crisis. And yes, those mistakes also lead us forward, but new problems arise as well, and these problems in retrospect are clearly mistakes— taking the wrong action—mis-turns off the straightest track for development. For example, the members of the drugged "flower-children" culture of the 1960s are now about 50 years old! The drop-outs of 30-some years ago, their loss of education, the children they spawned here and there, the responsibilities that were neglected, have all come home to roost, as we say, to focus in later life as conspicuous emptiness. Those kinds of poor choices were residually dysfunctional responses to earlier crises.

When we have to talk about such times of life and their effects in the present, we must remember that, under the pressure of new crisis now, the client defensively will want to hear only what he or she wants to hear. That is the tendency. By coming to the astrologer, the client has come to an oracle. At the very best, there is the hope for a miracle; at the very least, there is hope for reinforcement through companionship and information. Our solution here must be to involve the client with the parameters of development. As any counselor must do, we must educate as we inform.

In our discussion, we have made the point that crisis is necessary, that developmental tension must be creatively assimilated into our lives for us to grow energetically. Change is mandatory, and so we must deal with the accompanying stress. We have the mid-life crisis, we have the changes of menopause, we have the separation from the family home as we enter adulthood; we have numerous job changes; we have ever-increasing responsibilities; we have large concerns about politics, war, international community; and we have so many individual needs pressing for fulfillment throughout our lifetime. To live is a confrontation with busy-ness.

All of this requires energy within rigorous societal prescription. How can Mars function within the pervasive influence of Saturn? Is that the lesson we are all learning? This grappling with indecision and fear that we go through truly is our effort to keep alive the courage to be. *These are the ideas we have to clarify for our clients to sustain their growth in the midst of crisis.*

In my practice, I have found so often that *what* I say to a client about difficult things in the life process is often matched in importance by *how* I say these things, how I frame the issues of crisis. Let me share an example of this premise: the American psychologist whom I quoted earlier, Harry Stack Sullivan, used to teach young analysts not to interpret a dream as if it were etched in stone, as if it were law, as if there were no other possible meaning. He suggested that it is more productive—and, indeed, less threatening—to offer *two or three* possible meanings to the client, requiring the client to choose from among them. The sense here is that specific meaning is not as important as the opening of new possibilities, new psychic realities. In this way, routine ways of seeing things are left behind. New light is possible in dark areas, and the client is leading the way.

This principle applies to our management of astrological measurements. In inspecting past periods of development, we can suggest options of meaning from which the client can choose. In projections to freedom through crisis, we can suggest more than one way of seeing potential. In the process, new light falls into previously obscured sections of life; and most often, the new perspectives that are established reflect secure adulthood in the present, even under the threat of the present critical time of change.

So, part of how we say things is to remember always *the power of choice*, the luxury of options, that we can offer our client and which makes our client feel more in control in the midst of crisis.

In a recent consultation with a male, our dialogue covered his growing years in terms of feelings of estrangement from his father, focusing in on his deep fear of his father's disapproval. My client had recently been diagnosed as HIV positive. His job in a fine firm was secure, and a superb insurance program guaranteed that his medical costs monthly would remain at the barest minimum.

My client was literally bored to death, facing meaninglessness enroute to death. He wanted a better job but he could not ever again get hired into such a fine corporation with such all-encompassing insurance benefits. His horoscope showed strong excitation through Solar Arc Sun square Uranus supported by vigorous transits, crowned by the approaching transit of Jupiter over the Sun. Under this pressure for change and growth, all the energy was going inside my client instead of out. When energy is frustrated, fear is internalized, and depression dominates.

What could I say? Here my client had energy to burn, felt stifled, couldn't conceptualize opportunity, and was waiting for astrology to light up his life.

How I was going to talk to him about this worst of situations, this dark crisis, would be more important to him than reiterating his reality or discussing some kind of planetary intervention. My objective became to help *him* "invent" something, to create some kind of action that would give meaning to the lifetime he had left.

I asked him, "What if you could get another job with as good an insurance program as you have now, that would stimulate you more professionally; do you think that *would* make you feel better? Do you think that *would* solve the problem?"

My client had the choice to dig deep for his answer. This self-searching in new psychic channels took the place of imposed astrological dogma. The planets would not do anything; *he would.*

As I was preparing this introduction, I took on a most difficult consultation. I had not met the lady nor her husband, and my discussion with her was by telephone. Her crisis was intense; she had just discovered that her husband had been having an extended affair with another woman. The situation blew up. Emotional hurt and defensive reactions exploded. The husband was thrown out. He slept in his office. Locks were changed on the home doors, and this astrologer was called.

The simple astrology of the situation was startling: the wife had transiting Pluto on her seventh cusp and transiting Saturn squaring her Ascendant. The Secondary Progressed Moon was exactly on her seventh cusp as well, and there were background Solar Arc measurements of separation *and* new freedoms and opportunities.

The husband had the transiting Uranus and Neptune conjunction exactly on *his* seventh cusp, with background Solar Arc Pluto square Venus.

The woman, with her Sun and Moon in Pisces, the Moon in the 12th, was hurting terribly. The husband wanted reconciliation. The astrology in every way showed that the situation had exacerbated each person's deepest vulnerabilities, revealed that key needs had long been unfulfilled within the marriage, and that new opportunities for growth were beckoning for each of them *separately.*

Naturally, these people wanted to keep things as they were. She did not want to hear what I had to say. My work for an hour was not as Svengali astrologer but as artful communicator, regathering concomitants of self-esteem and reinforcing the future.

There's a simple teaching from the Sung hexagram of the I Ching, called "Conflict": it is that conflict must not be allowed to become permanent; *change out of conflict is essential*. It is this line of simple thought within a maelstorm of emotional panic that can guide us best to help others help themselves within the growth times of crisis. I see eight things we can do to reinforce our clients in times of need; these are the eight things I shared with this frightened woman:

1. *We must acknowledge the fears and vulnerabilities* the client faces in the situation. This clarifies self-perspective. So often, the acute shattering of the present is related to patterns of anxiety and specific fears, to "unfinished business" within the family structure of the early home, perhaps already repeated in earlier marriage(s).

2. *We should gently expose rationalizations* that are working to protect sensibilities, those plausible but usually untrue or invalid explanations of the crisis: the other woman was so much prettier than I; he is wealthier than I'll ever be; no one on the job ever liked me; my whole life has been torn up by the fact that I was molested as a child. The astrologer has got to sort these things out to determine what is real in the situation: "What if that were not the reason; might it be that the other woman made your husband feel strong, important, and energized, especially during this very pressured time in his work? Is that what he really needs?"

3. *We should help our clients ascertain their resources.* A woman who never finished college and hasn't worked for 15 years feels totally lost within the crisis of marital separation. It is a creative challenge to astrology to distill potentials, to give the client resourcefulness in the face of fear. In this case, I explored the symbolism of a peregrine Venus in Taurus that I felt had the potential to

run away with the horoscope! Sure enough, the woman had had courses at art schools years before, even marketed a cosmetic line, and most recently had gathered friends and ideas about getting into the motion picture industry. Here were ways out of the crisis into new growth. The client had been totally preoccupied with the problem so she had overlooked new potentials. Under anxiety, we limit our world.

4. It's very important to help the client see *how he or she presents him/herself to others.* So often, certain personality types lead into their image presentation with negative self-portrayal, complaining, braggadocia, even bizarre claims to specialness—"I've been abducted by UFOs many times!"—and set up reactions from others that become routinized one way or another throughout their life. People have so many fine things about them about which *they need to be reminded,* a success record, if you will, and the astrologer can actually make a list of these during the consultation and turn over the new image profile to the client! This is always a time of smiles; it's like a new photograph of words.

5. We must be careful to *project realistic time schedules.* Transits, especially those of Saturn, Uranus, Neptune, and Pluto, more often than not are obviously significant to time periods longer than the week or month of partile. The happenings at a time of crisis extend into time—from the past and into the future—conspicuously, sometimes ponderously. Critical times are complex, and the "time fallout" must be seen head-on and shared with the client, who is searching for a miracle-cure instead of building gradual change. We *can* stand pain when we know pretty well how long it is going to last and that it's for a good cause.

6. Often, astrologers must *eliminate the client's sense of being punished by crisis.* During crisis, rash emotional statements can resurrect primal feelings that life has not been right somehow and death of one kind or another is just around the corner. Statements like, "You deserve to

fail" or "I have never pleased you" can destroy confidence and fracture a fragile profile of resourcefulness and self-esteem. In a marital crisis, for example, jealousy can abound. Jealousy is always born out of some very specific fear, some very real vulnerability. One of the finest antidotes for jealousy is the understanding of the fear that spawned it, seeing it all as a knee-jerk reaction, realizing it has no end, and displacing the horror scene with some *beautiful* memory from the past. The mind always needs a rest during crisis. This is a great option for the client.

7. As much as possible, astrologer and client must *clarify new objectives:* is the crisis really about a career-change anxiety or something else, rather than a clandestine love affair? Does the client understand about the letting-go that is so important within the mid-life crisis? What is practical must displace what is morose.

8. The objective enroute out of crisis is to *define personal conviction about a new stance, a new perspective.* This is a gradual process. The client slowly begins to come around after he or she chooses a fresh alternative way of seeing the situation *and* life. Follow-ups by the astrologer help reinforce the growing confidence and conviction.

In crisis management, the whole effort is to reinforce the client in fresh ways for new ways of life. The crisis is necessary catalyst. Physical exercise is extraordinarily beneficial to relieve mega-stress and to help reorganize and restructure self-awareness. Behavior patterns are adjusting to new challenges, to new health. Old pains are giving way to revived strengths; needs naked and proud are reaching vigorously for fulfillment. We see time and situation telling us something.

I personally have had my crises, for sure! And I like to think that I am learning how to manage the anxiety and fears and pain productively. The anxiety and crisis of growth make life happen. It is so. And, in turn, in true Capricorn fashion, I can say that *I respect the concept of difficulty.* And I can say that nobody is very interesting who hasn't had the experience!

Christian Borup

Christian Borup has studied astrology since 1968, and has a diploma from the I.C. Astrology Institute (1978) and a professional diploma from The American Federation of Astrologers (PMAFA, 1983). He was chairman of SAFA (the organization of professional Danish astrologers) 1983–1986 and ISAR International vice president for Denmark 1991–1992. He has been head of the teaching faculty of the I.C. Astrology Institute since 1978.

The I.C. Astrology Institute was founded by the Danish astrologer Irene Christensen in 1956, continued by Birthe Kirk. Since 1987, Christian has been the owner and director. He is also the chief-editor of the well-known astrological monthly *Stjernerne* (The Stars) which has been published without interruption since 1956.

Christian has lectured widely in Denmark, England, France, Germany, Norway, Sweden and the former Soviet Union.

The Psychological Implications of the Birth-crisis

Christian Borup

Try looking at it this way: we are born, having no conscious desire or need to be so. The only gift we receive at birth is the knowledge that we shall die. That nothing lasts forever. Not even you! What happens in between these two very real and final turning points in life is up to us.

• Maybe a constant awareness of this terrifying fact, that time is always running out, is what we need in order to live better lives between the terrible two taboo transitions: Birth and Death. With capital letters! Remember that you are "naked when you come, and naked when you go"—and that "you can't take it with you when you go!" The finality of existence is forever linked to the process of life. And this starts with the Birth-crisis.

• And there you are! A living entity, that just "came down the chute" (as Bill Cosby so bluntly put it). You are ready for life—more or less. A figure in the population statistics. A person to be reckoned with in the future. And now all your troubles start. You have to get used to your new vehicle: the Body. The external pressure starts! You have to learn how to control your bodily functions and to communicate with the rest of the population. It's hard work being trapped in a body. Everything that happens after birth belongs to the realm of traditional psychology. What happened at birth—both in the heavens and in the Birth-crisis—constitutes the field of natal astrology. Your psychological make-up is already pinned down at birth.

The Birth Chart

This article is about the Birth-crisis and the importance of realizing that your birth made a deep impact on your subconscious. An impact that can never be erased. The coming into this life is the single most important crisis in a person's life. No matter how the birth happened, it is still a crisis: a crisis big enough to be the basis of a whole science called Astrology!

And that is why, an astrologer would argue, we are *not* naked when we come. We receive two divine gifts at birth. First of all, Life, and second, an important talisman and amulet: the birth chart—a personal map of our own individual universe, a map that can guide us through life. If we let it!

The Birth-crisis is reflected in the life of the person as a subconscious predisposition to perceive the world in a certain way. Like a pair of binoculars, the birth chart focuses the person's attention onto certain trains of thought and perception, and dims other ways of perceiving the world. Looking closely at the diopters and color of the binoculars' lenses (the content of the birth chart), we are given an explanation of the person's view of life, and in the consultation we try to communicate the reasons for this view to the client. (And of course the astrologer sees the chart through his or her own binoculars! So much for objectivity! But that's a completely different story.)

As astrologers, we just seem to accept it as a fact that the birth horoscope starts when we are born, and not when we are conceived. The birth chart is the basis of our art. When lecturing to people with no previous knowledge of astrology—and therefore no prejudices or preconceived opinions—I am always asked why astrologers use the person's birth chart and not a conception chart. In such a forum, the answer is that we don't know when the conception occurred. Research into artificial insemination might change this view and provide us with new possibilities. But still, most people are conceived "the old-fashioned way," and not by means of pipettes in Petri dishes.

Certain members of the astrological community have postulated the existence of the Prenatal Epoch and accepted the old rules of Hermes Trismegistus, but still most astrologers stick to the birth chart—because it's so logical to do so. The birth chart is astrological dogma, and therefore is unrefuted by us. So we call it a birth chart, *although all the genetic potentials of the little person being born have existed for nine months prior to birth.* An honest astrologer might say: "We use the chart of the birth, because we have to start somewhere! And this is—at any rate—where we all start!" But the sum total of the genetic make-up of the person already existed nine months ago! The real beginning and coming to life of the person starts at conception. The birth is nothing but another event—crisis—in a person's life.

To put it in another way: everybody's physical reality starts with the horary chart erected for the date, time, and place of birth: The Birth-Horary. And, as we know, a horary chart (a so-called inception chart) can be erected for any crisis or turning point in your life—even for when you decide to pose a horary question. But the birth chart is *the* starting point; the first major transition crisis in everybody's life; the confrontation with the world—with life. This horary is your first "hello" to the world, and it tells the story of the expectations you have of life. But, "What Do You Say, After You Say Hello?" as Eric Berne put it.

The Birth-crisis

The problem with the Birth-crisis is that nobody consciously remembers it. Various forms of regression therapy have made it possible to relive and remember the birth process; but there will always be a slight doubt with regard to the respective amounts of imagination and reality contained in these accounts. From regression therapy and the LSD experiments of Stanislav Grof, we learn that the subconscious picture of a tunnel, with light at the end, is a deep-rooted human experience that all people share, regardless of sex, age, culture, or century. This inner picture is a re-run of the birth trauma, the single first experience—and the only experience, except death—we share with all other living creatures on this earth. And from this first cause, our life evolves in a chain of cause and effect, based on the conscious and subconscious decisions we make on the way toward our death.

Everybody—at some point or other in life—thinks about where we are going, and where our decisions will lead us. The society and century in which we live are future-oriented. The same can be said about astrology. It is the future, not the past, that first draws most people to visit an astrologer. After being born, we tend to forget where we came from, and concentrate on where we're going. As if—like Lot's wife—we have reason to fear looking back on the mistakes we made.

Astrology is a very old form of psychology. For centuries it has been disguised in the veil of mysticism and occult teachings. Astrology existed long before psychology, and the birth chart always precedes therapy. The birth chart is you, and the sheer fact that you were born into a certain time/space-continuum gives you a tool and a predisposition that transcend any conscious mind-boggling psychological analysis you may later try to indulge in. The birth chart is pre-conscious. The birth chart is the first cause.

The Birth-myth

Most people have a story—a myth—to tell about their own birth. A story that the family—mother, father, and older brothers and sisters—have recounted about one's arrival here on planet Earth. This story explains to the child its *raison d'être*, and is a prologue of the life-quality to come.

The Birth-myth—as told to us and registered and stored in the conscious mind as one of the "facts of my life"—is a seemingly objective description of what you are supposed to know and think about your reason for existence. Most parents just see the Birth-myth as a funny or quaint story to tell at dinner parties, but to the child it has an almost religious sense of importance, because it tells about the coming into life of a hero: You! The Birth-myth is the child's own fairy-tale, the myth of its existence. The Birth-myth may be a funny story to the parents, and often the client likes to tell the story to other people in the same amusing and entertaining way he or she has heard it told, but the child needs a deeper explanation of why and how it was born. It needs to have a description of the "hero's" quest; a map of things to do and goals to reach for. It needs a Birth-myth, and many children who have never been told their own Birth-myth *make up their own myths* and fairy-tales about their birth, their conception and their parents. These birth fairy-tales often draw on the myths of the Collective Unconscious.

Humanistic vs. Horary Astrology

Since the publication of Dane Rudhyar's *The Astrology of Personality* in 1936, astrology has become more psychological. And now, in the 80s and 90s, the revival of horary astrology has provided us with new rules of interpretation. Although there seems to be an inherent contradiction between these two disciplines, I hope this article will show that they complement each other. I belong to the generation of astrologers to whom the psychological implications of a birth chart were self-evident. I grew up within a generation who believed that the inner world was even bigger and more unlimited than the outer world, or even the universe.

These days, the counter-reaction to the psychological revolution, which humanistic astrology started, is accelerating. Astrologers have a feeling that astrology has become psychology's younger sister, an appendix to psychology waiting for an appendectomy! Astrology is in danger of becoming nothing but a tool for diagnosing which form of psychological treatment a person needs. When this diagnosis has been made, the birth chart can be scrapped for ever, and psychological therapy begins.

But, in fact, astrology should be honored as the wise old sister she really is! The humanistic approach to astrology has drawn astrologers' attention to the inner psychological processes and has made an important and life-giving link to psychology possible. Many astrologers are beginning to feel that astrology can offer much more than just psychology. It did just three hundred years ago! But because we never look back, *we have forgotten our own tradition.* We never asked the question: where did astrology come from, why was *it* born, and how did *it* grow up?

To many humanistic astrologers, the new interest in the old horary techniques signals a "deplorable return" to the old-fashioned fate-ridden astrology, and a deletion of all the psychological implications in the birth chart. Of course, *this is not the case.* Astrology is a discipline of its own. And combined with psychological knowledge it transcends the artificial borders between the two disciplines.

Using the old horary interpretation techniques on the birth horoscope is of course no substitute for the usual astrological interpretation of the nativity. But used in conjunction with the Birth-myth, the horary for the birth gives us an invaluable tool.

I see no contradiction between the free will assumed in humanistic astrology and the apparent fatefulness of horary astrology. The answers given to horary questions might seem like fate-ridden answers, but the crux of the matter is that the person who asked the question could have used his free will to pose the question at another time, and be given another horary chart and perhaps another answer.

Modern astrologers are convinced of the existence of free will. Who can argue? If you believe in it, it's there! If not, fate rules your life. Giving the client the strength to believe in free will and in freedom of action is—to me, anyway—one of the main aims of astrological counseling. To give another person a feeling of control over himself/herself is another important gift. To feel you are in charge is a Gift of Life!

But, still, we are born. Whether we decided to be or not. And suddenly the tiny infant is there, thrown out of the protective shield of the womb. And often into a room with cascades of light, faces covered with masks, and all the hustle and bustle of efficient routine work done by cool professionals. The first skin sensation, of being touched physically, is often of a throw-away glove. Here you are, my friend. Welcome to planet Earth. We welcome you by measuring and weighing you, giving you a bath and, we hope, presenting you with a warm and loving mother.

The Moon

And here's the big surprise! A fact of life. A well-kept secret: Mankind is born of woman. Period! It is self-evident, but—as is often the case with self-evident matters—we take it for granted, and never question the implication of this fact. The Muslims are still waiting for the rebirth of the new Mohammed—who is to be born of a man. They will probably wait forever!

The mother and child are one for nine months. They share the same nourishment and blood circulation and hear the same sounds. All sensations are shared. The mother is the universe of the child, and the great traumatic separation at birth, as relived by thousand of people doing rebirthing or regression therapy, reminds us of the pain and anguish experienced by the child; no matter how harmonious the birth situation was. *At birth, you lose your link with the universe.*

The ultimate female/feminine energy in the chart is, of course, the Moon. Seeing and interpreting the Moon in the birth chart can give us an exceptionally deep understanding of what happened before, during, and after the birth. The Moon tells the story of our "Pre-Solar" existence—the existence we led before being "under the Sun's beams" (to revive an old horary phrase).

Gestation is the Moon-phase in life, a feminine existence we all go through. As it is put in genetics: "Ontogenesis mirrors Phylogenesis." Meaning that, during gestation, the child goes through the same developmental process as the human race has done. During gestation, the fetus lives through the whole Darwinistic evolutionary process, from single cell to mammal. Linking the Moon to the developmental process of giving birth to the Collective Unconscious is therefore based on a reasonable assumption.

And of course the Moon rules the womb and the Mother. The Moon is also memory in a very broad sense of the word, i.e., the storage of experience and perception. The Moon—on the subconscious level—has no filter or interpretative faculties. The Moon receives, records, and stores, like the RAM memory blocks in a computer. At night, your dreams replay the memory cells in an intellectual, illogical sorting order, for the consciousness to behold. And in so doing, we are reminded of the one-third of our life we spend back in the realm of the Moon: our inner feminine world where we live when we seem to be asleep.

And to draw from another source of knowledge within our field: in Hindu astrology the Moon even *takes precedence* over the Sun and the Ascendant. Why? Because the Moon shows the things you receive effortlessly (Moon), and not the things you consciously make an effort to get (Sun)! It shows the ease of living, the comforts of life and all the benefits a person reaps. Ask yourself seriously: "Have I earned what I get"? Who says you have to make an effort? The Moon position shows what you get, free of charge from the outside world, without doing anything—whether you have earned it or not. Just as the fetus receives its nourishment and security from the mother—free of charge.

The idea of having to deserve what you get is a typical Western-Christian culture myth. No wonder Hindu astrology places emphasis on the Moon. Therefore, if your Birth-crisis has been made more or less conscious, you will always feel you deserve what you get. There will be no reason to have a bad conscience because you are richer, more beautiful, more intelligent or even a better person than the next one. Don't worry! You deserve it. The Moon tells you so!

The Moon also shows the way your mother, family, and culture have subconsciously conditioned you to see things. The Moon is the perspective, the interpretation of reality, you are given at the moment of birth. If you make no conscious attempts to adapt and develop an understanding of these processes, the Moon energies remain unrecognized, repressed, and infantile. The contact with the past and the feminine qualities inherent in the subconscious will forever remain dormant. But still, the Moon will condition your choices in life, and you will not be able to choose freely. You will subconsciously focus on the *pre*-conscious programming, but still believe that you are using your own individual free will! In that case, the theme of your Birth-crisis will become the main theme of your whole life.

The feeling of belonging to this world is also stored in the Moon. The Sun gives you the possibility of making a personal impact on the world. *But the Moon conditions the way the world makes an impact on you!* During gestation—during your Moon-life—you experience the total passivity of being totally dependent on your environment. You receive input, but have no way of reacting. Later in life, you can easily become a very efficient, masculine, and outgoing Sun-person who is admired by all, but you can still feel lost and unwanted *inside*. Are you at home in the world? Does your mother love you? Does the world love you? Is the world "your oyster?"

Many books and articles have been written about these Moon data, but the root of the question, the Moon's strong linkage to the birth situation, has perhaps been vastly underrated. Even though you become famous, and make a big and important impact on the world with your Sun-personality, you may still feel like a lost child who does not understand why it is not happy with all its new toys. The feeling of belonging to and being a part of the World also comes under the sphere of the Moon. And your Birth-crisis and Birth-myth can provide vital clues about your life-quality and individual feeling of being alive. And isn't that what astrology is about? The enhancement of life-quality?

The Moon shows your subconscious reaction to the world, the reactions that take over when unexpected situations occur in your life. The Moon takes over, whenever something out of the ordinary occurs. You then have to draw on family and cultural behavior, i.e. the Moon. This will occur whenever you have no previous plan, knowledge, or experience from which to decide. And every minor or major crisis in your life is unexpected and new.

As John Lennon put it, "Life is what happens to you, when you're busy making other plans." If this were not so, a crisis would just be a dull, well-known repetition of an old movie you have seen far too often. *A crisis is always an invitation for growth. And it hides in the disguise of chaos,* often showing you that you have *not* matured or developed since birth! No wonder a crisis makes you depressed! But still, crisis makes you experience life anew. If you hurt, you are forced to realize that you are alive, and through that pain you often relive the first and primary crisis of your life: the Birth-crisis.

The Birth-crisis in Counseling

If we accept the fact that the subconscious is developed as a very fundamental and real entity during gestation, the fetus uncritically collects the feelings and the inner/outer experiences and perceptions of the mother. You could say that the mother filters the incoming data from the outside world, and by doing so already conditions the child to connect certain external experiences (as perceived by the mother) with a specific set of emotions and reactions. You could call this process the mother/family/culture/species-conditioning that takes place *before* and *during* your birth. You might come to the conclusion that the content of the Collective Unconscious (as defined by Jung) is created partly by this process. These are the subconscious reactions we ascribe to the Moon—the backbone reactions that are so natural to us that we seldom question their meaning or effectiveness; so natural, that it never occurs to us that we actually have the power and authority to change them!

The birth chart gives us information about what really happened in the birth situation, but the Birth-myth, as told to the child, gives us the myth/fairy-tale that the mother (and family) tries to impress upon the child. Ever so often, the implications and expectations that the Birth-myth tries to force onto the child are not realized by the child as an adult. This can give rise to depression and not achieving what you want later in life, because, deep down in yourself, *you feel that you have not deserved success.*

For the last ten years, I have always asked my clients to write and tell me about their Birth-myth before we were to meet for consultation. Often, clients have no Birth-myth, or have no knowledge of their parents. Often children fantasize about their own Birth-myth even if they already have one. They search for an explanation for their existence—a story that explains what they feel and why they are here.

If, for instance, the child feels the parents do not love it, it has to find an explanation for this fact. If the child has a strong feeling of being "worthy of this world," i.e., it has a strong sense of being an important person (as seen in the chart), the child might fantasize about being adopted. A very logical explanation for the narcissistic child: "If they don't love me, as parents are supposed to do, it must because they are *not* my parents." If, on the other hand, the child has a low feeling of belonging and deserving life, the explanation might be: "There is something wrong with me. I am not good enough. If I were a girl, and not a boy, they would surely love me."

These explanations are logical and self-evident to the child, and if no "reprogramming" occurs in adult life, this explanation lives on, and takes control of the person's behavioral pattern. The same situations are enacted again and again. And the adult person is unable to understand why certain themes in life occur again and again. If you always repeat the same crisis situation in your life, it might be because *each time you are confronted with a new situation, you subconsciously react to—and reenact—the Birth-crisis.* Because it gives a feeling of security, because it's a situation you can recognize if everything else fails, it reminds you of the fact that you are here. You seek the *feeling* of belonging to this world. The Birth-crisis reminds you of this fact. *You seek the Moon.* But it's always there in a crisis situation, and if no attempt has been made to make the Moon-energies conscious, they take control and repeat the birth pattern as established during gestation and birth.

When judging the birth chart as a Birth-crisis horary, I use the same rules and guidelines laid down by traditional horary astrology. In short, the significator of the child is the ruler of the Ascendant. The gestation and the experiences of the mother before, during and after birth, and the implication these have on the child, can be examined by looking at the aspects the Moon makes while still in the same sign.

But let us look at some case histories. In the first two, I will concentrate on the interpretation of the Moon, as a primary factor, while the last examples will also deal with other aspects of the birth chart (The Birth-horary).

Peter

In a letter to me, Peter (born 1967) describes his Birth-myth as follows:

"My mother always told me that my birth was quick and easy. She had 'decided' that I was to be born on March 19, and when the labor pains did not begin at the time she wanted them to, she drank large quantities of castor oil. And it helped! The rest of the birth took place without problems. It has always been my impression that the birth was very harmonious and surrounded by much love."

[Judging from this birth myth, it seems that Peter had a mother who really knew what she wanted!]

And in his letter Peter continues:

"It has been hard for me to find important events in the first 12 years of my life. O.K., my parents got divorced when I was about a year old, but of course I have no recollection of that. My first twelve years of life were for the most part very harmonious. My mother was a very firm and stable point in my life, and that made every negative outside influence relatively."

This is the way Peter describes his own Birth-myth—his personal explanation for his *raison d'être*. Taking his account for granted would mean that you had to accept that the conflict between his parents—resulting in a divorce when he was one-year-old—*did not exist* at the time of his birth. But let's look at his birth chart. Here, there seems to be a discrepancy between Peter's Birth-myth and his inner psychic reality.

The aspects the Moon makes—and has made—*during its travels through the sign it is placed in at birth show the events before, during, and after the birth.*

The mother is shown as a very mental/intellectual person (Moon in Gemini in the 3rd House). She plans that the birth is to take place on March 19, and when it doesn't look like anything is going to happen, she gives herself the same treatment you give yourself if you are constipated. Very practical indeed!

Unfortunately the story doesn't tell us why the birth had to happen on the 19th, and I forgot to ask, but maybe she wanted the child to be born on a Sunday. But it could also be that the mother wanted a Pisces and not an Aries child. And she got her will, except in one respect: the Ascendant is in Aries!

The chart shows a different story from the one that Peter tells us. In the old-fashioned astrology textbooks, the Sun-Moon square is often denoted as a sign of the parents' splitting-up. Seen in a more psychological way, the Sun-Moon square shows the inherent difficulty in combining the mother and father archetypes in the psyche. This often results in life presenting several choices, where the path of either the mother or father is followed. This is also the case with Peter.

His Sun-Moon square is exact in about 1 degree. This is consistent with the old horary rules of measurement: his parents split up 1 year after Peter's birth. Peter doesn't remember this, he says. He only remembers the "harmonious and loving relationship" shown by a Moon-Venus sextile *following* the Moon-Sun square. But it is his first loss.

The natal Sun-Moon square always creates problems in relating to both the feminine and masculine sides of the personality or, as seen from the child's point of view, whether to choose the father or mother as a role model. The applying sextile to Venus shows an almost romantic relationship between mother and child (also shown by the Venus-Mars opposition from the 1st to the 7th House). Peter describes his childhood as harmonious and we would say he was overly protected—by the mother. Until the age of 12, he is the only man in his mother's life. But at 12 years of age, the underlying catastrophe (seen symbolically through the Moon's first aspect, the square to the Sun) materializes: his mother meets a new man. This is his second loss.

At that time, transiting Pluto was in opposition to Peter's Ascendant. This was the timing mechanism. He lost his first partner: his mother. The disappointment made him "switch" the polarity of his Sun-Moon square.

His mother and her new boyfriend decide to move abroad, but Peter doesn't want to accompany them. He writes: "I then got the idea to go to the same boarding-school as my real father had gone to. And it was arranged that my father should take care of me on the weekends, though we almost hadn't seen each other for the last 12 years."

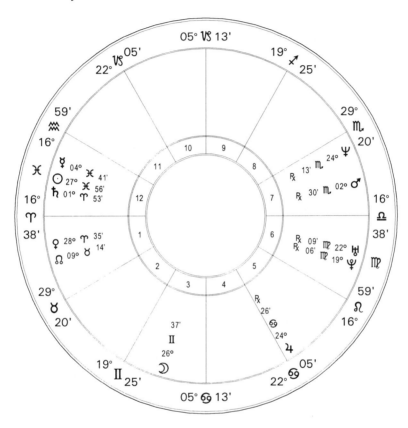

Peter
MC 05CP13 — Asc 16AR38
Sun 27PI56 12th House

Moon aspects

Moon	00GE00	2nd House			
Moon	01GE53	Sextile	Saturn	in Aries	in the 12th House
Moon	04GE41	Square	Mercury	in Pisces	in the 12th House
Moon	19GE06	Square	Pluto	in Virgo	in the 6th House
Moon	19GE25	enters the	3rd House		
Moon	22GE09	Square	Uranus	in Virgo	in the 6th House
Moon	26GE37	3rd House	at Birth		
Moon	27GE56	Square	Sun	in Pisces	in the 12th House
Moon	28GE35	Sextile	Venus	in Aries	in the 1st House
Moon	00CN00				

The Birth-crisis aspect is active at this point. He feels neglected by his mother or even cut off from her, and instead chooses the path of his father. Symbolically he does this by choosing the same boarding-school and by renewing the connection with his father. To ease the pain, he changes from a Moon-view of life to a tentative Sun-view. Because the Sun is placed in the 12th House, the realization of this fact has never entered Peter's mind. In a symbolic way, he chooses to go *into* his 12th House, carrying out a Piscean sacrifice and inflicting self-punishment. He "goes to prison" (as an astrologer of old would put it), simply to punish himself for not being able to keep his mother as a "partner" (the Sun is in the 12th in Pisces). The transiting Pluto opposing his Ascendant heralds the coming of puberty. The relationship to the mother is beginning to take on a sexual innuendo, which his mother probably feels subconsciously. And this frees her from the responsibility of making Peter the only man in her life. He goes to boarding-school, although he is afraid to do so, but as he put it in the consultation: "I had to learn to be a man."

Of course, Peter must have problems relating to the opposite sex, because at a very early age he has experienced a deep-rooted fear that he will lose his partner. He is a Pisces. The Sun and Mercury are in the 12th House, showing a shy, sensitive, and, in youth, often an insecure personality. But the ruler of the chart, Mars, is positioned in the 7th House in Scorpio, where "he rejoices" (as the old astrologers say). This is a very extroverted position which, combined with the opposition to Venus in the 1st House, shows a constant need to make an impact on the world. Possibly an impact with sexual undertones (Venus in Aries, and both sexual planets in the old Mars signs).

And meeting Peter was also a bit of a shock. He was a tall, well-built young man, almost 6′ 6″ feet tall, dressed as if he were trying to impersonate Oscar Wilde: he wore a wide-brimmed soft black hat and a black coat like those worn by the coachmen in a Sherlock Holmes movie, and carried a silver- tipped cane (British style) in his hand. He used his 7th House Mars to hide his inner feeling of unworthiness in this big, pompous show; and, of course, it also covered up the feeling of hurt and loneliness left with him by his mother's rejection. His style of dress was to signal that he was a special person, totally freed from the influences of his father and mother, which was, of course, *not* the case.

The rest of the letter from Peter is about the pain he feels every time a member of his family dies and the pain of losing his girlfriend (in 1987). Losing or giving up is a tough lesson for Peter to learn. It will always remind him that the subconscious part of him is still a child, and still feels the old, familiar pain of rejection.

In 1990 his grandfather (on the mother's side) died of cancer. He writes: "When my grandfather died, I felt the creation of a new deep tie between him and me. I felt an obligation to carry on the ideals and values he represented to me: integrity and the will to fight for justice." The loss of a person he loved gave him something to strive for. Understanding his Birth-myth and its implications will in time give him the power truly to believe in himself, without the need for the idle display of his individuality. In time, he will realize that there is no need to hide inside a cloak of vanity.

Stella

Stella is a good example of how a harsh Birth-myth leaves its mark on a life. Stella was born in 1923, and was 65 years old when she came to me for a consultation in 1988.

In her letter, she describes her Birth-myth as follows: "My mother often recounted: 'The town hall clock struck 12 at the moment of your birth.' I was baptized at home shortly after birth since I was nearly strangled at birth because I was born with the umbilical cord around my neck. My parents had previously lost a new-born boy—who was unbaptized—before they had me."

What is she trying to tell us with this story? She was hastily baptized at birth as a Protestant, because the parents feared that she would not survive (a custom very rarely carried out in my country). It is as if this Birth-myth puts her under an obligation and almost demands of her that she *be* the unbaptized boy who was not permitted to live. As if she were born with an obligation toward God, because it was a miracle that she survived! But what comments does *the chart* make on this Birth-myth?

The question is whether any of the crises this woman had experienced in her life would have made any less impact if she had been told about the expectations put on her tiny shoulders already at birth. The worldly expectations of the mother are very often shown by the Moon in the 10th House, i.e., the mother having great plans for the child's future. These are often plans the mother herself had no opportunity or not enough ability to fulfill.

The most important aspect the Moon makes is the square to Pluto in the 12th House. This aspect tells the story of her birth: she almost died. And because of this *she has allowed death and loss to play a very important role in her life.* Not being able to handle this square, she has had many periods of hospitalization in psychiatric wards (Pluto is in the psychic 12th house of hospitalization), while yet always being active in the work sphere, having quite high-ranking jobs and a leading position—just as her Moon (mother) in the 10th expected of her.

Something happened in connection with this birth which has not merely to do with Stella being born with the umbilical cord around her neck. There may have been a basic repugnance/ aggression on the part of the mother (Moon in Aries in square to Pluto in the 12th House), of which the mother was not conscious. When Stella was one year old a younger brother was born, nullifying the necessity of her being the incarnation of the dead boy-child. An explanation of the mother's aggression might be that, when Stella was almost three years old, the Moon-Pluto aspect was exact. And Stella's father was killed in an accident! (In the Birth-horary, the Moon had traveled the orb that approaches 3 degrees, thus making the Moon-Pluto square exact.)

With this chart, Stella would be prone to consider it to be her fault and responsibility that the father was killed, because she feels an inexplainable resentment emanating from her mother. The relationship with the mother is, on the whole, difficult and, just as with Peter, there is a Pisces Sun, which tries to adapt its ego to the family's demands.

Stella writes: "For the most part, my life has never been harmonious or particularly happy, not even when I was a child. My father was killed in an accident, and at the age of 25 my mother was a widow with two children, and never remarried. I myself was barely three years old, my brother was two. Her understandable bitterness about her fate greatly influenced my start in life. I left school and was apprenticed in 1939, and eight days later war broke out."

It is practically always the case with Moon-Pluto aspects that they indicate *an extremely strong mother fixation,* which in women's charts gives strong mother-daughter conflicts. And we very often see a general life-theme where the person wants to explain his or her life by means of the great political events which take place out in the world. There seems to be a natural urge to identify oneself with mass movements and the atmosphere, characterizing the influences from the collective and from society.

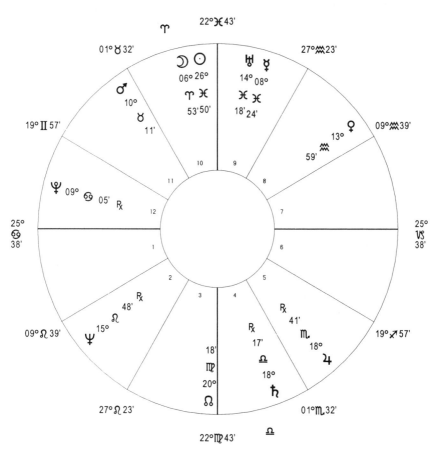

Stella
MC   22PI43 — Asc   25CN38
Sun   26PI50   10th House

Moon aspects

Moon	00AR00	10th House			
Moon	06AR53	10th House	at Birth		
Moon	09AR05	Square	Pluto	in Cancer	in the 12th House
Moon	13AR59	Sextile	Venus	in Aquarius	in the 8th House
Moon	15AR47	Trine	Neptune	in Leo	in the 2nd House
Moon	18AR17	Opposition	Saturn	in Libra	in the 4th House
Moon	00PI00				

All of this is wholly in keeping with Pluto's fundamental meaning. With Pluto you are subject to these collective mass influences in an often uncontrolled manner. During World War II, Stella's brother was in a concentration camp in Germany, and her mother just managed to escape being killed during the Allies' bombing of the German headquarters in Copenhagen.

Stella chooses to interpret other events during World War II as being extremely important to her personal life, even though, from an objective point of view, they are not. But the Moon-Pluto square becomes a *symbol of her Birth-crisis*, and she therefore chooses to interpret events in this way. On the whole, Moon-Pluto contacts always seem to raise the question of whether you have "deserved" to be born.

Very often, Moon-Pluto squares involve a constant feeling of guilt, and in this case, original sin. Stella converts to Catholicism in 1954, probably in an attempt to explain the sensation of catastrophe which she feels throughout her life in line with the aspect. In this "rebaptism," she at the same time rebels against her parents' baptism of her at birth. By converting, she tells her parents that their action had no significance, that she is not the son they awaited. In 1965, the conversion results in a family drama with the mother as the protagonist. But as Stella expresses it, "I never let my mother discover that she was the real cause of the showdown." And she never let on to her mother that she knew the crux of the matter was her Catholic persuasion. In a defensive and reversed way, her rebellion had at last succeeded.

Who dares to challenge a Moon in Aries squaring Pluto in the 12th? Stella didn't, but she let her emotions out on her younger brother—the "incarnation" of the boy-child she could never be herself.

But please remember that not all Pluto aspects contain the implications we see in Stella's chart. Remember that in this chart the Moon-Pluto square is especially strong because the Moon *only receives this one aspect and because it is the ruler of the Ascendant in this chart.*

Let me give a few illustrations from Stella's list of life events, to give an idea of her inner condition.

"In 1940 I fell in love with Harold, who knew nothing about it. He was ten years older and engaged. Our ways parted, and in 1943 I learned that he had enlisted in the German army, as a Danish officer! Not until 1947 did I decide to forget him. My brother was in a German concentration camp for the whole course of the war."

Note the constant awareness of the political situation (the mass principle of Pluto) and the personal implications Stella reads into them. She mixes the private and collective projections of the square, and tries to interpret them within her own framework. She actually confesses that the man she loves—in a symbolical way—*is the tormentor of her brother*. She wants to confess what a terrible person she feels *she* is. She even loves Harold after the war ended—the war that almost killed her mother!

In 1975, she tries to forget an unhappy—and secret—love affair by plunging into physical activities and excessive work. She never tells the man of her great love for him. But, as she writes, "At the end of 1975 this man crosses my path again, and I experience the greatest love of my life, but am tied down by work, and therefore nothing can come of it."

At last, there seems to be a possibility of success and happiness. The man she loves wants her, *but she decides to work instead*. She is unable to break her habits at this time. She still tries to fulfill the expectations of her mother (Moon in the 10th). But she has a plan! At that time, there are ten years until she can retire, and she decides that this great love will have to wait until then. Not until then does she feel *that she will have deserved him*. On January 1, 1985 she retires, so now there will be time for love. Two weeks later she has a date with the love of her life, but she waits in vain. She assumes that he has dropped her, and does not try to contact him. She adjusts to the loss. She did not deserve him, anyway, she thinks. Two weeks later, in a round-about way, she receives an explanation for his absence: he had died of a heart attack a month before!

Stella's chart is a good illustration of the fact that *a person does not choose the options that can bring happiness or fulfillment*. It is a typical example of how the Birth-myth and the Birth-crisis can expand into an enduring habit pattern, which the person never consciously considers. The Sun's position in Pisces and the Ascendant in the water sign of Cancer lead to the person choosing the role of victim as a life pattern: a person caught in this web of circumstances can not break loose by herself, simply because she cannot see that there are other options. Hopefully the astrologer can help her break this vicious circle.

In her letter to me Stella describes how at the beginning of 1975 she met, by chance, the well-known Danish astrologer, Irene Christensen. Stella recounts: "Great was our mutual amazement when it turned out that we were born on the same day, I at 12 noon, and she at 12 midnight. I remember quite clearly a certain sentence she uttered: 'One day I will cast your chart myself.' It never got to anything since not until the month of August did I send for my birth certificate, at a time when I had difficult decisions to make, and later I did not have the energy to get my chart done. And when, at the beginning of 1976, I read about Irene Christensen's death, I felt so strange, understandably enough, that I simply did not dare to do anything more about it."

A clipping from a woman's magazine from 1976 accompanied Stella's letter. The heading reads: "Death did not come as a surprise to astrologer Irene Christensen. She had herself predicted the date. It was to be February 18, on her 1st wedding anniversary." In actual fact, Christensen did not make any such prediction. The media just liked the story. But again Stella uses the mass-media to justify *her* actions—or rather her lack of them.

Not until 12 years later, in 1988, did she set up a consultation with me (I am currently carrying on the Irene Christensen Astrology Institute, as Director). Her mother had just died 10 months before, freeing her from her Birth-myth, making new developments possible. But could she trust her inner feelings? The progressed MC was approaching a sextile to the Sun. Was it her own death Stella wanted me to predict? Or was it a new life?

Alice

Alice came for a consultation in 1989. At that time, she was 43 years old. In her letter to me prior to the consultation she wrote as follows:

"My time of birth is not to be found in the public records, nor in those of the district medical officer, and even if it were found, it would not be correct, since my birth was very dramatic. According to the entries in my father's diary at the time of my birth, it was a question of whether I would enter the world at all. I quote from my father's diary:

Sunday 5/26

At 5:30 a.m. the labor pains were so strong that we called the midwife, Mrs. D., who however couldn't come and therefore sent Mrs. H. She gave Agnes (my mother) a morphine injection. In the evening Mrs. H. came again and since the pains were even stronger, she again administered a morphine injection. She would come again some time on Monday.

Monday 5/27

Strong pains from 1. p.m. Called Mrs. H. at approx. 4:45 p.m. She wasn't at home but her husband would try to get hold of her. Since she still didn't come, I called again, but she still hadn't come home. The husband said he would call a children's nurse. She came quite quickly and thought that the birth would soon occur, and therefore the midwife had to come.

Mrs. H. still had not come home, and her husband therefore sent for Mrs. D. She came "and not a moment too soon," as she said. Almost immediately she sent for Dr. R.W. He arrived at approx. 6:45 p.m., and I walked back and forward in the living-room and could do nothing to help.

At 7:20 p.m. Dr. R.W. came in to me and told me that I had got a daughter. She had had difficulty in coming to life, since she had an inordinate amount of fluid in her lungs, but thank God they managed to remove this water. But it could easily have been a different story."

The following is what Alice's mother remembers about the actual birth:

She comes round from the anaesthetic and hears Mrs. D. ask Dr. R.W., "What time is it now?" The answer given is 7:15. Then my mother asks whether there was anything wrong. "No," is the answer given. So therefore we can't approximate the correct time of birth more closely than 7:15 p.m.

The hard and especially long birth is shown by the Moon's own exact square to Saturn. And as is often the case, the birth is characterized by delays and problems in getting hold of the midwife. (Often, the mother is also incapable of participating actively in the birth.) And when this child is finally born, it is apparently dead and has difficulty in surviving. The Moon's square to Saturn is the Moon's final aspect before becoming *void of course*. Often it is a sign that the life-force energy is not at the baby's disposal *after the birth*, an influence that requires outside action.

The exact Moon-Saturn square in Alice's chart indicates potential periods of depression not explainable by outer events, but which are often triggered by an unconscious re-experience of the Birth-crisis. It is my personal conviction that the Birth-myth/crisis is capable of illuminating the causes of the so-called endogenous depressions.

For instance, in her list of events, Alice describes 1988 as her worst period, where a heavy and deep depression overpowered her. She did not seek help for this depressed condition, such as is often the case with Moon-Saturn squares. It as as if she says: "I managed to be born, and I shall cope with whatever happens to me now without help." The MC by secondary progression has reached the opposition to the Moon and the square to Saturn. Thereby the Birth-myth *is activated*, and demands that a decision be made with regard to the life goal and the meaning of the person's life.

Alice is a qualified lawyer, but has never worked as such. The Saturn position on the 9th cusp indicates a striving toward educational status, but the square to the Moon (the Birth-myth) makes it difficult for her to explain to herself why she feels this urge. Expressed in another way, with a Birth-myth like hers she does not feel that she herself has determined her career. She needs a support, probably a man (in the Birth-myth illustrated by the academic type, Dr. R.W.) who is the only one who can save her life *after* the birth. This Dr. R.W. has, in Alice's subconscious, grown to be a sort of god, who is the only one with the necessary wisdom to save her. Such a projection can make it difficult for her to reach decisions on her own.

In her letter, she continues: "In 1967 I saw for the first time the man, A, who has since had such a great influence in my life, right up to Spring 1989, that I regard him as my guardian angel."

She calls A her guardian angel, but he is just another of the personalities Dr. R.W. has assumed in the course of her adult life.

In 1988, "I fall into conversation with the man, B, to whom I have had a very strong relationship since June 1989." And at the end of 1989 she makes an appointment with a male astrologer (me), and poses the following questions: "I feel that I am standing at a crossroads, what shall I do? I have a degree in law, but I have never used it. Shall I go into this field again, as B thinks I should? I know

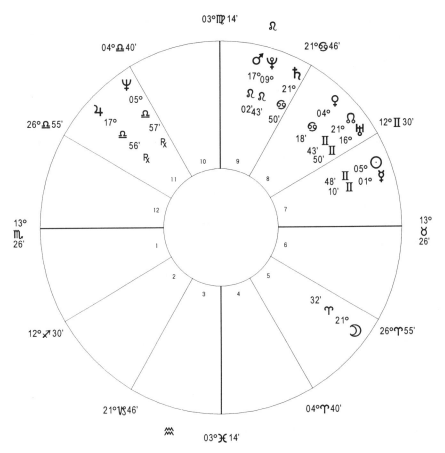

Alice
MC   03VI14 — Asc 13SC26
Sun   05GE48 7th House

Moon aspects

Moon	00AR00	4th House			
Moon	02AR44	Square	Venus	in Cancer	in the 8th House
Moon	05AR48	Sextile	Sun	in Gemini	in the 7th House
Moon	04AR40	enters the	5th House		
Moon	05AR57	Opposition	Neptune	in Libra	in the 11th House
Moon	09AR43	Trine	Pluto	in Leo	in the 9th House
Moon	16AR50	Sextile	Uranus	in Gemini	in the 8th House
Moon	16AR53	Trine	Mars	in Leo	in the 9th House
Moon	17AR57	Opposition	Jupiter	in Libra	in the 11th House
Moon	**21AR32**	**5th House**	**at Birth**		
Moon	21AR50	Square	Saturn	in Cancer	on the 9th House cusp
Moon	26AR55	enters the	6th House		
Moon	00TA00				

that astrologers can't do charts for third parties, but you must be able to tell me whether I am still under A's influence or whether I should do what B suggests, both as far as work is concerned and personally. Or whether I should do something quite different?"

Just as her Birth-myth shows, Alice seeks a male guiding image, who can "remove the fluid from her lungs," i.e., remove feelings (water) from her intellect (air), and get her to breathe (think) freely. She asks which of the two men she is "under the influence of," as though she can not imagine not being under anybody's influence. Again, a manifestation of the Moon-Saturn square.

Alice will have to understand the connection between her Birth-myth and the guiding figures giving her advice, who have hitherto been the wise men in her life. It is her father's point of view (his description of the birth) she assumes. The mother's version is presented as though the mother had no idea what was going on in the birth situation. Her mother comes around from the anaesthesia and hears Mrs. D. ask Dr. R.W. what the time is. Mrs. D. can't even answer that! All the women in this Birth-myth commit mistakes or can do nothing (Moon void of course). This applies also to her mother, who is in an anaesthesia stupor. Only the man, Dr. R.W., can help.

No wonder that Alice never practiced law! No wonder that Alice continually seeks strong protective men to control her life, instead of trusting herself enough to make her own independent decisions. If she does not learn this, she will still prefer to let the so-called wise Saturn men in her life control her goals. A was, of course, a Capricorn, while B is an Aries.

Short Case Histories

The following short case histories demonstrate some of the interpretation possibilities the combination of separating/applying Moon-aspects and the Birth-myth can give.

Petra

Petra's Birth-myth has some of the same themes as Alice's, and has also had a considerable impact on her life. In 1989, Petra is 45 years old, and she writes:

"I was the first child born to my mother, and I have been told that owing to the war it was difficult to get hold of the midwife (I

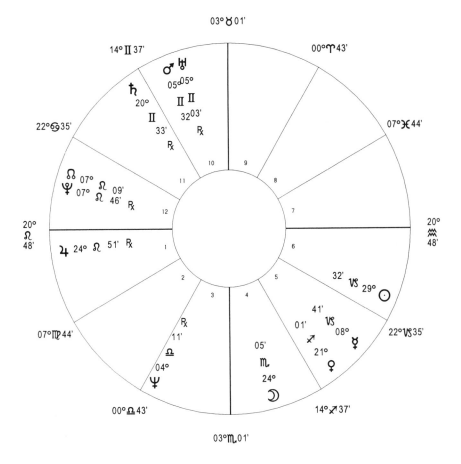

Petra
MC   03TA01 — Asc   20LE48
Sun   29CP32   6th House

Moon aspects

Moon	00SC00	3rd House			
Moon	03SC01	enters the	4th House		
Moon	07SC46	Square	Pluto	in Leo	in the 12th House
Moon	08SC41	Sextile	Mercury	in Capricorn	in the 5th House
Moon	**24SC05**	**4th House**	**at Birth**		
Moon	24SC51	Square	Jupiter	in Leo	in the 1st House
Moon	00SG00	Sextile	Sun	in Capricorn	in the 6th House

was born at home). My mother lay for a long time without help
and could not give birth to me, so when the midwife finally
arrived and I was born, I was apparently dead. Nobody can

remember whether it was a matter of seconds or minutes." The birth chart shows an applying Moon-Jupiter square. Again we have a case of a void of course Moon in a very difficult birth almost costing the life of the child, mainly because the midwife could not be called in time. (Although the Moon-Sun sextile is right on the signline, i.e., when the Moon is in 0 degrees Sagittarius and the Sun in 0 degrees Aquarius, I still consider this to be a void of course Moon.)

In her description of the Birth-myth, Petra in actual fact expresses her fear that she has suffered brain damage during the birth, that her ability for higher intellectual activities (Moon-Jupiter) has been impeded. And it would be a good basis for a talk about her Birth-myth if she were to blame her violent birth for the fact that she never got around to acquiring the higher education (Jupiter) which deep down she feels she deserves (she has Jupiter in the 1st House and a Leo Ascendant). Instead, she has chosen to aim at the Moon in the 4th House, but when she has a consultation in 1989, it is a year after her marriage broke down, and three months after her husband has moved in with another woman. She misses him and is disappointed about his poor treatment of her and the 2-year-old daughter they have together, whom he "apparently isn't interested in seeing."

The feeling of deep loss is often associated with the Birth-crisis. Here the sorrow is reflected in the projection of her own pain onto her two-year-old daughter. A child not loved by her father—exactly as she never was (Venus-Saturn opposition). It is particularly difficult for squares in fixed signs (the Moon and Jupiter) to admit loss and lack of control, and this is also true in Petra's case.

Karen

Karen was born on July 16. She writes: "My mother cannot remember the time precisely, the birth being complicated. My mother tells me that I should really have been born in the middle of August according to the doctor's and midwife's calculations. In the middle of June my mother fell ill and there was the risk of a miscarriage, but she improved and so I was born on July 16—a month too soon. A twin, which my mother thinks came just after me, was also born but was dead upon birth, probably having died in June when my mother became ill. They had difficulty in keeping me alive in the first few weeks after the birth."

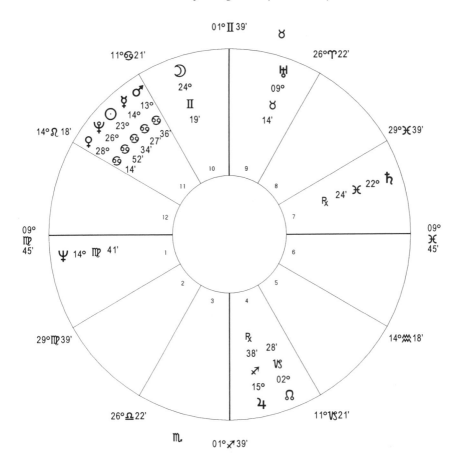

Karen
MC 01GE39 — Asc 09VI45
Sun 23CN34 11th House

Moon aspects

Moon	00GE00	9th House		
Moon	01GE39	enters the	10th House	
Moon	14GE40	Square	Neptune	in Virgo	in the 1st House
Moon	15GE38	Opposition	Jupiter	in Sagittarius	in the 4th House
Moon	22GE24	Square	Saturn	in Pisces	in the 7th House
Moon	**24GE19**	**10th House**	**at Birth**	
Moon	00CN00			

The Moon had left the square to Saturn (the mother's illness) 2 degrees before, and was now void of course (she almost dies at birth). Additionally, the relationship to the partner will always play a big role in Karen's life. She married in 1955, and was unhappy on her wedding day. Her list of events is characterized by many love affairs and relationships that are suddenly broken off, because she is *disappointed by the partner*. Her Birth-myth does not mention the father, and the Moon's square to Saturn in the 7th House is the classical aspect for seeking fulfillment of the father-archetype through the partner, and also for an early break with the parental home.

Note: For the following short case histories, important for analytical content, we will not use the full chart; the text will make the telling aspects clear.

Liv

Liv was born in 1956. She has a Moon-Pluto opposition which is right on the Descendant-Ascendant axis, often showing a birth where the person's life is at stake. The Moon is void of course in very late Aquarius and has to cross the signline to reach first the opposition to Pluto in Virgo and then the opposition to the Virgo Ascendant (just a distance of 2 degrees). Liv almost died at birth, and that is the reason for her name, Liv, meaning "Life" in Norwegian. With this Birth-myth, the mother expects the child to give life to other people. And that's exactly what Liv does. Liv is a well-known theater actress, and of course she has specialized in deeply Plutonian character roles.

As she says, "When I act, I don't feel that I have reached my goal until I hear the public sniffle." She projects her own Birth-myth onto the audience, and Pluto's tight conjunction with the Virgo Ascendant connects her with the deep unconscious forces affecting those people who experience her performances. Such a Pluto aspect demands that you concern yourself with the deep unconscious forces that reside in all human beings (Pluto's mass principle). But Liv often asks me if she is supposed to be an actress, or if it would be better if she did something else. Moon-Pluto *always questions your reason for being here on earth,* and every time she feels she cannot transmute her inner heavy emotions, she feels as if she is not doing her job properly. She feels she has no right to be here. She always feels she has to make an impact. She has to touch the emotions of others. And if she feels she is faking (i.e., not being deep enough) guilt is the result, as always with Moon-Pluto.

Frej

Frej has the same Moon-Pluto opposition on his horizon axis as Liv, but Frej's Pluto is on the *Descendant*. His Moon is in Capricorn, exactly conjunct the Ascendant. Frej's birth was hard and long, and he almost died at birth. His mother fixation has been incredibly strong (the Moon's first aspect is the square to Venus). It is so strong that he always says that his life did not begin until his mother died. Unfortunately (as Frej himself says), she did not die until he was in the beginning of his 60s.

The applying square to Venus out of the Plutonic opposition might also explain his homosexuality. Frej is 78 today, and he says that the last four years of his life have been by far the best. He is a qualified dentist and has for many years been involved in the training of new dentists at the Dental College. He hated having a private practice. "I was relieved every time a patient cancelled an appointment."

Frej always says that he is not good at anything (Pluto rules his 10th House). That he can't do anything (he also has Sun in Pisces square to Pluto), and that he definitely can't teach. Yet all the pupils he has had through the years feel great respect for his teaching abilities and his personality. Additionally, he has great artistic abilities as a sculptor, designer, musician, and astrologer, activities which bring him into contact with his own deep Plutonian wells, but which he practices in solitude (as opposed to Liv who has Pluto on her Ascendant). So even the Moon-Pluto opposition prevents him from seeing his own talents, still he has given generously of them through the years, but he refuses to allow himself the satisfaction of being proud of what he has to offer.

Louise

"My birth took place normally. However, it was artificially induced, since this suited the family better. I remember my childhood as being normal, though I had no particular attachment to my father. However, this has changed slightly in recent years."

In Louise's chart, the Moon is in the 8th House in Pisces, 1 degree from the opposition to Saturn (the poor relationship with her father), and also shows the implications of the Birth-myth: that she was not born until it suited the family's routines and plans. This birth has structure and control, and Louise has done much to structure and control *her own family*, as her Birth-myth dictates.

The Moon's next aspect is a conjunction with Mercury. Louise's problem has always been that she is inclined to give practical considerations too high a priority when reaching decisions in her life, since the Sun, Moon, and Mercury are in the 8th House. It is easier for her to reach decisions on the basis of her 2nd House Saturn (practical considerations, i.e., when it suits others) instead of searching her heart for her obscure emotional considerations (Sun-Moon-Mercury in Pisces concealed in the 8th House). She therefore makes use of astrology as a means of obtaining clarity with regard to her more hidden and obscure needs, wishes and motives.

Harriet

Harriet's mother was only 19 years old when she gave birth to her. The birth took place at the home of Harriet's maternal grandparents. Harriet recounts her Birth-myth: "My mother was irritated about having to give birth at this time. She was more interested in seeing the 'Six-Day-Race' on TV." In Denmark in the 50s and 60s, the Six-Day-Race—a team cycling event which continued without interruption for six days—was a point of focus for the whole nation. The mother was extremely absorbed by the bicycle race on TV.

Harriet recounts, "My mother said that she was glad that she managed to get the birth over and done with so she could see the end of the race." Today, Harriet still thinks that racing cyclists are "repulsive," and likes best to switch back and forth between channels instead of concentrating on one program. Harriet has chosen a partner who is interested in films and video, and who therefore spends much time in front of the TV. He wants peace and quiet when he's watching films, and he often complains that Harriet can't stop interrupting and initiating conversations in the middle of a film. *Harriet is still seeking the undivided attention and love which her birth situation did not provide.* The Moon's first aspect is a square to Venus in Aquarius in a 2 degree-orb conjunction with the Descendant: *not getting the love and attention one needs.*

Birgit

Birgit had a consultation with me in 1987. At that time she was 72 years old. And she was ready for a change! By secondary progression, her MC trined her natal Uranus, one of the most important planets in her Birth-myth.

She writes: "My mother gave birth to all her six children between 9:50 and 10:10 a.m., says my brother. And then I, who was the youngest, was born with a caul, a membrane which envelops the child at birth, and which neither Dr. Howitz or the midwife had experienced before."

It should be mentioned, that Birgit uses the Danish word for caul, which is "armor of victory," a term that in Danish folklore always has indicated a victorious and lucky person. With this Birth-myth, Birgit tells us that she is special and remarkable. The Moon's separating trine to Uranus and applying trine to Mercury (close to the 11th House cusp) tells the same story. And at the time of the consultation, the same Uranus was activated by secondary progressions.

For 10 years, Birgit has lived in the same little town as her two children, but she wants to "strike camp" and move to the capital, where her friends (Uranus-Mercury) live. She wants to disengage herself from family duties. But at the same time she has a bad conscience about leaving her children in the lurch, in that every second weekend she acts as a babysitter of her grandchildren. Her Uranus wants out, and the only reason she consults an astrologer (another Uranus-person) is that she wants him to tell her it's all right to let it out; i.e., that it's all right to set aside the usual expectations people have of a grandmother as a person whose primary function it is always to be at her children's beck and call to act as a babysitter, a person with no life of her own. She does not want to be like all the other feeble-minded grandmothers. She wants to have fun with her friends again! This is a typical case, when Uranus is activated by transit or secondary progression—no matter what age you are!

Her Birth-myth tells us that she considers herself to be a unique Uranian person. She even chooses to reveal the name of the famous Danish professor who helped deliver her (Uranus as the "name-dropper"). And "Dr. Howitz was sooooo surprised" at her caul, of which he had probably already seen a few hundred or so.

There is no mention of her mother, or any other details about the birth situation itself. She only remembers the story of how amazed and impressed the professor and the midwife were by her caul—the objective proof that she is different, and something very special. Moon-Uranus contacts often give an estrangement from the mother, and also transfer the same quality to the mother-role the person herself will play later in life.

And now, two examples [data from *Today's Astrologer* AFA Bulletin data-section, courtesy David Dozier], from a series of articles I wrote about "Strange and remarkable births," published in the Danish astrological monthly *Stjernerne*. The first two are examples of babies being killed shortly after birth. Both have *very* void of course Moons.

Bob

In this example, there is an accumulation of planets in the 1st House, which seems surprising, since this should ensure ample vitality and reserves of strength, representing the personality and the body. This was not to be in this case!

Bob was born of a 20-year-old woman in a dormitory bathroom. He was a healthy child. Immediately after birth his mother smothered him. He was then placed in a plastic bag and thrown into a garbage can in the hall outside the school dormitory.

Seven planets in the 1st house apparently provide no guarantee for the survival of the physical body (1st house/Ascendant)! But what has Bob's birth chart to say about the event? The big stellium in the 1st House in this case results in a *surprising lack of aspects in the chart*. Most of the planets (Venus, Uranus, Mercury, Neptune and Saturn) are in Capricorn, while the Sun and the Moon, which are so important for the personality, are in Sagittarius. The Lights need to cross into the sign of Capricorn to reach the other planets in the 1st House. Only Pluto receives a weak (having a large orb)—but very collective—sextile from Saturn. All these strong planet energies are therefore "imprisoned" in the 1st House. It is difficult to transmit the energies from the 1st House out to the rest of the chart.

Even Jupiter, which rules the Ascendant (Bob), forms no traditional aspects with the other planets. Jupiter is in the 8th House (the life/death house), and receives no help (aspects) from the other planets. The Moon is the 8th House ruler, and is *void of course* and very late in sign. Despite the accumulation of planets, *there is no power.*

The Sun and Jupiter are in mutual reception, however, which in traditional horary astrology is a positive and affirmative sign. Perhaps in this case it merely shows that Bob was a healthy child.

"Other people" (7th House) can't help, because Mercury (the 7th House ruler) is both besieged and squeezed in between Uranus and Neptune, retrograde, and moving toward an exact conjunction with Uranus. Thinking is fast but not particularly clear.

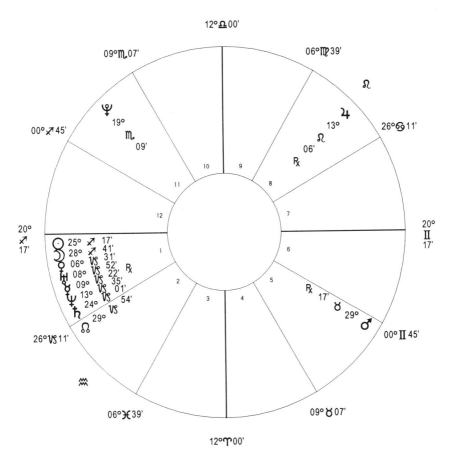

Bob
MC 12LI00 — Asc 20SG17
Sun 25SG17 1st House

Moon Aspects

Moon	00SG00	12 House			
Moon	13SG06	Trine	Jupiter	in Leo	in the 8th House
Moon	25SG17	Conjunct	Sun	in Sagittarius	in the 12th House
Moon	**28SG41**	**1st House**	**at Birth**		
Moon	00CP00				

But what about Bob's mother? The Moon is in Sagittarius and void of course ("It comes to nothing"). We have seen many other examples too, where the child did live after all. But in Bob's chart, the Moon is very close to the signline, tired of the long migration through Sagittarius, and therefore without strength.

The mother is preoccupied with her studies (Moon in Sagittarius) and feels divided (Moon close to the Capricorn signline) and lacking in will (unaspected Sun) to do anything other than what she does. Most likely, she acts on a reflex (Mercury/Uranus), and has no emotional connection to the child (the Moon can't "reach" the planets in Capricorn, across the signline). The mother wants to forget the father and enter a career (Moon into Capricorn). The subsequent court case, where the mother was accused of homicide, put a stop to this, however.

Rhiannon

On December 8, 1990, around noon, 24-year-old Becky Wildman suddenly had very serious and painful stomach pains. Her husband, Jamie Wildman, called an ambulance, which at full speed drove Becky to the acute gastric ward. Becky and Jamie were amazed to learn that there was nothing the matter with Becky but that she was in the ninth month of pregnancy and had labor pains!

Her husband Jamie looked on in bewilderment when Becky at 3:33 p.m. gave birth to a fine, healthy girl. Indeed a surprising birth!

What worried the parents most was whether the child had been harmed because, during the whole pregnancy, Becky had carried out hard physical work and had taken contraceptive pills! She had had normal menstrual periods throughout the whole pregnancy.

In the course of the pregnancy, Becky's weight had increased from 145 to 172 pounds, which she had merely ascribed to her "normal" fluctuations in weight. Becky is barely 5' 1" and, if the official average weight tables are to be believed, Becky's normal weight should lie somewhere around 110 pounds. She had felt *nothing* during the pregnancy, and nothing seemed to be different from usual. Becky's daughter, who was later christened Rhiannon, was born vaginally, and was a normal, healthy, and pretty child.

In the Birth-horary, it is shown that the birth went quickly—and that it *was* surprising. Mars is very close to the Ascendant, which has just passed over it. The ruler of the situation (the Ascendant ruler, Mercury) is in tight conjunction with Uranus (sudden events and surprises). This conjunction is placed in the 8th House, the house for life/death and birth processes. The Moon (which in horary astrology also shows the underlying cause of the event) is in the 5th House, the house of children, and has just passed the trine to Neptune in the 8th House (the birth) and is on its way to a square to the Sun (the meeting between

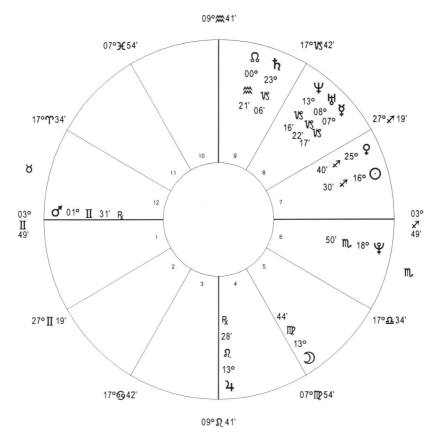

Rhiannon Wildman
MC 09AQ41 Asc 03GE49
Sun 16SG30 7th House

Moon Aspects

Moon	00VI00	4th House			
Moon	01VI31	Square	Mars	in Gemini	in the 12th House (cusp of 1st)
Moon	07VI17	Trine	Mercury	in Capricorn	in the 8th House
Moon	08VI22	Trine	Uranus	in Capricorn	in the 8th House
Moon	13VI16	Trine	Neptune	in Capricorn	in the 8th House
Moon	13VI44	5th House	at Birth		
Moon	16VI30	Square	Sun	in Sagittarius	in the 7th House
Moon	18VI50	Sextile	Pluto	in Scorpio	in the 6th House
Moon	23VI06	Trine	Saturn	in Capricorn	in the 9th House
Moon	25VI40	Square	Venus	in Sagittarius	in the 7th House (cusp of 8th)
Moon	00LI00				

Rhiannon, the Sun, and the mother, the Moon). The birth situation itself is thus well described by the horary chart.

But this chart is also little Rhiannon Wildman's birth chart. What connection is there between the birth situation and the life she can expect? The Ascendant ruler (Mercury) describes a person who wants to be—and is—different (Mercury conjunct Uranus). And this "differentness" starts at the very moment of birth.

Strong Uranus influences often give the individual a feeling of being a foundling or of not properly belonging to the family. In their urge to be special, people with these strong Uranus influences may often make up fantasies about their own appearance in the world. I have encountered many examples of people with Uranus in the 4th House with aspects to the personal planets who thought that they had been born into the wrong family, been exchanged with another baby by mistake, or—in the most exaggerated case—that the person in actual fact "came from Outer Space."

When we examine Rhiannon's mother image (i.e., how, according to the chart, she sees her mother, the Moon), it seems as though she sees her as a hard-working person (Moon in Virgo), at the same time something of a dreamer, never really present on the physical plane (trine to Neptune in the 8th House). We get a picture of a mother who "lives in another world," and who seems to be partially out of contact with reality—perhaps also with her own body! And perhaps without real contact with other people. The same aspect also corroborates the use of contraceptive pills (Neptune represents chemical substances) during the whole pregnancy. This mother has borne and nourished another human being in her physical body without knowing anything about it! If she felt anything, she must have pushed it aside (into the 8th House!).

The same influences may make it difficult for the mother to accept her child's extroversion and need for contact with other people (Sun and Venus in the 7th House in Sagittarius, the Sun trine to Jupiter). The Moon (the mother) is in square to the Sun (the child's contact with her surroundings). It is in this area that mother-daughter conflicts will be enacted in the future.

It is the unaspected Mars in the 12th House, in "backwards" conjunction with the Ascendant, which "starts" the birth. Mars has no aspects and is in the hidden 12th house. The fact that Mars is unaspected seems to indicate that Rhiannon will have a great need to make an impression on her surroundings through the expression of masculine energies, so in her early years she will be a real tomboy (the Sun is also in the 7th House). But under any circumstances, extreme nervous unrest is shown in the chart (Mercury/Uranus, Mars and Sun/Moon), and the childhood years will probably be characterized by activity, energy, wildness, and a tendency to unruliness—however, without this getting out of hand. Symbolically this can be perceived as Rhiannon's urge to contact the physical world, into which she was abruptly "thrown." Incidentally, the family is named Wildman!

Finally, it should be pointed out that Rhiannon Wildman's chart is not special, different or outstanding in relation to charts of normal, unsensational pregnancies and births. The above potential "problems" could just as well appear after a quite ordinary pregnancy and birth. But still there is a clear connection among the interpretation of the "Birth-horary," Rhiannon Wildman's birth chart, and the Birth-myth. And in this case, there is indeed an astounding story to tell the child. It is a story which—in relation to its strange course—has a happy ending. Also for little Rhiannon Wildman in the long view. After all, she isn't the only person in the world with a Sun-Moon square in her chart, is she?

Epilogue

In closing, let me emphasize that the birth situation can be *interpreted* as coming or originating from the mother. But the mother is not to be blamed! The birth chart conditions us to focus on certain traits possessed by the mother or projected onto someone else. The problem is that it is so easy to project onto the mother, *because she is there from the very beginning.* We don't know why we are born. Maybe the unborn child "chooses" the mother. Maybe it doesn't. We only know for a fact that a child has been born, and that that child receives a birth chart when this happens. The physical mother is just a symbol of the child's inner processes, a physical object that is to fill the child's predisposed Mother-archetype—to express it in Jungian terms. The mother is only an external symbol of the child's internal make-up. But the Moon belongs to us, to our chart. It is part and parcel of our own emotional life. And as we have just learned: the Moon gives what it has to offer, whether we deserve it or not. But the handling of the Moon energies in our own chart is our responsibility and our quest in life. Life has so much to offer if we let it!

Gloria Star

Gloria Star is an astrological counselor with over eighteen years experience. She has integrated her study of traditional concepts in nursing, education, and psychology with an extensive background in astrology, metaphysical study, holistic health, alternative therapies, yoga, and meditation. Her first book, *Optimum Child: Developing Your Child's Fullest Potentials through Astrology* (Llewellyn, 1987) offered insights into developmental astrology. She is also a contributing author of the Llewellyn anthology, *Houses: Power Places in the Horoscope* and has written the annual *Sun Sign* books for Llewellyn since 1989.

Gloria spends much of her time presenting very popular astrological workshops and lectures for local groups and at national and international conferences. She also maintains a busy counseling practice in both her home in Clinton, Connecticut and in the Oklahoma City metropolitan area.

Family Crises in the Early Years

Gloria Star

Imagine your beginnings, your primordial essence, the joining of your parents, the spark of life which kindled your formation as a human being. Feel your cushioned ride within the womb of your mother, then your emergence as a singular individual into the exposure of the outside world. See the swirl of images, as you struggle to make all the adjustments necessary to breathe, your attempts to translate what you see into something meaningful. Feel the warmth of your mother's touch, the strength of your father's arms. Remember the largeness of the world, inhabited by giants who gesticulate and speak in bombastic phrases or who dance and utter melodious tones. Feel yourself growing larger and stronger. Remember. Come to the time of a major change. Let the pictures in your mind stop and recall how you felt. This is the impact of life before you, as the child, realize the impact you are having upon the world around you.

Through the influence of individuals such as Eric Erickson, Alice Miller, and Joseph Chilton Pearce, childhood needs and emotions have been brought into a clearer focus. Although astrologers have traditionally dealt primarily with adults, the analysis of charts for children has become increasingly important, since many adult clients also want to understand the needs of their children. Additionally, we are realizing the impact of early life experiences upon the psychological make-up of the adult. And we can see the pattern of these experiences illustrated through the astrological chart. Since the family is the first support group known to a child, many of the dynamics of the child's personality are framed by the issues and crises within this system.

A child's psychological boundaries develop gradually over time; and in the beginning, every life experience is part of the child's sense of self.

During the early impressionable years, a child has not learned mechanisms that allow for the maintenance of individual integrity. If Mommy and Daddy are blissfully going through the day, the child feels this calm as part of the self. If Mommy and Daddy are in the midst of turmoil, the child feels the turmoil as part of the Self. But we also know that each child has a core level of personality and needs and will perceive his or her experiences differently.

When examining a natal chart, we can look at the potential of each individual to use her or his energies to create particular realities. Astrologically speaking, we know that different patterns are likely to result in different responses. And we also realize that these patterns, as defined by the natal chart, are likely to repeat themselves over and over again, confirming an individual's concept of self and reality. In childhood, there seems to be greater flexibility when shaping the self into the patterns. Even in the midst of major upheaval, history has shown us that a child with proper support can bounce back and can use the change in positive ways.

As with any astrological experiment with cycles and change, the backdrop for the experience is the individual, whose energy and personality are illustrated by the natal chart. Look first at the patterns in the natal chart for indicators of the individual ego strength and emotional need systems, since the crises or changes will occur within the individual's own frame of reference. Someone else, an outsider, even a parent, may not see the situation or feel it in the same way. Many parents have realized, long after the fact, that something that had little significance to them created havoc in the emotions of the child.

Significant family crises are usually apparent, however, and will affect every member of the family unit in some way. From the loss of a family member to the addition of new family members, each critical point reshapes the psychological dynamics within the family. Since a child in the early years, before age six, has not yet developed the mechanisms to deal with its feelings or the power to step in and create change, most family crises seem to be foisted upon the child, who, unwittingly, *must* cope.

Because of its vulnerability and interdependence, the child may feel that she or he is the cause of the crisis. This is especially significant during periods of loss. If you are looking back on those years with the help of your astrological chart, then you can understand why you feel about some things the way you do. You can recreate those images and begin to foster healing within your inner child. But if you're examining the chart of a child who has not yet lived long in the world, then you have the power to provide additional support and understanding during the periods when the child is likely to feel most vulnerable.

Childhood Needs and Basic Development

During different ages, a child's needs develop gradually, eventually resulting in a sense of personal identity. In early infancy, through five to six months of age, a baby struggles with staying alive. Simply existing takes all of a baby's energy. Life began in an environment different from the outside world, where the child and the mother were one unit. Trusting this new environment takes a bit of adjustment. Not only is the body coping with the assimilation of food, adjustment to temperature changes and new discomforts, but the infant is also trying to find ways to have all those needs met. The parents need to offer the attention and nurturance required by the infant to support its growth and they need to establish a feeling of trust with the infant. The need to feel safe and secure is paramount during this period. *Absolutely everything makes a lasting impression in these months.*

Once the baby develops sufficient physical coordination to move about—rolling around, crawling, pulling up—the adventure of finding out what exists in the outside world stimulates most of the baby's actions. Nurturance and safety are still important, but knowing how the brightly colored toy on the carpet tastes and using all the senses to learn as much as possible enlarge the baby's framework. Going for the object of desire develops the initiative to keep exploring. During this first year of life, the baby has moved from a helpless mass of human parts to a moderately coordinated creature who feels more a part of the world. And once the baby begins to walk, the excitement of getting around and seeing, touching, tasting, and feeling more of life continues.

During this period, the parents provide protection and nurturance and ideally show delight at every new development. It is also during this time that the child learns about the need for outside limitation.

At some point between eighteen months and three years, babies become toddlers who start to separate other people and objects from themselves. This is often a difficult stage, since this separation means a loss of a part of the sense of self. Temper ensues; the toddler is rebelling. Communication improves with the development of speech, and interactive skills improve; through these tools the toddler can also grasp more information. At some point near the second birthday, the child begins to exhibit the emotions of shame and guilt and incorporates these feelings into decisions about behavior. Interaction between child and environment extends as far as the child can perceive. And the child needs encouragement not only to explore and trust this outside world but to search for ways to trust the self.

Personal identity becomes more noticeable in the child between the third and sixth year, when interaction with other children and defining reality become key issues. These are years of definition of the self. The child may think that its actions and thoughts are causative, and this magical thinking can be the basis for creative activity, but it can also be detrimental if it is negatively supported. Now, the child has developed into an individual who can talk about thoughts and feelings, but these may still be on the borderline between the child's inner reality and the external world.

The Impact of Family Crisis on Development

With appropriate, supportive parenting, a child can move through the developmental stages with fairly smooth transitions, gaining confidence and positive self-affirmation. But interruptions in the structure that has provided the support can create a multitude of difficulties, depending upon the level of development the child has reached and the type of support the child receives during a change. Additionally, a significant alteration during a particular developmental phase can have long-lasting effects on the child's behavior and ability to relate to others once she or he matures.

It is possible for the child and family to emerge on the other side of the crisis with enhanced awareness and positive transformation. For example, a family that relocates in response to career opportunity for the parents is involved in the crisis of adapting to a new circumstance while grieving over the loss of their previous life situation. We have learned from studies of stress levels during changes, that *even positive changes carry the weight of stress.* A vacation can bring on crisis! But a child, who may have very little input concerning these changes may feel completely vulnerable and overpowered by what, to the parents, is a step forward.

There are some situations which can not change without the benefit of crisis. Rather than anticipating a negative outcome, the realization of change and the level of bonding a crisis situation can provide are often necessary precursors to a healthier family. For example, a family in which one of the parents is alcoholic will experience a crisis if that parent seeks to change and recover from dependency. But the effect of this change can result in a more honest and supportive relationship among all family members.

Identifying and Measuring Family Crises: The Natal Chart

To determine the child's sense of support, it's necessary first to examine the natal chart for clues to the child's areas of vulnerability or strength. Through this exercise, it is possible to discover the inner aspect of the child that can be targeted to provide sustenance during times of stress. Learning to trust what is within the child is always a large task for parents, since a child's limitations are often more apparent than its strengths.

When I first met Susie, our focus during her astrological counseling sessions involved her disappointments in love relationships. With several disappointments and losses in relationships behind her, she was then involved with a gentleman who seemed to be rather distant.

Through exploring the dynamics of her chart, it soon became apparent that she had been unhappy in her relationships since her early years. The powerful pattern of the fixed T-Square involving the Sun and Mercury in Aquarius in the 10th House, Jupiter and

Saturn in Taurus in the 1st House and Pluto in Leo in the 4th House led me to question her regarding her feelings about her parents and their impact upon her sense of faith in herself.

The need to feel good about being alive is primary when building a strong sense of self. I have frequently seen the Sun-Saturn-Pluto aspect pictures involved in the psychological dynamic that can result in a feeling that the individual should not be here, a deep feeling that existing is somehow wrong! Although the parents may not perceive that they are sending this message, a child's experience of receiving the message is often quite different. It is rare for a parent to say bluntly, "don't exist" or "you don't deserve to exist," but actions or other words can impart this feeling to a child. Abandonment issues are frequently paramount in this energy dynamic. I was curious about Susie's reactions to personal relationships based upon her early childhood.

In Susie's experience, she remembers "from the beginning" hearing stories of her mother's development of diabetes mellitus during her pregnancy. Susie's mother continued to manifest problems with diabetes following Susie's birth, and always seemed to be ailing. Her mother's suffering seemed to be inextricably tied to Susie's existence.

As Susie described her feelings about her mother's stories of physical suffering, she shared that she had always felt responsible for her mother's pain! As a result, she experienced deep guilt about having what she wanted, since someone else had to suffer so greatly just so she could exist. The strong tension from the parental axis also indicates a lack of support from the father, whose absorption in his work and worry over his wife's physical problems always seemed to overwhelm Susie's needs. Susie was left in charge of taking care of Mommy from a very early age. It seemed there was nobody "taking care of Susie."

The consistent challenge of such tension in the personality would *require* that the child feel a strong support system from the parents. When counseling parents whose children show this dynamic, I encourage them to be aware of the projection from the child that the world is not a safe place, and the feeling from the child that they may not be wanted.

There are other aspects and planetary indicators from Susie's chart that indicate a difficulty in openly expressing her needs, especially noting the Moon's placement in the 8th House and

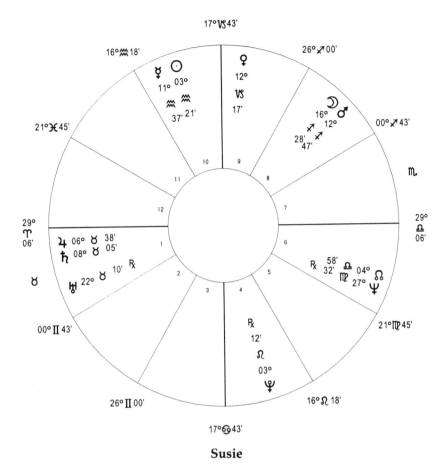

Susie

Venus in Capricorn. However, there is a strong feeling of self-preservation indicated by the trine from Venus in Capricorn in the 9th to Saturn and Jupiter in the 1st. She does have the capacity to maintain her own values. But I felt we needed to safeguard against her sabotaging her own feelings in favor of an overriding mistrust of herself, symbolized by the fixed T-square.

In working with Susie, we focused together on the situation from the "logical adult" viewpoint. Through looking at the circumstances objectively, she could easily see what had been happening during her formative years. And it was only from this perspective that we could begin to define and defend the needs she felt as a child. Allowing the infant Susie, the small child Susie, to speak was not easy, but through inner child work, she is uncovering greater faith in her abilities and is determining a more productive quality in her interpersonal relationships and in her career.

Susie's natal chart shows the potential to perceive a lack of support of her sense of self from her environment. Although this picture could have been illustrated in many ways, the inner experience of the child was one of feeling that existing was somehow *not* okay. Through exploring different cycles later on, we'll locate the times which underscore the events that confirmed this inner feeling.

It is crucial to identify the patterns and planetary placements that indicate particular vulnerability for a child before projecting the cycles on the natal chart. In contrast, the strengths and areas of resilience are also of special importance, since these are the elements that can suggest the best ways to deal with the more traumatic issues.

Managing the Crises Represented by the Cycles

By exploring the cycles represented by the transits of the slower moving planets, eclipse cycles, the Secondary Progressions (with special emphasis on Sun, Moon, Mercury and Venus) and Solar Arc directions, we can identify the times when a child may feel more vulnerable to crises within the family. Although each cycle represents developmental change, some are more indicative of crisis. As with any astrological cycle, event timing may either precede or follow the exact period of the cycle. An individual whose chart contains a strong Uranian focus may always seem to be a bit ahead of the cycles, whereas an overriding Saturnian influence may slow the realization of these developmental processes to some extent.

Transits to the Angles

The slower-moving transits of Saturn, Uranus, Neptune, and Pluto to the angles (ASC, IC, DSC, MC) of the natal chart are often key trigger-mechanisms for crisis. These axes are crucial, since they are indicative of the child's relationship to the world *through parents.* Although the ASC does illustrate the child's projection of self into the world, in the early years, this point corresponds to the career axis of the parents (using derivative houses, the 10th from the 4th). For example, a parent may undergo a career change while the child experiences a transit of Uranus over the ASC. However, Mars transits are also interesting to watch, since they often provide the actual ignition of an event or change. Careful observation of the times of action may indicate that a circumstance was set-up during one of the slower cycles, but that it was during a Mars transit when a situation was activated.

The transits of Saturn and the transpersonal planets to the Sun, Moon, Mercury, Venus, or Mars do not always mark a period of family crisis. However, these planets transiting to Sun and Moon can indicate *shifts in the child's ability to identify with the parents in some way.*

♄ Saturn's transits to the angles (conjunction more than square) represent times during which the structure of a child's life is challenged in some way. There may be restrictions imposed that were not previously in place. But it is during these times that the child may also feel a strong sense of loss or inhibition. Depending upon the developmental age of the child, these transits will have different effects. Under the age of two, a child is likely to feel the loss of the presence of a parent and can sense that there is less to trust about its environment. During this time, the child needs to be reminded of its safety and support by the caretaker, whether that is parent, grandparent or day care.

From age two to three, this transit would be a strong indicator of the types of restrictions that could lead to increased feelings of shame. The child needs to be supported in its decisions about right and wrong. But this transit can be more difficult from age three to six, when the child feels more responsible. Because children of this age engage in magical thinking, they are likely to interpret that *they* are the cause of any difficulties, problems, or losses. The support system must show the child where its responsibilities begin and end.

♅ Uranus' effect during transits to the angles (conjunction more than square) is disruptive and can be upsetting to the child who is unprepared. Radical changes, such as a move, can alter the child's viewpoint of the world. What may seem to be planned to the parents can be revolutionary to the child. Uranus can also bring an enhanced feeling of freedom, but a younger child is usually not prepared for shock-waves of freedom. This needs to come gradually, through supportive guidance and encouragement.

During ages two to three, when the child is testing the environment and breaking away from the mother's constant protection, a Uranus transit to the angles can be indicative of too much too soon. Even a precocious child may not have the emotional stability to deal with the sweeping changes this transit can bring about. A crisis can result from the sudden change of career for the parent, from an unexpected move or disruption in family life. The parents and support system need to safeguard the child's feeling of belonging. The most likely result of these cycles can be the nagging feeling that the child is a misfit, a stranger in a strange land.

♆ Neptune's transit to the angles during early years is possible only if the natal placement of Neptune is in fairly close proximity to the angle. Individuals with Neptune near the angles of the chart often have problems with boundaries, and for a child this is highly exaggerated, since the child interprets everything as part of the self until about age three. This transit can be doubly difficult for the child who has Neptune very near the angle and experiences the retrograding transit of Neptune back into the cadent house and then again over the angle. This period may be a blur for the child. What was real becomes unreal. A parent may have an illness or may be pulled away from the child and can seem to disappear. This crisis can damage the child's sense of trust, but can also result in a feeling of disconnection from the world. This can be a seat for great anger. Losing that feeling of connection can result in the child opening the boundaries even more in an attempt to re-connect or bond with the parent. During this cycle, the support system needs to be made as real as possible for the child. Consistency is paramount. Tangible contact is necessary to offset that feeling of "where am I?"

P Pluto's transit to the angles during the early years is also dependent upon this planet falling in close proximity to the angle in the nativity. The influence of this energy is often felt at a very deep level, and corresponds to a powerful opening of the psyche. A young child experiencing this transit can feel highly vulnerable during this time. The child may feel overpowered by changes within the family. Family crises marked by Pluto transits may be buried deep within the psyche for many years, and can become the root of long-term guilt, resentment or fear. A move during this time can leave the child feeling completely uprooted. A parent's opportunity in career may bring greater income or influence, but might leave the child with a feeling of being less important than Mom or Dad's job. During this transit, the support system needs to give the child a sense of power. If the child feels powerless during this time, the resulting resentment can form a blockade to the parent or family which remains forever.

Solar and Lunar Eclipses

The effect of eclipses is one of increased awareness of the experiences symbolized by the luminary, planet, or angle that receives an aspect from the eclipse. Of special significance during the early years are Solar Eclipses that conjunct an angle of the chart. The enhanced awareness of the child during this time may facilitate an opening of the psyche that allows greater sensitivity. The transits of planets following up an eclipse seem to have great significance, and may carry a longer-term impact.

For example, a Solar Eclipse to the ASC followed by Jupiter transiting the ASC may bring about a change that expands the child's sense of the nature of the world. A grandparent could move into closer proximity to the child or spend more time with the child. This could lead to a feeling that life is filled with greater abundance, or it could stimulate a positively enhanced period of self-confidence with far-reaching effects. Conversely, a transit of Saturn to the ASC following a Solar Eclipse to the ASC may have a more profoundly limiting influence than the transit it would otherwise impart. Any loss or separation during the Saturn transit could be more strongly felt by the child.

With the effect of the accompanying transiting Nodes of the Moon, which intensify the "feeling" level of an individual, these eclipse cycles seem to have an impact on the subconscious levels of the psyche. An angular transiting Solar Eclipse accompanied by a family crisis such as the death of a grandparent, an environmental change, or other changes that seem to be part of "normal" cyclic change for an adult *can bring a devastating shift in the nature of a child's reality.* Becoming aware of the timing of these cycles can clue the parent and supportive individuals to this period of increased awareness and vulnerability for the child. Keying into the child's age-related developmental cycles during these times helps the parent amplify the types of support most crucial to the child at that age.

The Lunar Eclipses may also be clues to the planetary influences that are most significant for the child during the months to come. While the eclipse of the Sun often opens to more externalized events, the Moon's eclipses stimulate that same opening within the psyche at a deep subconscious level. A planet or angle contacted by a Lunar Eclipse signals a period of greater sensitivity to that particular energy. The child's support system may seem to have a weak link during this phase, and the eclipse pinpoints the area of susceptibility requiring special attention.

Managing Crises Indicated by Solar Arcs

Solar Arcs are among the most effective tools for projecting into time. When working with the chart of a child, I seek out early Solar Arc directions to help the parents determine those times *which are likely to be experienced as more crucial from the perspective of the child.* Not only are the arcs to the angles important, but the Solar Arc aspect from planet/luminary to planet/luminary indicates especially powerful periods of change.

Most natal planetary aspects are not "perfect," but are still considered to be valid and effective within a particular orb of influence. These orbs may range from a few minutes to several degrees (e.g., in Susie's natal chart, shown on page 61, the Sun and Saturn are in square aspect within an orb of 4 degrees 44 minutes). The effect of the natal aspect within the individual is considered to last a lifetime, but it is at the time during which the aspect, when projected by Solar Arc, reaches perfection that this aspect may have its greatest impact. For an individual to resolve the issues surrounding the nature of the aspect, it is often helpful to trace back to the time the aspect reached its "perfected" degree by Secondary Progression (for the Sun) or Solar Arc direction of the planets, i.e., the projection of the Sun's SP arc from the planet's natal position. This is especially true of the more intensive aspects—conjunction, semi-square, square, sesquiquadrate, and opposition.

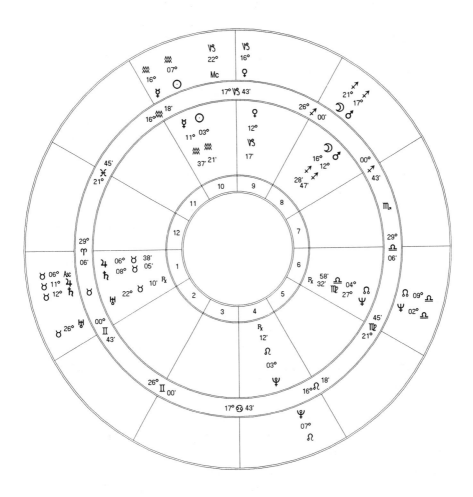

Susie

In my work with Susie to help her uncover the core of her feeling that she was responsible for the unhappiness and suffering of those she loved, I suggested that we move back in time to a period from age three (when SA Pluto squared Jupiter) to about age 4 to 4-1/2 (when the Sun progressed to square Saturn and SA Mars conjuncted the Moon).

When talking about the events of her life during this time, Susie's voice modulated, becoming lighter and more childlike. She described staying home with her ailing mother during the days and remembered her father's instructions to be sure that her mother was okay. One day, at about age 4-1/2, Susie and her mother took an afternoon nap together on the bed. When Susie awoke, her mother had fallen into a diabetic coma. Susie, who was instructed to telephone her father in an emergency, had also been ordered not to leave the house under any circumstances. Upon finding her mother unconscious, Susie felt a powerful panic overtaking her. She could not remember her father's telephone number at work. She stared at the phone, trying to recall, but drew an absolute blank. Her only thought was to get help.

Susie ran out of the house and began knocking on the doors of neighbors. Finally, a neighborhood friend answered. Susie explained that her mother was asleep and she could not waken her. The neighbor followed Susie home and, upon checking her mother, immediately called an ambulance. Susie's father was also contacted. He rushed home, and was furious. Susie felt that his rage was directed toward her. He took her into the back room and spanked her for leaving the house. Her mother was rushed to a hospital, where her condition stabilized.

Susie felt totally responsible for her mother's severe condition, and felt that her father held her accountable. The power of this experience had ingrained itself into Susie's consciousness to such an extent that she even felt responsible when, years later, her own husband died. Her comments were that, even though she "knew better," she felt that anyone she loved was doomed. In actuality, Susie was the one who felt doomed, and in her desire to get permission from an outside source for achieving success or happiness, she met only partial success.

In addition to the Solar Arc directions at that time, at age 4-1/2, Susie was also experiencing the impact of a Solar Eclipse to her IC and Saturn moving across the IC by transit. All these cycles were indicative of a major family crisis which would have a lasting impact. In Susie's case, the impact was one of deciding that she did not like having to be held accountable for others, but that she seemed unable to escape it! The resulting reaction formation had been part of a series of destructive co-dependent relationships, a situation she has been working to resolve over the last few years.

In the chart of John F. Kennedy, Jr. (on page 71), Mars in Cancer in the 11th House opposes Saturn in Capricorn in the 5th House. The need to be in control is often paramount with individuals who possess this aspect, but with Mars retrograde in Cancer, it is highly probable that learning direct assertiveness has not been easy for him. At the time of his father's assassination on November 22, 1963, Saturn directed by Solar Arc had fulfilled the opposition to his Mars. Not only might this indicate a time when the child would feel more marked restraint, but the feeling of powerlessness that could accompany such a cycle could strongly undermine his sense of personal control. One of the most potent images flashed in news magazines and on television during the time of President Kennedy's funeral was that of his three-year-old son saluting as the caisson bearing his father's coffin passed in its procession down Pennsylvania Avenue. That salute from the innocence of a child struck the heart of a nation which seemed to lack the means to ease the pain of a broken dream.

Solar Arcs to Angles

At the time planets reach an angle by Solar Arc, a child is more acutely sensitive to the influence of this energy and its impact upon the parents and familial structure. Since young children are especially prone toward projecting their energy into their environment and the people within it, most cycles that involve the connection of planets to an angle will be felt as external, rather than internal influences. However, the internalization process does occur, since the child is not reasonably free of the identification of the external/internal dilemma until about age seven. Each planetary energy may be projected into the environment in a particular way. Considerations for these projections could be:

Sun   = Father
Moon   = Mother, Caretaker
Mercury = Siblings, other children
Venus   = Mother
Mars   = Father
Jupiter = Aunts, Uncles, Teachers
Saturn   = Either parent, teachers, older relative in the home
Uranus   = Playmates
Neptune = Storybook and movie characters
Pluto   = Heroes, Mother
ASC/DSC
and Rulers= Grandparents

A child with a planet in a Cadent House near an angle would naturally feel the influence of this planetary energy as having a powerful impact throughout the life. *But during the year* when this planet reaches the "perfected" conjunction with the angle by SA, the essence of the experience of that energy would play out in some way. Frequently, a family crisis can occur during one of these cycles.

As an example, SA Saturn coming to conjunction with the Ascendant could symbolize a time when the child feels a stronger restrictive influence from a grandparent, or possibly even the loss of a grandparent. At the very least, the inner fear behind the cycle could be that a loss would occur, and the support system would need to answer this vulnerability by bringing a sense of nurturing stability and structure to the child. The child's inner fear may involve a feeling that the freedom and spontaneity of childhood are somehow inhibited due to some restricting influence. Early responsibilities could be foisted upon the child, which could result in the internal impression that life is filled with many "should's," and "have-to's" rather than possibilities.

To analyze further the signal for family crisis for John F. Kennedy, Jr., several factors provide clues to his increased susceptibility during 1963. The Lunar Eclipse on January 9th on the axis of 18 degrees 59 minutes Cancer-Capricorn may have presaged a feeling of breaking away or cutting away. This developmental age represents a period of beginning to break some ties with the parents and a motion toward exploring the world with greater freedom. This

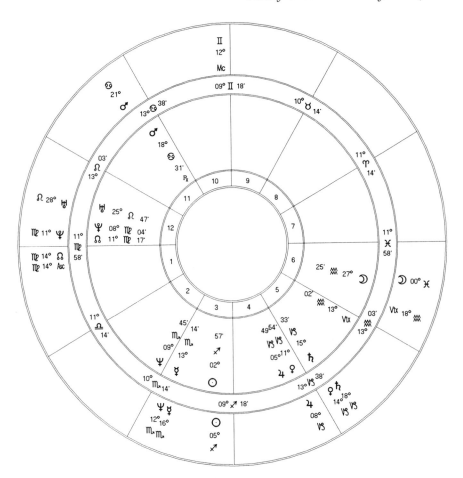

John F. Kennedy Jr.
Nov. 25, 1960, Washington DC, 12:22 a.m. EST
77W02 38N54
(with Solar Arcs, age 3)

breaking away can be healthy, and is a necessary part of self-identification. But a child also needs to feel a continued support and closeness from the parents. Although there were ample numbers of caretakers in the White House during those days, the psychic vulnerability John Jr. felt was undeniable. When Jacqueline became pregnant shortly after this time, the detachment may have continued. (This pregnancy resulted in the death of the child from hyaline membrane disease a few days after his birth in August of 1963.) The polar Lunar Eclipse on August 6 at 14 degrees 06 minutes Capricorn continued the theme of emphasis of the Mars/Saturn opposition, amplified by the SA Saturn-Mars in November.

Pluto in the 12th House conjunct the Ascendant provides a clue to a personality which is influenced by the experiences of unfathomable change. This planet, conjunct the Moon's North Node, reached the conjunction of the Node at the end of 1963 by Solar Arc. With the SA motion of Pluto moving closer to the exact conjunction of the Ascendant, we could assume that the entire environment would change due to some major family crisis during the third year. The transit of Uranus over the natal Pluto adds further texture of sudden change to the portrait. The deep disconnection due to the sudden death of the father occurred too soon to be understood and assimilated by a three-year-old child.

Uranus' transit over Pluto and Pluto's transit over the Ascendant continued to bring a series of changes into the life of this child. The unsettled nature of these cycles may have been numbing for such a young child, but certainly had a deep impact upon his psyche. Not only had he lost his father, but his entire life circumstance was detoured and disrupted several times in the months following the tragedy. He had become a casualty in the destruction of America's Camelot.

Secondary Progressions and Early Family Crisis

Since the Secondary Progressed motion of the planets is relatively slow, the most valid timing tools for crises in the early years involve examination of the Secondary Progressed Moon and Sun. The Moon's motion during childhood years keys times of inner evolutionary change and can also signify times of evolving awareness of changes in the external elements of the child's life. Extending the symbology of Sun and Moon to Father and Mother, respectively, the timing of aspects from these progressions to the natal planets and sensitive points frequently illustrates periods of shifts in parental activities.

The Moon by secondary progression moves on the average one degree per month. The child with a slower or faster Moon-speed will experience these shifts later or earlier. In the early years, the Moon symbolizes the experience of attuning to daily habits and the development of response patterns that help to answer the child's needs. When projected into the environment, the Moon always involves a child's sense of the mother. Of crucial importance are the aspects from the Secondary Progressed Moon to the angles, since all the angles are related to parental activity and environmental modifications.

Other indicators of modulations in the child's awareness evolve as the Moon changes signs by progression. Each ingress represents the development of a *different viewpoint*. Once the Moon forms its first square to its natal position by secondary progression (about age 7-1/2), the period of early development reaches a turning point, and the child is ready to step into the world with a stronger sense of inner strength.

The Sun's progressed motion marks consistent development of the self. But the child does not yet fully own the qualities represented by the Sun, and is likely to project these into the environment as Father and everything associated with his activities. When the child is confirmed by the father in positive ways, then this ego identity slowly begins to take shape during the natural cycles of separation and change throughout the developing years ahead. However, it is quite plausible to use the Sun's progressed aspects to determine actions by the father which may precipitate crisis in the family or for the child.

Combining Influences to Manage Family Crisis

Children's lives are often caught up in the drama of their parents' psychological warfare: they are caught in the cross fire. With little power to speak out for themselves, their needs are frequently left to the interpretation of what their parents want for them. In the chart of Baby D, the planetary picture suggests that the need for personal recognition is quite strong: her Scorpio Sun in the 10th House conjunct Pluto and square her Leo Moon in the 7th is illustrative of her feeling of being in the cross fire of differences between Mommy and Daddy. Additionally, the conflict suggested by the square from a final degree of Mars in Pisces to Uranus and Saturn would indicate a great feeling of unsettled energy.

The mother conceived this child long before either she or the father were ready to marry. The parents felt that their relationship was not leading to marriage, and the mother decided to go forward with the pregnancy without planning to marry the father. The father, however, wanted to play an active role in the life of the child and continued to spend a great deal of time planning for his fatherly activities. He promised to help take care of the child's needs and, at the least, be financially supportive. Shortly after the baby's birth, the couple decided to marry. This choice was carried out when Uranus by SA moved into exact conjunction with Saturn in the 12th (about six months, at 5 minutes of arc per month) and when Saturn by transit conjuncted Baby D's Ascendant.

The parental marriage never quite solidified, and within two years the turmoil reached such great proportions that the couple decided to separate. In the interim, the baby had been spending a great deal of time with the paternal grandmother, who had made a place in her home for the child while both parents continued to pursue their educations. Once the parents separated, this arrangement continued, and the baby spent increasingly more time with the grandmother. When the father completed his educational obligations when Baby D was 1-1/2 (SA Uranus reaching the perfected square to Mars), he began to spend more time with his daughter and began to build a career.

At the same time, with Neptune transiting Baby D's Ascendant, her periods of separation from her grandmother became increasingly more difficult. The child began to develop respiratory distress and bronchitis during her time with the mother, and the paternal grandmother spent much of her time attempting to convince the mother to avoid smoking around the baby.

Because of the increased sensitivity to her environment suggested by Neptune reaching the exact conjunction of the ASC, I suggested that the child would be reacting more strongly to everyone's emotional outbursts, although the increased physical sensitivity was also a concern. Grandma was worried that her own increasing attachment to the child would create more problems, but her concern for the emotional and physical well-being of her grandchild was also intensifying her dilemma. Everyone around this child was in some sort of turmoil, and the young child was feeling all of it!

By the end of that year, the parents had decided to file for divorce, and a custody battle began while transiting Jupiter in Leo was square to Baby D's Sun and Pluto. In the temporary support hearing, the judge ruled that the child would spend equal amounts of time with both parents, but the "home" of the child was not parental! The child was shuttled from maternal grandparent to paternal grandparent, never living with either parent. Baby D seemed to show a preference for the paternal grandmother.

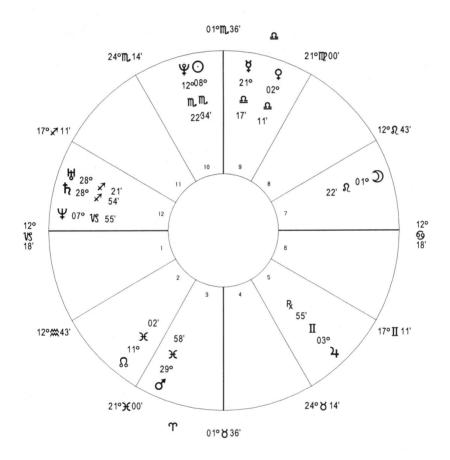

Baby D
Oct. 31, 1988, Chandler, AZ, 11:44 a.m. MST
111W50 33N18

In February of 1991, when Baby D was about 2-1/2, this new arrangement was firmly in place (transiting Uranus conjunct her ASC and Saturn opposing her Moon), and the child continued to experience greater physical symptoms when separated from the paternal grandmother. Baby D's mother was showing stronger hostility toward the father, and continued to raise her financial demands in the divorce, and the father seemed ever stronger in his resolve to gain custody of his daughter.

Meanwhile, what about the child? Although she had been examined by psychologists, physicians and judges, she was still too young to speak about her strongest needs. Her vacillation in her home environment came at a time when she was in deep need of greater stability (while transiting Saturn opposed the Moon and squared the Sun, as well as squaring the MC-IC). The conflict suggested here seemed to cry out for the mother to take a more active, caring role, but it was the paternal grandmother who became the security base for the child. Throughout this period of conflict, there has been some positive support of the child, although her feeling of trust in herself and in her environment may have been undermined by the nature of the conflict. This can be particularly difficult if the child looses contact with the one person who has been consistently present, her paternal grandmother.

The final decision in this case will be made in March of 1992 (after this writing). It is interesting to note that the Secondary Progressed Sun finally moves into the exact conjunction with Pluto in August of 1992, a time when Baby D (and everyone around her) may feel that circumstances are beyond her control. The judge will be deciding her fate and seems, at this time, to be leaning toward joint custody with the home being that of the mother.

I anticipate that the child's needs for a sense of personal empowerment may require closer interaction from the father. If the father disappears during this cycle, the impact could be one of tremendous grief and despair. Hopefully, the power of healing and restoration suggested by this cycle will be balanced by the resolution of conflict between the parents and a mending of the wound suffered by the child during their extended battle.

Child of the Flower Children

Rachel was born while her father was still in medical school. She was the apple of her mother's eye. Rachel was an exuberant, although fretful, baby and was precocious in her development. Several months prior to her birth, her father had begun to experiment with hallucinogenic drugs with his medical school buddies, but the mother was not willing to get involved in drugs because of her fears about their effects on the baby. However, a few months after Rachel's birth, the mother decided to try smoking marijuana, which she continued to use on an irregular basis during parties or other social occasions. The father's use of marijuana and other hallucinogens increased more rapidly. Despite this, the father did well in school and everything at home seemed to be normal to the casual observer.

The mother had left her job a month prior to the baby's birth, but was eager to return to work part time when Rachel was about nine months old. At this time, the Secondary Progressed Moon squared the Midheaven; Mom had gone to work part time, and the parents hired a nanny who stayed with Rachel while Mom was away. Mom began to work full time in August 1972 (transiting Saturn opposing Rachel's Mercury-Jupiter), but the same nanny stayed on to help. By the late summer of 1973, the Secondary Progressed Moon had reached its conjunction with Neptune. Rachel's mother and father were both experimenting with LSD and mescaline, but no incidents of abuse or harm to the child occurred.

What did occur was a gradual undermining of the parental relationship. With transiting Uranus square to Venus, Rachel was beginning to test her mother's patience by refusing to cooperate with the daily schedule. Her beloved nanny decided to retire, and Rachel was moved to a private Montessori day-care center. Her sensitivity to her parents' conflict was further amplified by the SA Saturn in exact opposition to Neptune.

The parents decided to try an "open marriage," but once again, had different ideas about the meaning of the arrangement. The father's idea of openness was to tell his wife that he had been carrying on a long-term affair since they had married six years previously. The mother retaliated by wooing one of the father's friends into a sexual liaison that lasted about a month. The parental marriage continued to disintegrate. The family was in the midst of a major crisis.

The parents decided that a separation might prove beneficial, and had also begun marriage counseling. In addition, the mother was working with a therapist to help her resolve her own internal issues. She noticed that Rachel had begun to react to the stress at home by withdrawing and becoming less responsive toward her mother. Mother initiated a series of bodywork sessions with a nationally respected rolfer who was developing gentle techniques for working with young children. Rachel's response was remarkable, and she began to be more openly expressive about her feelings toward her mother. By the time of the Solar Eclipse at 17 degrees 51 minutes Sagittarius in December 1973, conjoining Rachel's Sagittarian stellium, the parents felt that the marriage was doomed. The parental separation occurred in February 1974, when transiting Jupiter transited the IC and Mars opposed the ASC.

Since Rachel's parents were open to new ideas, they decided to divorce, with Rachel remaining in the home of her father, since mother's income was less substantial (father was to complete medical school in June and take on a commission in the Air Force Medical Corps). Rachel spent afternoons after pre-school with her mother, and stayed with each parent every other weekend.

Father was relocated by the military out of state following medical school, and he and Rachel's mother decided to live together again. Mother left her job, moved in with Rachel's father in July, and the family seemed to be healing its old wounds. However, the father had fallen in love during his previous period of separation, and he could not decide which woman he wanted.

With SA Moon moving to the ASC in Rachel's chart (at about age three), Mother decided she would move into her own apartment nearby. Within two months, she went back to her previous job in another state and reentered school the following fall. Rachel came to stay with her mother for a while during the summer, and it was at this time that the mother worked with Rachel in therapy to help her express her anger and hurt toward her mother for leaving.

This exercise seemed to bring back the strong bond they had always felt and gave Rachel's mother the assurance that the child was not following a tendency to repress her feelings (as is often the case with a 12th House Moon in Scorpio!). Mother, Rachel and the therapist worked from the idea that Rachel needed to avoid the feeling that she was causing all the turmoil in her life, but also wanted to give Rachel a strong sense that she was safe. Rachel's mother encouraged the father to keep Rachel in a creative pre-school program, which he did, giving her plenty of time for socialization and objectification of her needs. Mother and daughter maintained consistent contact via weekly phone calls, letters and numerous visitation periods. Father and his new love married, and Rachel was joined by three new siblings in the late summer of 1975. (SA Uranus sextile the Sun.)

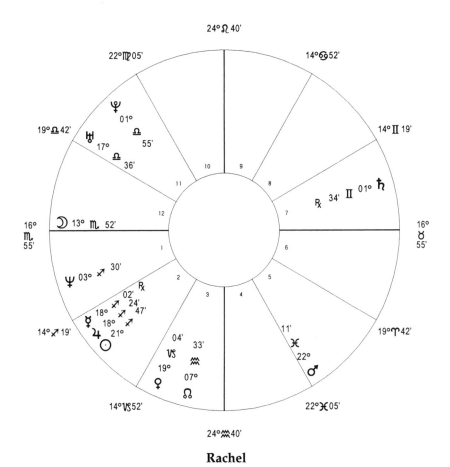

Rachel

With transiting Saturn square the ASC and Mars conjuncting her Sun in December 1976, Rachel's father was under investigation by the military and was soon court-martialed. His new marriage had become a shambles, and his second wife and her children had left him. Rachel's mother traveled to spend the greater part of December with her daughter. Shortly afterward, Rachel's father was sentenced and incarcerated by the military for misappropriation of drugs and behavior that defied military regulations. By late January, with transiting Saturn square her Moon, Rachel had come to live with her mother. In September of 1977, Rachel's mother attempted to file for full custody of her daughter, but received threats from Rachel's paternal grandparents about counter-custody suits if she attempted to proceed. Her mother, still in school and working, did not have the resources for a long legal battle and dropped her custody suit. (By this time, Saturn was transiting over Rachel's MC.)

Rachel continued to live with her mother until the end of the year, at which time her father, now released from military prison and dishonorably discharged, promised to mend his ways and began a new direction in his medical practice. He vowed to help Rachel and her mother stay in close contact.

By May 1978, with transiting Uranus conjunct her Moon, Rachel's father had hired a live-in nanny to help care for Rachel. As "fate" would have it, he fell in love with the nanny. Rachel spent the summer with her mother, and when she returned to her father's home in the fall found a very different situation waiting for her.

While Uranus transited in conjunction with her ASC, Father had decided to move. However, the father's new love did not like his new rural location, and Father did not like the separation from his beloved. He and Rachel moved back to the city in the spring of 1979. During the summer with her mother, transiting Uranus once again conjuncted her ASC. Daddy had decided to marry again. By the fall, with transiting Saturn square her Sun, she had a new stepmother, but also began to feel that she had lost real contact with her father.

Rachel's life did begin to stabilize after this time, and she and her mother have continued to remain close. Rachel lived with her mother during high school, and, and with her mother's gentle persuasion has been open about her feelings of abandonment, despite her "understanding" of the situations that existed. Her feelings toward her stepmother have wavered over the years, and she is just now beginning to deal with her issues with her father. Throughout the tumultuous experiences, Rachel has adapted. However, she does seem wary of commitment in relationships and is working to find some measure of direction for her own life.

Embracing Crisis as an Indicator of Growth

Family crisis arrives in many forms, and can be handled in creative and positive ways to help the family and the individual achieve a stronger sense of personal empowerment. As astrologers, we have superlative information to help guide clients through precarious times and we can use our understanding of the strengths and liabilities of an individual to offer hope and confirmation. Although most individuals seem to deal with family crises years later during their processes of self-discovery as adults, we do often have an opportunity to help objectify a child's situation *at the time of a crisis.* By avoiding prejudicial conclusions and working with the situation as it exists, astrologers can offer a family the insight necessary to minimize disruption and insecurity and maximize the realization of growth.

When analyzing the chart of an adult for early family crisis, we have keys to unlocking the pain, confusion, or doubt of the inner child. Through clarifying the times of crisis, clients can create the images and recall the memories necessary to free themselves of the heavy burdens of guilt, shame, and disappointment that may be inhibiting the fulfillment of needs. It is crucial for us astrologers to operate from a nonjudgmental standpoint, acknowledging the validity of the feelings of the child and avoiding the negative process of blame or other scapegoats.

We may not be able to divert family crisis, but we can utilize these experiences to promote greater stability and positive self-confirmation, rather than allowing them to undermine the integrity of the child. Whether examining these situations retrospectively or currently, we can search for the power that will allow the individual to emerge as a whole person.

Diana Stone

Diana Stone is actively involved in an astrology and counseling practice in Portland, Oregon, plus ongoing lecturing and writing projects. Her book, *The United States Wheel of Destiny*, was published in 1976. A health crisis in the 60s had precipitated her studies in healing, psychology and astrology. In the 70s, she trained as a psychodramatist and did postgraduate studies in Transactional Analysis and Gestalt therapy. A transpersonal crisis in 1980 preceded extensive involvement in shamanic practices, healing rituals and rites of passage. Diana currently specializes in work with teachers and healers coping with the psychophysiological transformation process. She is also an articulate teacher, translating her personal shamanic journeys into an eclectic model of healing and therapy.

Root Causes of
Mental Crisis

Diana Stone

There I was, floating blissfully out of my body. This ultimate peak experience was shattered as the realization exploded into my consciousness that I was dying. I screamed in my earthbound brain, "I have a son to raise. I can't go now!" I skidded back into my body.

I emerged from that personal crisis onto a path new to me but one well worn by ancient travelers. The world's earliest doctors were the shamans and saints who were called by profound crises to reshape their lives around a larger self. The stories of their odysseys through affliction give life to the Wounded Healer archetype. My blind faith in allopathic medicine brought me to the brink of death. This frightening episode precluded all other choices for me except to explore alternative options for healing.

That was twenty-five years ago in the late 60s, and I have continued to cope as best I can with physical, mental, and emotional crises. It has been clear to me for a long time that illness and disease have meaning far different from what I was taught to believe from traditional medical and psychological models. So it is as God's guinea pig that I share with you some of the ways I identify and manage others' mental crises in my astrological practice.

Let me tell you about John. John is a favorite client of mine whom I have known for many years. When John made an appointment out of concern for his youngest son who had just dropped out of college, I thought back to the time when I had first discussed the boy's natal chart with his father. The boy was then about six years old and a delight to everyone. Through the years, I enjoyed hearing about the progress of this exceptional child.

What a different story I heard from John this day: John and his wife had divorced, and the children lived with their mother. Brandon (not his real name) seemed to have fallen apart in his junior year in high school. His once perfect grades had slipped to failing. He hung out with a bad crowd. This latest departure from college was his third because of an apparent inability to apply himself. John was at his wit's end and concluded his story by saying he believed Brandon's troubles stemmed from his mother's reluctance to discipline the boy since the divorce.

I studied Brandon's chart and asked if the personality changes had followed a head injury when Brandon was about fifteen years old. John thought back and, with surprise, recalled just such a sequence of events. The boy had been knocked unconscious in a football game, and the injury was serious enough to require hospitalization. After the following discussion I will point out what I was looking at in the chart that defined the problem for me so quickly.

Brandon's case is typical of many others I have diagnosed from the horoscope. I learned about neurological problems such as Brandon's when I, myself, developed symptoms suggesting an increasingly worsening case of dyslexia. At my worst, I could barely make a telephone call without transposing the numbers. Luckily for me, I discovered Florence Scott when I accompanied a friend of mine to an appointment with her. Florence diagnoses and treats neurological disorders at the Hope and Help Center in Woodburn, Oregon, near Portland where I live at the time of this writing.

After working with Florence for a time and reading the materials she recommended, I was shocked to discover another world, that being the silent world of the brain, injured by accidents, birth trauma, illness and developmental problems.

That world languishes generally undiscovered because neurological dysfunction masquerades as psychological problems. Despite the best efforts of therapy, however, these problems just don't go away.

Brain injury is masked as well by the broad symptom picture that belies a single cause. It is not unusual for one patient to suffer from insomnia, weight gain, memory loss, and lowered body temperature requiring an enormous expenditure of energy to deal with tasks that others perform effortlessly. The uncountable thousands who seemingly recover from injuries may still suffer from subtle intellectual and behavioral effects that seriously impair their ability to work and interact normally with other people, leading experts to label this situation a "silent epidemic."

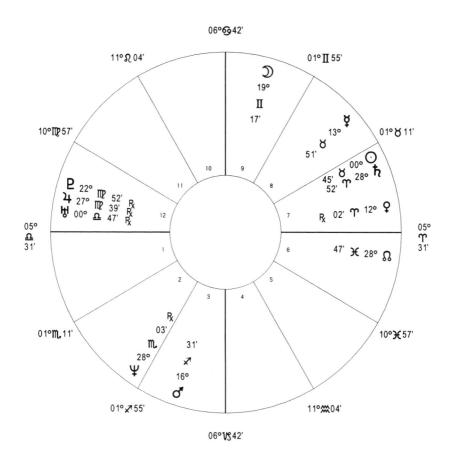

Brandon

I work professionally as an astrologer, but I have had many hours of formal training in psychology and counseling. I ordinarily see several clients for weekly therapy sessions. This turned out to be fortunate, because I could translate my personal experience and knowledge immediately to a clinical environment. Did I ever hit pay dirt!

Despite dedicated work by both myself and certain clients, some problems just did not respond to therapy. Once enlightened about the world of brain dysfunction, I have since referred perhaps two dozen people to the clinic for evaluation and therapy. Not once did I misdiagnose a case. Testing revealed severe neurological disorder in every instance. It was amazing to watch the changes that followed when patients were started on a treatment program. I saw cases of alcoholism, depression, violent rage, and other severe disabilities turned around in a few months! Therapy with these clients progresses rapidly. Better yet, it is possible to differentiate clearly psychological issues from neurological issues.

After working with Florence Scott for several months, I felt I had met a kindred spirit. Her specialized program of physical therapy enjoys about the same acceptance by the medical establishment as astrology does, which is to say it is summarily dismissed. Florence presents papers at international symposia and, when she documents case histories, establishment medicine listens in disbelief. She rehabilitates people who are written off as hopelessly debilitated.

As tempting as it is for me to get carried away in my enthusiasm for this bastard child of traditional neurology, let's look at this from the perspective of the astrologer in practice. Astrologers have the advantage of operating freely outside the confines of the AMA-type models that hamstring most practitioners inside these systems. We can chart *our own* course and need not be intimidated by other professions that enjoy acceptance by the majority. I don't mean there is not a place for everyone. There is. I am simply using my experiences to show that astrologers can solve problems which extend beyond the belief systems of established protocols.

All the clients I have referred to the Hope and Help Clinic would have to be described as utterly despondent. They suffered with their symptoms for many years, often since childhood. Neither traditional medicine nor psychiatry had a clue about how to deal with these patients. Worse yet, they were frequently written off as hysterics, hypochondriacs, or hopelessly incurable. They were fired from jobs, spouses divorced them, and their self-esteem was destroyed. They turned to astrology as a desperate last resort. Yet with proper diagnosis and treatment, these people reclaimed their lives.

There are several other types of dysfunction that I diagnose in addition to the neurological problems already discussed; more about those later. I mention this to make the point that I have ventured my way through new territory enough times now to be able to offer some guidelines to those of you who are willing to tackle some issues normally assumed to be beyond the scope of astrological practice.

Most astrologers who identify a group of people suffering a particular dysfunction would eventually look for some common astrological indicator. I am no exception. I was curious to see if I could find some repeating patterns in the horoscopes of victims of neurological disorders. I discovered an involvement with the signs Gemini and Sagittarius to be present *in every case.*

The Gemini/Sagittarius polarity is frequently seen on the angles in charts where neurological problems are substantiated. In my own chart, Gemini and Sagittarius are on the Midheaven axis, and Mars is in the 7th House. My problems were not from an injury, however. My mother had kept me in a walker as a baby, and I never learned to crawl. Crawling and creeping are developmental stages necessary for proper neurological functioning. My Mars is in Pisces opposing Neptune retrograde.

I have two other cases in my files where there is a rising Neptune and where the clients developed neurological symptoms as an adult. This makes me suspect that a 1st House Neptune indicates some problem in the developmental history, and that problem may well be neurological *if the other indicators are there.* Neptune in the 1st House can also indicate an underdeveloped endocrine system. I have the advantage of working with my doctor-husband. I send my clients to him for the confirming diagnoses, and my cases of endocrine disorders number in the hundreds. This is why I say Neptune rising cannot be depended on by itself to indicate neurological symptoms; there should be other corroborating testimony in the chart along with it.

The most damaged person I have encountered to date is an elderly woman in whose chart Gemini is on the Midheaven with the Sun in Gemini and the Moon in Sagittarius forming an exact opposition in angular Houses.

We know that the majority of neurological problems are the result of a head injury. Not surprisingly, these are charts where Mars is a strong indicator. Look for an angular Mars, particularly in the 1st House. The chart of a male client has Gemini and Sagittarius again on the Midheaven axis. Mars is in a critical degree, zero degrees Cancer, in the 4th House.

I like to use Solar Arc directions because it is easier to eyeball the chart for clues when an accident may have happened. This is how I interpreted Brandon's chart, the boy I mentioned earlier and whose chart is reproduced on page 85. This is a classic: Gemini and Sagittarius are heavily emphasized by the Moon opposing Mars within that axis. Not only that, the opposition occurs in the 3rd and 9th Houses, the natural houses of Gemini and Sagittarius. The timing is indicated by Uranus in a critical degree, zero degrees Libra. By Solar Arc direction, the aspect between Mars and Uranus should activate at about fifteen years of age, the difference in degrees between the two planets [i.e., advancing Mars to square with Uranus–Ed.]. Brandon was born in 1969 and his father said the football injury occurred in 1984 or 1985. Uranus retrograde and in the 12th House describes the close call, the hospitalization, and the long delay in diagnosing the hidden cause; Mars describes the impact of the injury; both planets corroborate physical contact in sports, with Uranus ruling the 5th.

One of my favorite cases involved a couple who were acquaintances of mine. The wife is an astrologer and, over a couple of years time, she complained bitterly about her marriage. She eventually issued her husband an ultimatum: get help or get out. He came to see me as a client. As he described his marital difficulties, I recognized the typical confusion of many brain-injured persons who really do not understand what is happening to them.

I asked if he had suffered head injuries. He described several motorcycle accidents! I personally had to haul this man over to the clinic to be tested. He was suffering severe problems. A personal therapy program was designed for him—it makes me wonder how many divorces issue from undiagnosed brain injury. Believe me, these people really do appear to have psychological problems. In fact, the couple I just mentioned had been in therapy together and, not surprisingly, the husband was completely unresponsive.

It is always gratifying to help somebody, but even more so when you can help a loved one. At the time I write this, my brother, Duane, has been living with me for six months. He suffered a severe mental breakdown while living in a different city. Most of his life, he has been a successful corporate executive with a six-figure income. For the past five years, though, from all outward appearances, Duane's life has fallen apart. I suspected he was manic-depressive, and a psychiatrist here in my city confirmed the diagnosis. He prescribed Lithium, commonly used in treatment of this disorder. The drug brought the bipolar mood swings under control quickly. In this emergency, I was very thankful for that.

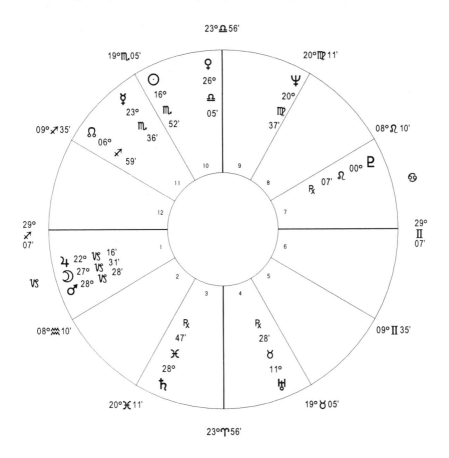

Duane

For most people, I am convinced that that would be the end of the story. Since Duane is living with me, I, of course, had been observing him closely day by day. As I did, I came to realize there were other serious symptoms *not* associated with the manic-depressive pattern. Based on the information I have given you, look at Duane's chart and guess what I decided about his situation.

There are Sagittarius and Gemini on the horizon! And, not only do we see a 1st House Mars, but it really packs a punch when conjoined with the Moon and Jupiter. That 1st House stellium is under stress in the chart. It's in square aspect with Venus and opposed to Pluto, all in dynamic angular houses. The transiting position of Saturn had activated the T-cross when it traversed the latter degrees of Capricorn and the early degress of Aquarius. Further stress came from transiting Pluto simultaneously crossing his Scorpio Sun! I'm sure you know what my conclusion was. I took my brother to see Florence Scott for a neurological evaluation. He would really be prone to head injuries with that 1st House Mars, wouldn't he?

As children growing up on a farm in Iowa, my father finally relented after endless pestering and bought us a horse. He refused to help us break the spirited animal, so the horse and we rapidly discovered what each other was made of. My brother was thrown from the horse and knocked unconscious as I watched in horror— on three different occasions! I escaped the same fate because I was more cautious, bespeaking my Mars in Pisces.

A footnote to the manic-depressive patterns: in earlier research, I concluded that this problem was part of the Gemini/ Sagittarius polarity as well. I pay particular attention to a stressed Jupiter. Duane has the signature for both the bi-polar swings and the head injury. It was not much of a leap to speculate whether one caused the other. Florence Scott is quick to say she regards this and many other psychiatric disorders as having originated with head injuries or other traumas that have had a neurological impact. My hope is that, after completing his physical therapy, my brother's problems will be healed at a fundamental level and he may someday discontinue medication.

It is too early to report on Duane's case, but Florence has similar cases in her files where complete healing occurred. I am confident that this time it will be no different. Recently, I was reading a report in one of my husband's current medical journals (he's a holistic doctor) that researchers have discovered no difference between Alzheimer's Disease and what was known as Senile Dementia. The suspected cause is *head injury*, setting off the terrible sequence leading to the typical horribly disabling symptoms.

Of course, not every chart with an emphasis on Gemini and Sagittarius or a distressed Mars indicates a neurological problem. So, how is it possible to tell whether it does or whether it doesn't? There is no way to tell for sure *from the chart alone,* and that is why I caution against rigid interpretations. Some knowledge and experience of any subject, not just neurological problems, is in order before one can then pick up the additional clues from the client and the chart for confirmation. Medical astrologers, for instance, do not speak totally out of context of some knowledge of the body and what makes it tick or get sick.

Transformation of Consciousness

Another sort of crisis that can be extremely disruptive involves a rebirth process or transformation of some kind. For centuries, information about the transformation of consciousness was sketchy at best, existing only as veiled references in ancient texts, and those were mostly in the East. The world has changed dramatically since I began my astrological studies and practice in the 60s, but nothing has been more revolutionary than the exploding interest in consciousness. The most shocking development of all, however, was that the fabled transformation of consciousness happened *to me.* Its mysteries were reinterpreted into the context of contemporary Western consciousness as I worked along with others in the crucible of my counseling room.

Transformation of consciousness is a contender for the granddaddy of mental crises. Somehow the glorious accounts of spiritual geniuses and their enlightened lives paled against the harsh day-in and day-out realities of coping with this strange malady. The year transformation hit bottom for me was 1982. I was in terrible shape. What still astounds me is that nearly all the clients I saw that year were wandering in the underworld of transformation as well. It proved to me that counselors attract clients who are facing similar situations in their own lives.

I could sense when a client was experiencing this extraordinary state. There was a surprising similarity in the way it was experienced: a sense that one's life is totally coming apart. Unfortunately, that is all too often literally true. It is terribly difficult to cope with the outer life coming down around your ears, when the inner life is completely disorganized. There is an awful sense of disorientation and loss of identity. I yearned for a year's respite in the "Home for the Transformationally Disabled!"

Don't for a moment believe this to be just another variety of psychological problem. Transformation is in a class by itself. For that matter, some typical treatments for psychological problems can seriously jeopardize a case of transformation-related complications. Particularly destructive are some of the medications prescribed for psychiatric ailments.

Transformation is a process of spiritual rebirth. From Yoga, we have borrowed the word *kundalini* to describe this process, particularly the aspect of a life force unfolding through the body's Chakra system. It involves altered states and perhaps psychic openings, but it is not simply that. I have observed this phenomenon to last from a few months to years, sometimes many years, passing from one stage to another.

Someone undergoing transformation has experiences far removed from normal life. Yet, close observation of these individuals definitely precludes a diagnosis of psychosis. In most of the cases with which I have had direct contact, the persons were previously involved with intense growth experiences or spiritual disciplines. The most remarkable feature of these cases to me is that, despite the great difficulty in coping with rebirth, all the people have some sense that they are embarked on a meaningful spiritual adventure.

There is now a growing body of evidence to support the idea that transformation and rebirth are valid experiences despite the skepticism of prevailing psychiatric models. Dr. Lee Sannella, in his book, *Kundalini—Psychosis or Transcendence?*, has collected case histories and attempted to classify symptoms. Dr. Sannella raises an issue in which clinicians are most interested: how to make the diagnosis. Despite our added advantage of information from the horoscope, astrologers would do well to consider his comments carefully.

Dr. Sannella says that this is a situation where "it takes one to know one." A person who has experienced a spiritual awakening can intuitively sense the state in another. In a few cases where patients were admitted to a mental institution suffering psychotic symptoms, these people knew who among them were "really crazy" and those who were not. They reported that others in the institution population made the distinction as well. Dr. Sannella goes on to say that clinicians themselves have a finely tuned sense of what is psychotic and frankly states that this "smell" of psychosis is primarily how diagnoses are determined. This is a startling statement if one perceives psychiatric diagnosis as an exact science!

I hope this point is well taken by astrologers. As far as my experience is concerned, that certain click in the gut is the essential catalyst. Yet, as potent as it is for the intuitive sense to "recognize" root causes, I do not mean that this sixth sense comes only when individuals have personally experienced identical problems. I have given workshops about these subjects for astrologers who have experienced neither neurological problems nor transformation. As often as not, I hear from a few students who have undertaken to educate themselves further and network with other appropriate healers. Interestingly enough, these people report that they, too, develop an instinct for sniffing out these same problems—not wanting to belabor this point, I do want to dispel the belief that diagnosis can be made for certain *from the chart alone.* It takes a combination of the astrologer's experience, knowledge, intuitive sense, and then the very considerable power of the horoscope itself.

After repeated descriptions from clients experiencing the dark night of the soul, trips into the underworld, and rebirth sequences, it is not hard to imagine that the crises of transformation are associated with the mythology of Scorpio and its ruling planet, Pluto. I have worked with Chiron for several years now and am convinced that powerful transpersonal crises are associated with the symbolism of that body as well.

Transformation is promised in the natal horoscope when there is a strong accent on these astrological indicators. Look for Scorpio on the Ascendant, Pluto in the 1st House, the Sun or Moon in conjunction aspect with Pluto or in the sign Scorpio. The same is true for Chiron—whenever a client experiences disturbance of this sort, Pluto is likely to be very active and intense in its transit cycle when the trouble begins. It can also be indicated when difficult transits from other planets are made to Pluto or planets in Scorpio.

Once a crisis is diagnosed as a transformation, an effective strategy is to explain to the client what it is and especially what is isn't, i.e., a hopeless psychological breakdown. Ordinarily, I describe the death, transformation, rebirth sequence. The initial stage, death, requires of the client a tremendous letting go in the life. Ordinarily this is very painful and difficult. Themes of loss run rampant through the life. Many things highly valued may be snatched away: career, money, marriage, health. There sometimes is an actual death in the family or circle, but not necessarily so. Inner emotional patterns may call for changes beyond what the client feels is his or her capacity to handle. Then follows a time of extreme disorientation. The rebirth stage feels very fragile, often requiring an uncharacteristically reclusive lifestyle for a time.

Experience suggests utilizing support, strength, and understanding as the best approach. I have repeatedly been given strong positive responses from clients when I asked them to accept their symptoms as part of a powerful and *ultimately positive* process. Because of my own confidence and acceptance of the condition, the client is soon able to accept it as well—you need to remember that these people are overwhelmed by an experience about which they have no understanding. The stress is compounded when there is strong negative feedback from those around them. This I ordinarily expect. Helping someone to understand the process as therapeutic and not pathological may be the most valuable help we can give.

A classic case involved JoAnne, a client of mine whom I had seen a few times for routine consultations about family matters. Now, the woman was describing the kind of painful picture I have come to expect from a transformational crisis. What gave me a reason to suspect that's what it was? It is not possible to describe exactly how the knowing comes together, but it is not completely mysterious either.

First, she had been in crisis for a long time, a couple of years. Also, she herself is a therapist, knows her way around the psyche, and is experienced at working through such emergencies. Indeed, she had been working very hard to bring herself out of it. Also, she had done some very creative work earlier in her life. That is usually true, too. One of the most revealing clues, though, was her steady involvement in spiritual studies and practices preceding her crisis.

There was another element running through the client's troublesome symptoms. When I confronted her with it, she readily acknowledged it. I asked whether underneath all the turmoil she sensed a powerful spiritual movement of great significance. Nearly all my clients undergoing rebirth get in touch with a certain ecstatic sense of purposefulness even in the darkest of times. I pointed out to her that she had been working on her growth process for many years and embraced her spiritual path with total dedication. It made no sense that this could be a psychological breakdown. The pattern simply did not fit. What did fit was the transformational emergency state often resulting from a journey such as hers.

My confidence in diagnosing any pattern, after the other criteria have been satisfied, rests ultimately on the confirming testimony in the horoscope. I don't want to imply that the "smell" of a pattern, however powerful it is, is enough for me when there is astrological evidence available. Even when the natal patterns of particular problems are not known, the astrological cycles are invaluable by themselves. Any powerful configuration activated by Pluto in the case of transformation can be trusted if the other evidence in the life concurs. Spiritual rebirth is so comprehensive and complex I don't pretend to know how to recognize its potential in every case. I do know that, if I didn't have astrology as a guide, I would feel terribly handicapped in my work with people.

I would like to share one more incident that happened in this case with JoAnne. Before she talked to me, the woman had written a letter desperately seeking guidance from a well-known author of metaphysical books. I read the letter she had received in return. It was most patronizing and insulting. The letter implied that the woman wanted to be sick somehow, and if she really wished to get well, she would. Even if that were true, there are certainly more helpful ways to handle the situation. Some aphorisms were suggested that in the face of this woman's situation fell far short of the sort of help she needed. I found the author's reply grossly inappropriate in light of my client's original letter, which was extremely articulate. This author writes extensively on the subject of transformation, and while I can understand her hesitancy to make a definite diagnosis from a letter, I would at least expect her to suggest more practical and encouraging possibilities.

My client was devastated by the letter, although I am sure the author's comments were unintentionally negative. Does this sound like a cautionary note about *our* responsibilities when people are in crisis? There are many root causes for life's assortment of ills. It is imperative to avoid a too reckless or casual attitude when the welfare of a client is so critical.

It is clear that transformation is a complex subject, far exceeding the space here to cover completely. Yet, as spiritual disciplines increase in popularity in the West, transpersonal crises are sure to escalate along with these practices. If you want to learn more about this, the time and energy will likely be well worth your efforts. More and more people will need your help desperately. There is no better source of information on this subject than the Institute of Transpersonal Psychology, established by Dr. Stanislav Grof and his wife, Christina. There are a newsletter, seminars, books and even a doctoral program. Write to the Spiritual Emergence Network, 250 Oak Grove Avenue, Menlo Park, CA 94025. Don't be put off, much of the information is written for the layman. Astrologers should have no trouble with it.

Psychic Experiences

One of the problems an astrologer is likely to hear about from clients, that other professionals don't, relates to psychic experiences. I assume that, if you are an astrologer, you are involved in something pretty weird yourself. Many clients have come to me in extreme agitation because of personal psychic episodes such as flashes of insight that *turned out to be true*. Even more disturbing is that the precognition generally involves events of a violent or tragic nature—if you haven't already discovered that casual assurances about this matter fall on deaf ears, you soon will. People in crisis about their psychic nature should be taken very seriously, even if the astrologer relates to the subject in perfect comfort.

As I write this, visions of Barbara dance in my head. She is a client of mine with whom I shared more than one hysterical session over just this issue. Surprisingly, these took longer to resolve than some of the more spectacular cases. Here is an opportunity to compare this client to JoAnne, exposing the startling difference in managing situations such as Barbara's where there is not the same access to an underlying spiritual transformation.

There is a happy ending for Barbara. Her psychic abilities no longer terrorize her. As a matter of fact, she works with doctors identifying physical illnesses that otherwise have confounded traditional diagnoses. Isn't that a perfect expression for her horoscope patterns: the Moon conjoined with Neptune in Virgo in the 12th House opposing Mars, a singleton in Pisces in the 6th House?

Let's remind ourselves that Western culture does not suffer psychic openings gladly. Adding the negative reaction of individual families, just the right environment is then created to convince psychic individuals they are evil, crazy, sacrilegious, possessed, or too different from others to be accepted in society! Calm reassurance from the astrologer is a good beginning step in bringing this situation under control. Clients tell me my unruffled response was their first positive experience with anyone with whom they shared this problem.

Avoidance is never a good strategy and it certainly doesn't work to repress psychic material. It just makes matters worse. This is why so many people pick up on violence and tragedy only. They are trying so hard to turn off their psychic function that only powerful calamities can get through. If this issue is handled properly, the nature of the psychic material changes dramatically to more helpful everyday information. The occasional catastrophe can be seen as a useful warning system and does not loom so large.

What about the client with religious messages mixed in with their psychic faculty? Some people believe psychic abilities are the handiwork of the devil. It's a sticky issue, but I have succeeded with it by tackling it head on: I simply say that psychic function is natural to everyone. It is here to stay, and they are going to have to deal with it, whatever it takes. I don't think anyone wants to believe they are taken over by demons. I encourage you not to be put off when the client tells you there is a religious issue involved. Treat it as a counseling situation rather than walking on eggshells around a sacred cow.

Probably little needs to be said about spotting the psychic patterns in the horoscope. This belongs to the world of the water signs, pure and simple. The majority of the work in managing psychic opening usually involves unraveling the messages from parents, however, rather than simply determining from the chart if the person is psychic. Those messages must be ferreted out and worked through if this problem is ever to be resolved.

The astrological chart is an invaluable aid. Here are some examples: if the Moon is in the 9th House, this can indicate the parent who supposedly speaks for God. This is ordinarily some sort of power play used to manipulate the child. The same is indicated when the ruler of the Ascendant is in the 9th House, increasingly so if the planet is Neptune or Jupiter. I rely most heavily on the Ascendant sign and 1st House to give me information about what might have been going on in the client's early life.

Gemini rising in the psychic person's chart seems to be particularly troublesome. This sometimes describes an overly intellectual family absolutely intolerant of a psychic child. These are the clients who end up believing they are crazy. Because of my involvement in psychic work, my sister-in-law has believed me crazy for years. Her horoscope has a Leo ascendant with the Sun in a stellium in Virgo. For her, *anything* to do with the right brain is suspect. The strong Mercurial emphasis in charts like hers definitely mitigates against the intuitive.

If the astrologer can skillfully show the client what the parents' messages were, it becomes obvious that these messages are more problematic than the actual psychic outbreaks that have become fearsome. In one of my cases, a woman told me of her many psychic intuitions as though she were revealing some unspeakable sin. I pointed out that the underlying problem was actually a message from her parents saying psychic abilities were proof of evil demons attracted by her so-called transgressions. I shuddered when she told me about the relationship with her husband: he is a minister who is probably crazy himself; he found out about her psychic abilities and routinely punishes her by forcing her to stand naked in a very hot shower while he scrubs her with a steel brush and bleach.

Obviously, a very powerful part of this woman's psyche still believes herself to be cursed by demons— deservedly so. It is no surprise that the abusive husband was attracted into her life, probably in hope of redemption or rescue. If something is true, you will see the thread of it repeating all through life. Put all the pieces of the puzzle together and click!—a nice, neat story comes into focus, in which everything makes sense. Your client may be suffering because of it, but pleasure or pain is not the determining criterion when trying to figure out what is *really* happening.

When I work with clients who have a strong psychic sense, not necessarily just those who are having problems, I am frequently asked how to develop this extrasensory ability. This is a tough question. Everyone has his or her own specific gifts and is seldom psychic across-the-board, so to speak. Classes and teachers are hard to find. A prevalence of psychic training that is inept or even dangerous obscures the picture even further. Portland is fortunate to have a Silva Method class available for people who need a tried and true and safe place to get started. Perhaps this experiential seminar is available near you. If not, a little sleuthing in your community or metaphysical book store may yield enough information to help clients take the next step.

Now about Possession

After seeing how Hollywood has treated the subject of possession, it makes me wish there were some other word for it. I am talking about possession as when a person is "taken over" by an entity on the other side of the veil, not as in "possession is nine points of the law." I have worked with this phenomenon for many years. I ordinarily by-pass arguments about whether possession really exists or not. I can't prove it one way or the other. I only know from experience that when certain cases are recognized and treated as possession, *dramatic and sudden recovery occurs where all other options have failed.*

I will get to some of the ways astrology figures in with this, but first I want to provide some background on a subject that is so poorly understood. There appear to be degrees of possession. When there is total possession, it is a case of multiple personality. Ordinarily, though, the primary personality is not completely overwhelmed. That kind of possession might better be described as a strong influence from outside the person. However, when it comes to possession, a little bit goes a long way. People who suffer this strange affliction normally see their lives reduced to a shambles. Battling this phantom adversary may be the single most overriding constant every day of their lives. Whatever success or progress might be achieved is very hard won.

I have performed many routine exorcisms (I cringe at the word, but I guess I'm stuck with it). My friends like to tease me about performing "routine exorcisms." Nonetheless, there is more mileage to be gotten from routine exorcisms than any other therapy I know. Unimaginable anguish is sometimes relieved in twenty minutes or so. At the risk of oversimplifying this, the treatment is basically energy work in an individual's energy field. The Catholic church retains its exorcism rituals to this day. I understand that its methods are quite a lot more involved than what I generally do, but when you charge clients by the hour you learn to work fast!

So what, you might ask, are non-routine exorcisms? What I am referring to are the multiple personality cases. I have worked with two full-blown multiple personality cases. One woman, Doris, had five personalities. Some knew about the others, but Doris was not aware of *any* of the others. I occasionally received late night phone calls from one of the other personalities, tattling on Doris. However amusing some of the incidents were (we both laughed at them), Doris suffered terribly in her life. She was a recovering alcoholic and drug addict when I met her at age fifty-two. She had been in and out of mental hospitals and all kinds of therapies, none of which brought relief or peace of mind.

Because of my work with exorcism, I am, of course, more aware of what some of the horoscope patterns could be indicating. The Sun in Doris' chart is in the 12th House pressured by an exact square aspect from Saturn in the 4th House. I approach a 12th House Sun as ego and identity issues. I seldom confront my clients outright about meanings because I believe it is not possible to know for sure without some judicious questioning. I could describe my counseling style as knowing what questions to ask.

Normally the problems with a 12th House Sun will fall more in the range of "putting one's light under a bushel basket." With Doris, however, the ego and identity were challenged by a constant threat to their existence. I never actually mentioned possession when Doris came to me for that first consultation. Because of the questions I asked, something stirred her at a deep level, and she entered weekly therapy with me.

My strategy in these cases is not to disturb the possession at first. Multiple personality people have difficult and entrenched secondary psychological problems as a result of the possession. Also, I have found that possessions do not just happen at random. There is a reason the door is ever opened in the first place. In the majority of cases, the situation comes from severe abuse in early childhood. More recently, drug abuse is the culprit. Whatever the reasons, those basic issues must be worked through first.

If not, the exorcism can be successfully performed on a short term basis only. If the other layers are not dealt with, the possession returns again and again, each time weakening the personality further.

From this perspective of working through the layers of psychological issues, the chart is utilized in the same way any practitioner is normally used to doing it in his or her practice. After bringing the other personalities under control, and working through psychological patterns for a year, I was ready to confront Doris about the possession. I rarely go ahead and eliminate the possession without first discussing it with my client. It is not my favorite thing to do, as you can imagine. Yet I am always shocked by the client's reaction: in every case I have ever worked on, the "other" person always tells me he or she had really known what the problem was all along. I think they really did, but dared not admit it even to themselves. In fact, victims of this terrible affliction are enormously relieved that I have discovered it and, of course, are even more relieved when I do something about it.

In Doris' case, the exorcism took about half an hour and involved an inner psychic process I have evolved over the years. "It" physically attacked me, but she was easily subdued and I don't mean to imply I was in any real danger.

The most incredible consequence of the exorcism was that Doris appeared instantly to lose about twenty pounds. It was amazing! When she went to her next AA meeting, everyone there who knew her were dumbfounded to see how much weight she had lost. Yet, the scales indicated *no* weight loss. I think this demonstrated that other people subjectively sensed the influence of the possession when they interacted with Doris. The idea of possession, however, was a foreign concept or, even more likely, an unacceptable one to them. The conscious mind attaches the subjective awareness to something else more in line with the conscious belief system. This happens all the time. Consequently, when the possession was eliminated, the reality was that Doris had "lost weight." Doris went through about six weeks of extreme confusion and disorientation. This is typical when the case is as extreme as this one.

Mark, my other multiple personality, was handled similarly. It was again about a year before the possession issue could be confronted. Mark instantly acknowledged his agreement with my diagnosis. Mark had been periodically debilitated by allergies as we worked together. I referred him to a naturopath, and the doctor ordered extensive tests. Shortly after the test results came in, I did the exorcism. Suddenly Mark's physical condition completely changed. The tests were readministered. The results were all different, and there was no sign of allergy ever after that. Also, some of his personalities smoked, but Mark as the primary personality never did. The doctor was certainly mystified by that case. He said the incident with Mark was like working with two completely different people.

I am happy to say that Mark and Doris have remained stable for many years now. Doris retired from her career as a teacher and enjoys extensive driving trips all over the United States. Mark, now in his thirties, has his own business and enjoys a successful live-in relationship.

As for the possession cases, I first encountered material on the subject in the Huna literature. Huna was a system practiced by ancient kahunas in the Polynesian islands. Very few authentic kahunas remain today and those who do work underground. [Most people are unaware of this, but Jose Silva who developed the Silva Method was a long time student of Huna. I recognized the Huna principles the first time I went though the Silva course.]

Max Freedom Long retrieved part of the ancient system and has written about it in several books. The most popular of his books cover the basics; *The Secret Science Behind Miracles* and the second book, *The Secret Science at Work*. More contemporary literature on this subject is M. Scott's Peck's excellent work *People of the Lie*. I have referred the latter to many of my clients. It is not generally understood that possession comes not only from disembodied entities but from people very much in the flesh. Peck's book powerfully exposes the reality that there can exist among our close relationships malignant influences beyond our abilities to cope without special understanding and help.

Don't get the idea I am encouraging all astrologers to deal with this issue without knowing for sure what they are doing. The material here on possession is included to extend awareness *beyond* the existing narrow limits as to the many underlying causes for mental problems, and to dispel the notion that every condition is a psychological problem appropriately treated by conventional therapies. I am not a degreed or licensed therapist.

Yet, I have developed techniques to deal with exceptionally serious crises which are beyond the ability of most professionals either to recognize or treat successfully.

For those who strike out and explore non-traditional ideas responsibly, I support their efforts with confidence. What I do is not magic. I have simply come to realize over the years that many clients consult the astrologer as a last desperate cry for help. I figure I have nothing to lose. I simply have not allowed my belief system to diffuse my compassion for people who suffer so terribly and who may well have no place else to go.

Past Life Awareness

Now I will tell you about a client of mine who died a horrible death by suffocation as she lay pinned beneath the rafters of a burning building. This story has a bizarre twist to it in that *I discussed the tragedy with the victim herself!* No, she is not a ghost. The untimely death occurred in a past life. I came by this past life information psychically as I investigated the reason for a debilitating claustrophobia in the young woman's present life as Paula. I can do psychic work myself if it seems appropriate to examine past lives for my clients. After that one consultation, the claustrophobia for which Paula came to me for help was gone.

Paula's case is not singled out for its extraordinary fast and obvious results. There are many other instances in which the retrieval of past life trauma has suddenly released a layer of energy in the memory banks. There is another client, Penny, who, when I first met her, was inexplicably terrified of being cold. She locked herself out of her house once and so feared getting cold, she became hysterical. The neighbors heard her screams and called an ambulance. I looked at this problem psychically and connected with a past life in which she had frozen to death. The moment I saw the reason for her fear, and before I could even say a word, Penny let out a scream. Her whole body shuddered. She looked at me wide-eyed and said, "I am not afraid of the cold anymore!" That was many years ago and the only concession she makes to her old fears is an insistence on being cremated when she dies.

Only in certain instances do problems give way so rapidly to past life therapy. These are situations in which the past life memory is not interwoven with a more complex psychological pattern. Any competent psychic or regression analyst can handle this sort of situation. Now I will address some other issues related to past lives which are not so simple and straightforward. These cases require special handling.

Let me begin by identifying some different ways past life material is retrieved in the first place. Under certain circumstances, clients themselves may spontaneously recall earlier lives. A hypnotherapist can regress individuals and lead them in an altered state through past life recall. A third alternative is for a psychic to read the past lives and recount them to the client as I described earlier.

To make the comparisons, I will refer to a case in which one client experienced spontaneous recall, regression under hypnosis, *and also* a consultation with me. My first contact with this person, Sandra, was through her very agitated phone call to me. She was referred by a regular client; one for whom I have done some psychical past life work. Sandra's spontaneous recall had not been a comfortable experience for her, to say the least. Apparently she was thoroughly confused and overwhelmed for quite some time before she called me.

Specifically, Sandra explained how an overpowering awareness had engulfed her consciousness, precipitating a "memory" of her life as Billy the Kid. Questions came tumbling from the phone one after the other so fast that I could hardly get a word in. Her reaction is familiar to me and typical of people who have spontaneous recall. Their first concern is often not the recalled material, but rather, "What is happening to me?"

The first step in treating a client in the midst of this sort of crisis, is calm reassurance. Sandra shared this story with family and friends, and their uninformed reactions were compounding the problem. This is ordinarily the course such cases take at first.

Sandra was obsessed with knowing whether or not she really had been Billy the Kid in a past life. She wanted to be regressed. I referred her to a skilled hypnotherapist—I regret that decision now. If I had it to do over again, I would have pressed for her to come in for a consultation with me at the outset, which is what eventually happened anyway.

As it turned out, the regression left her as unrequited as a bride left at the altar. By the time I finally saw her in person, it was evident that she had been a very busy lady indeed. She had located an organization which apparently devotes itself to the study of Billy the Kid. Not only that, she had signed up for a tour throughout the Southwest to visit sites significant to Billy's life, his birthplace and other places.

It isn't that the regression did not confirm her past life memory. In her mind, I think it did. However, it did not remove her obsession with this matter nor restore peace of mind. The reason it didn't is because the psychic material knocking at the door of her awareness was not being processed properly. The material itself was simply being identified over and over again. The mystery really was why Billy the Kid was intruding on this woman's consciousness—it is cases like this which challenge our detective skills and are the most gratifying ones to crack.

When Sandra came for her consultation with me, I was not interested in simply looking at this past life. Therein lies the trap in this matter of past lives: *it doesn't make any difference if a past life is really a past life or not.* It is easy to buy into the client's urgency about "proving" it one way or the other, but a past life memory from the counselor's perspective is *just another way the psyche presents something with which it wants to deal.* If it presents it as a past life, accept it at face value and get on with it.

Look at the content of the story the client reports. Identify the main theme. The main theme in Sandra's story is fairly obvious to anyone with some experience handling symbolism. Billy is famous as an outlaw. I asked myself why the psyche wanted this woman to access the outlaw pattern. I got to the bottom of it with one question, "Have you lived under too much control from others?" *That was the story of her life!* There was a tyrant father, a strict Catholic parochial schooling, and a controlling husband. Now we could get on to the real issue in her life and process the experience. It was time to "break the law" laid down by dictatorial others in her life.

Sandra asked me whether she should pursue her avid interest in Billy and go ahead with her tour. She was having so much fun with it that I saw no reason to discourage her from accessing the energy in this way, just as long as she worked through the real issues it exposed in her life. I will never know for sure if Sandra was once Billy the Kid, but I can tell you one thing, I will never challenge her to a shoot-out. She accompanied a friend to a target shooting lesson, picked up a gun for the first time and shocked on-lookers with her natural ability as a sharpshooter.

Once the patterns coming from the unconscious are recognized, the next step is to find the corresponding symbolism in the chart. Sandra's horoscope revealed the patterns of control we would expect from heavy Capricorn and Saturn emphases. Comparing any psychic information about past lives with the horoscope is always of special interest to me as an astrologer. The stories of the past lives are not confined to just one House, the 12th House for instance. Whoever we have been determines who we are now and who we are now is represented by the *whole* chart.

I trust that a client's spontaneous recall of a past life signals the next step in the process of personal growth. I do not trust the information to be as useful when it comes from regression. That is not to say there isn't something to be gained from personally reliving a past life. Too often people only access the past lives with the highest energy levels, the ones in which there is unusual violence and tragedy. It is similar to the problem I mentioned about psychic opening. The inexperienced person may not always bring forth the most significant material, being drawn instead to the most sensational. The real drawback in the case of regressions may be that the past life material is simply recalled and not *processed* in relation to the significant psychological patterns of the client.

I realize that most astrologers are not psychic as well. This need not necessarily rule out working with someone who is, however. There are some dependable psychics who might be interested in exploring past life therapy in partnership with the astrologer. Even though I am capable of doing it all myself, there is another psychic with whom I work sometimes. In complicated cases, we do some powerful work together.

Unresolved Psychological Problems

Let's move on to more familiar territory and examine crises that are primarily involved with unresolved psychological problems; ones in which conventional therapies *are* in order. It is important to recognize that there may be several lanes of "traffic" to cross before a particular difficulty is reached. At any given time, traditional therapy is the treatment of choice. At other times, though, some of the earlier issues I have addressed can suddenly burst upon the scene.

In my brother's case, you will recall that a psychiatric diagnosis of manic-depression existed along with neurological problems. Duane was/is also in the midst of spiritual emergency. Several years ago, he experienced a sudden psychic opening. Luckily, I was able to explain what was happening and guide him along. It was soon apparent to me that Duane was taking the swan dive into full-blown transformation of consciousness. His journey has been very difficult, but also powerful. In the past few years, my brother has developed into a brilliant psychic and healer and, in many other ways, there is evidence of a transformation in progress.

At one point, it was necessary to retrieve some absolutely critical past-life information. So, my brother's problems certainly reveal the complexities that can be involved in just one case. It is also clear in his case that there is a tremendous advantage in knowing alternative therapies and working with suitable treatments.

The horoscope is a gold mine of information when it comes to dealing with psychological patterns. Astrologers routinely interpret the natal chart in terms of the client's psychology. This is a revolutionary change from the event-centered model used until relatively recently. For example, Saturn used to be interpreted primarily as limitation in outer life affairs and regarded as malefic. The holistic astrologers now speak more to the processes involved with issues of authority figures, emotional inhibition, and feeling over-responsible. Such issues are presented as things to be resolved within the context of commitment to an on-going personal development and not fated patterns that can never be changed.

Neurological problems, transformation, psychic opening, possession and the like aside, nearly all consultations with a client begin on the level of the client's psychology. This is true whether the course of treatment eventually includes other exotic problems or not. Yes, it would be helpful if every counselor developed the expertise and instincts to diagnose a wider range of problems. Yet, if this isn't coupled with a) mastery of horoscope interpretation, b) the ability to translate those interpretations to a client's psychological patterns and behaviors and, c) clear communication that the client understands, it all falls down like a house of cards.

I will tell you why this is true and share with you my suggested step-by-step procedure; but first I will tell you why everything collapses without a foundation of skill in working with the client's psychological patterns. It is because no matter what the problem is, the reality of dealing with it will come down to a stepwise psychological *working through* the unresolved, unconscious baggage we all carry.

Transformation may sound cosmic and foster images of walking with spiritual giants. People come down to earth soon enough when they realize they are going to work through the same tedious "stuff" as the unenlightened. It is appealing to imagine the exorcist grandly sweeping away all problems. The reality is that, however obscure, the reasons for the possession in the first place will be worked through just the same as problems of a more pedestrian nature will be.

It is absolutely necessary to stay centered if you choose to deal with the issues I have discussed. Very often, glamorous events such as psychic openings totally take over the client's consciousness. It is imperative that the counselor stay in control. I have dealt with many extraordinary events in my personal and professional life. Yet, in my work with clients (and myself) I am probably less likely to deviate from solid psychological issues than most traditional therapists.

Using psychic development as an example, the first thing that happens is a release of unresolved issues from the individual's unconscious. You can count on it. These people may as well have entered therapy for all the difference it makes. *No one has any business trusting his or her psychic work until there has been some psychological house cleaning.* Whatever the issues, I consistently see to it that my clients toe the line of the matters at hand, and I refuse to get sidetracked.

I promised to give you a step-by-step method for working at the psychological level. I developed this model over many years in my private practice. I teach this in all-day workshops and, even then, time is short. Space here is more limited still, so I can't elaborate. I call this the Diana Stone Applied Astrology System. Pretty neat name, don't you agree?

Briefly, I call my system Applied Astrology to differentiate it from the typical consultation wherein the astrologer reads patterns from the horoscope and interprets them to the client. In my system, the astrologer listens with a trained ear to the client, identifies patterns from the client's conversation, translates the patterns into astrological symbolism, finds it in the horoscope, and then leads the client through a process of understanding the pattern.

Let's start with the astrologer listening to the client with a trained ear. You get a trained ear by understanding one thing, namely this: whatever story the client tells you actually represents a decision he or she has made *to have those exact circumstances manifest in life.* If the person does not like those particular circumstances, this simply means that the decision was made at an unconscious level. Those decisions are not made without a reason, so the task is *to find* that reason.

The trick is to determine just what is the story that the client is telling you. My client, Marcy, told me about her relationship with her husband. Essentially it was boring and lacked passion. She complained that there was no communication, even about everyday affairs. Marcy's chart has Saturn in the 1st House, the house of childhood. To summarize briefly, I asked Marcy if anyone had ever paid any attention to her as a child, if she had anyone to talk to. She hadn't.

So what *is* the client's story and what was the childhood decision? The client's story is that she is isolated and overlooked, and more to the point, some part of her has created this situation deliberately. The story is what is *actually* happening, *not what the client does not like about what is actually happening.* It is no accident that this pattern is duplicated all her life. The childhood decision was about what relationships are like for her. She unconsciously decided she was overlooked and isolated in relationships. Interestingly, the same pattern prevailed in her isolated and boring government job as well.

It would have been a mistake to buy into Marcy's reality. She was focusing on her husband. I shifted her perspective to understand why she chose this type of relationship which she was certain to choose to fit the childhood decision about relationships. The marriage is not the real issue, *only the reflection of the actual problem.* Nothing will change until Marcy, herself, can accept intimacy and change the way she sees herself inside—this may be a therapy issue and not necessarily something the astrologer will take on. The astrologer's job is diagnosis. Yet the client's first question is so often, "How can I change this?" I tell them nothing can be changed unless it is first understood. After it is understood, and only then, is the decision of what to do about it in order. In so many cases, just explaining the dynamics of situations like Marcy's is enough for my clients to go ahead and work things through for themselves.

Another example concerns my client, Laura, who is absolutely beside herself about her boyfriend of three years. She wants to get married but he keeps changing his mind about commitment. First the relationship is on, then it is off. What is the client's story here? Remember, the story is actually what is happening. Do not focus on what the client wants to happen. What is happening is what the client has chosen to happen at an unconscious level. What actually is happening to Laura is her decision to have on-again, off-again relationships. The next step is to find this pattern in the chart. That means you must know enough astrology *to find corresponding patterns to the person's story.* On and off relationships are ruled by Uranus. Uranus must be somewhere in the relationship patterns. Go find it, and you will have the answer.

Laura's chart has the Moon conjoined with Uranus! The Moon is always an indicator of the emotional life and also rules what we learned about relationships at our mother's knee. Uranus rules the connect-disconnect pattern. I asked her if her relationship with her mother had been an on-again, off-again affair. It had been. Somewhere in childhood, she had decided about the nature of relationships. *Her boyfriend is a player in her drama,* not just a coincidental bad choice. It is *she* who made the decision that relationships would be a sometime thing. No matter how many boyfriends came and went, she could expect a replay of some version of this theme. The astrologer might look at relationship cycles, or examine the man's chart, but the fact is that Laura's romantic life will *not* change until Laura works through this pattern.

Clients typically talk about their concerns and what is happening in their lives. It is at these times that the dynamic process of the consultation is at work. What are otherwise patterns and behaviors operating outside our client's waking consciousness are communicated in the counseling environment. If the real meaning of the dialogue is not recognized, a great deal of valuable information goes by unnoticed. It may not be what we tell our clients that most leads to life changes, but, rather, *how effectively we deal with what they are telling us.* It is so important to emphasize again that no matter how far and wide the life experience may roam, no matter how esoteric or mysterious some problems may seem, it is the ability to catch hold of the issues, the root causes, as they present themselves, that puts the helpful astrologer front and center in the client's life drama.

Bibliography

Clow, Barbara Hand, *Chiron: Rainbow Bridge Between the Inner and Outer Planets.* St. Paul, MN: Llewellyn Publications, 1988.

Groff, Stanislav. *The Adventure of Self-Discovery.* Albany, NY: State University of New York Press, 1988.

Sanella, Lee. *Kundalini: Psychosis or Transcendence?* San Francisco: H. S. Dakin, 1976.

Robert Hand

Robert Hand has been an astrologer since 1960 and a full-time professional astrologer since 1972. His books include *Planets in Composite*, the masterful *Planets in Transit, Planets in Youth, Horoscope Symbols* and *Essays on Astrology*. He has explored heliocentric, sidereal, uranian/cosmobiological and *in mundo* techniques, and uses a synthesis of these along with more usual techniques in his practice. He has a BA in history from Brandeis University and did graduate work in the history of science at Princeton. In 1976 he began writing astrological programs for microcomputers, and in 1979 he founded Astro-Graphics Services, Inc. (now Astrolabe, Inc.) and Astrolabe Software, to make the beneifts of computers available to astrologers.

He currently serves as national chairman of the National Council for Geocosmic Research, is a patron of the Faculty of Astrological Studies, and is certainly one of the most celebrated astrologers of our time.

Saturn, Action, and Career Crises— Introductory Concepts

Robert Hand

We have to begin by completely understanding that what we call a "career" is simply one component of a much more complex and important aspect of one's life, *its direction*. What is each of us here to do? What is our role in life? And even more fundamentally, who is each of us as an individual? When we meet someone for the first time a common question is, "What do you do?" We are not asking merely how this person spends time. We use the question of career to help us determine who this new person is and what kind of role this person plays in society and perhaps even what this person's role might be with respect to ourselves.

All of these issues are connected with the 10th House of the horoscope. In modern astrology we tend to think of this House almost solely in terms of career, but in older astrologies it had a much broader meaning, much more in accord with the issues I raised in the previous paragraph. If we go back to Lilly, for instance, the chapter on the symbolism of the 10th House is entitled "Of the Honours or Dignities of the Native." Then, most of the discussion that follows relates to whether the "native" will gain a preferment (appointment to a church position) and how long he will keep it, etc. Much of the other material has more to do with what we call social class than with career as we know it. Only after a good deal of this does Lilly come to a discussion of profession or career.

If we go back further to Ptolemy, we find another term associated with the 10th House. The Greek word is πραχεως, praxeos, from which come our words *practical* and *practice*. It is usually translated as "employment," and this is a perfectly valid translation. However, what the word really means at its root is *action*. The Robbins translation of Ptolemy actually entitles the chapter on profession as "Of the Quality of Action."* The clear implication of this word is that what we call career and the astrological correlates that we associate with career are more properly to be used to describe the quality of what one's life *does. What is the proper **action** of our lives?*

One of my personal irritations with popular renditions of Eastern religious and philosophical ideas has to do with the word, *karma*. As used by most persons in ordinary conversation, it has a strikingly Judaeo-Christian quality suggesting reward and punishment for good and evil deeds meted out by a moral deity. What the word, *karma*, literally means is also "action" in exactly the same sense as *praxeos* in Ptolemy. In Hindu astrology, the 10th House is referred to as the House of karma.

I have found it interesting to ask astrologers trained in the Western tradition what they think, based on their understanding of karma, might be the House of karma according to Hindu astrology. I have invariably gotten as answers the same group of three houses, the 4th, the 8th and the 12th, not necessarily in that order. Two of these are regarded as difficult houses even in Western astrology and as positively evil in Hindu astrology, such is the negativity imputed by Westerners to their peculiar notion of karma.

To the Hindus and the ancient Greeks, karma–praxeos–action meant the sum total of the energies that the life would generate, what the individual would do and what chain of events would follow from these energies. Clearly this is much more than the narrow matter of what one does for a living! In this article, I will use this expanded notion of life-direction and action as the basis for discussion of crises involving the 10th House.

A question arises: is each individual's action and purpose a constant thing or an evolving set of processes resulting in changes of direction and life purpose? As a point of personal faith which the reader may feel free to accept or reject, let me state that I believe each life has a single, overall, unified theme that consti-

---

* Robbins translation, p. 381.

tutes its action and direction. However, I do not believe that this means a successful life should find its one path early and stick to it for life. To the contrary, I believe that the changes one goes through in "finding one's path" are really stages in the evolution of a *single, integrated path*. The changes are not fundamental ones but, rather, changes of outward form.

It is also very clear that the unifying theme of a life may not be obvious to either the individual or others around him. It may require a retrospective examination late in life by the individual or even by others after the individual's death. And it is *particularly difficult* to perceive the inherent unity of an individual's "action" if one persists in evaluating it entirely in terms of a "career."

Therefore the type of crisis that we will examine in this article has to do with turning points in the expression of the overall action of a life and with periods in which the individual is called upon to define the nature of the action, to manifest it, and to make necessary changes in its form.

There are two additional basic principles that must be understood. First of all, in one sense, *one can not fail to find one's own life direction or action*. The individual *always* finds the path because it is, in a real sense, one's destiny. One can fail to realize that one is on the proper path and one can also fail to understand what the path consists of. In fact, it is relatively rare that an individual understands completely the nature of his or her action. Only rather extraordinary individuals seem to have a developed sense of destiny (which means, by the way, simply knowing what one's destination is or where one is going). Most people, even quite intelligent and conscious people, spend their lives moving along their paths, not understanding what they are doing and where they are going.

Second, while it is not possible to fail in finding one's path or in manifesting one's action, it is possible to manifest it *at a very low level*, a level at which most of the energies that are released are negative and anti-evolutionary or produce a great deal of turbulence, either within one's own life or in the lives of people near to one. This is not so much a consequence of ignorance as it is of either not knowing or not accepting a path and, consequently, fighting or trying to do something else or go somewhere else. Severe crises of life direction and action may be the results of this kind of energy conflict and may be the occasions in which individuals can readjust and realign energies so that what follows in life is more productive and possibly more conscious.

Third, it is not so much the function of the astrologer to tell a client what his or her life direction and action may be, as it is to describe to the client what kinds of energies the proper action should manifest and to suggest ways in which the energies can manifest more smoothly, leading to personal and spiritual growth. The astrologer should not take the position of passing judgment on the nature of a client's action. The full understanding of the life direction and action of any individual is in the hands of something that is far beyond our comprehension and knowledge. Call it God if you like.

> Canst thou bind the sweet influences of Pleiades, or loose the bands of Orion? Canst thou bring forth Mazzaroth in his season? or canst thou guide Arcturus with his sons? Knowest thou the ordinances of heaven? Canst thou set the dominion thereof in the earth?
>
> *Job 38:31-33*

One last point before we proceed: What is a crisis? It is not a disaster. *It is a turning point.* And in particular it is a point in which the past has minimum hold upon the present, but the present has a maximum hold on the future. One may in a crisis actually have more freedom than usual, but the consequences of one's actions at these times may strongly determine what will follow. Always keep this in mind as we proceed with this article.

The Tools

Saturn—The first consideration in our analysis of life-direction crises is the planet Saturn. Traditionally, it has been regarded as the "greater malefic." In modern astrology, Saturn has undergone a significant rehabilitation. Modern astrologers recognize that it is an essential energy that is present in every aspect of life. Without it, we would have nothing. However, we should not go too far in rehabilitating Saturn. It is a genuinely challenging energy. It is not evil, merely difficult. It represents real limitations on freedom. It is the structural aspect of one's existence which cannot be changed without great difficulty or pain. When Saturn is strongly operative in one's life, one is often forced to move in ways and directions that one would not choose as the easiest or most pleasant. Very often, Saturn, which traditionally rules heavy weights, serves much the same function as placing a heavy weight upon a structure in order to test its strength. A structure that is sound and well designed passes the test. One that is not collapses.

Now all of this is positive and allows a creative life, even if the path is not always pleasant. So, where does Saturn get its bad reputation? Were the ancients simply unable to stand up to its demands without caving in? Is modern humanity more enlightened now that we can regard Saturn in this kinder light?

We are *not* more enlightened! What we are doing is *ignoring* the other side of Saturn. Saturn is not only an energy that tests the validity of an existing structure; it has another role. It is also *the structure itself.* Saturn often comes to us in the two forms simultaneously. In one form, it is our personal structure, in the other it is that which challenges our personal structure. In early life especially, Saturn is an external energy that challenges immature structures within the developing self and forces them to become mature and solid, or destroys them. The end result of the encounter with the external Saturn is the development of the internal Saturn, the inner structure. The problem is that the encounter with the external Saturn may favor structures which succeed in overcoming short-term challenges but create long-lived, self-limiting behavior that makes an inner prison to confine the self far beyond what is necessary or desirable. It is these confining structures within the self that have no real positive role in individual development and do not assist us in the pursuit of proper action that constitute the negative part of the Saturn complex.

However, for us in this discussion, the important thing is that Saturn's structuring quality *is* a major factor in timing life crises that have to do with life-direction and action. Very frequently, a Saturn transit will correspond with difficulties in one's career (to focus for a moment on the narrower definition of one's action). As we shall see, certain cycles of Saturn have a great deal to do with the long-range growth and manifestation of one's action.

The Other Planets—Like most things in astrology, we ultimately find ourselves looking at everything in the chart whenever we focus on anything. Every element in the chart, signs, planets houses, aspects etc., can be read as pertaining to every issue in life although each element must be interpreted somewhat differently according to the issue upon which one is focused.

However, in traditional astrology it was held that certain planets "ruled" certain professions. One could not succeed in a profession unless the governing planet was favorably situated in the natal chart so that its energies could assist the native in pursuing the career. If the governing planet were not favorably situated, the native would have a hopeless time pursuing that career.

There is considerable truth in that ancient notion. Individuals are not free to follow any life direction that he or she might choose. And fortunately, most people will not choose a mode of action that is completely unsupported by the symbolism of the natal chart. It is not so much that the planet governing life direction and action does *not allow the individual to choose* as the individual will *not be inclined to choose.*

The work of Francoise and Michel Gauquelin showed a statistically significant tendency for certain planetary placements to correlate with careers. However, in their later work they discovered that the correlations between *temperament types* and planetary placements were even greater. It quickly became clear to them that temperament types tended to choose particular professions and that the most successful individuals were those whose professions were most in accord with temperamental inclinations. They also found that the more successful in a profession an individual was, the more probable that the "ruling planet" of the profession would be in a significant place in the chart. I do not believe that I belittle the important work of the Gauquelins when I say that this is an intuitively plausible result according to traditional astrology.*

However, let us not oversimplify matters. The Gauquelins were trained as psychologists and, like many modern psychologically

---

* However, the places that the Gauquelins found to be significant in "determining" profession, were not precisely those that astrologers would have expected. But the planets *were*, for the most part, the ones that astrologers would have expected. [See *How to Use Vocational Astrology for Success in the Workplace* for an overview of the Gauquelin research; Llewellyn Publications, 1992–Ed.]

oriented astrologers, they saw psychological traits as the means by which astrological symbolism manifested. There is a more traditional view which I support: psychological traits are merely one of the ways in which astrological symbolism can manifest. One can also experience the symbolism through objects in one's surroundings or through situations and events. This is what makes a simple correlation between planets and life paths difficult. One can be involved in a path that is not traditionally associated with the planets that one would expect to "rule" the path, but there can be aspects of the path, events, circumstances, physical surroundings or even, as we have said, objects that *do* manifest the symbolism we would expect. So even though the path itself may not seem appropriate to one's planets, the proper symbolism *is* being manifested in the way the individual follows the path. So the path "works" for the individual.

This also should make it clear that the traditional rulerships of planets over careers must be used carefully. An individual who has a strong need for order and detail and who does not like disruption may do very well working for a revolutionary organization as an accountant or manager of logistics. This person would not be fond, however, of actually being personally involved in the "revolution." The astrologer should always find out what an individually actually *does* in the course of his or her work. The astrologer must go beyond the simple symbolism of the career, itself, to the *action* involved.

The 10th House and the Midheaven—The 10th House is the house of "action," itself. We have already seen that this is more than simple profession. The 10th House and its cusp,* the Midheaven, are extremely important parts of the chart. The 1st House and the Ascendant get more attention from most astrologers, which makes sense if astrology is mainly concerned with personality description. However, if one is more concerned with the life direction and path, the *action* as we have defined it, then the 10th House and the Midheaven are more important than the 1st House

---

* In most systems of house division, the Midheaven is the cusp of the 10th. However, there is at least one popular system in which it is not: the so-called Equal House system in which all houses are 30° equal divisions of the ecliptic from the Ascendant. However, even in this system, one should note the position of the Midheaven and regard it as an important influence on life direction.

and the Ascendant.* In particular, transits to the Midheaven by both conjunction and aspect and transits through the 10th House are very important in timing crises of life direction.

Planets in the 10th House should also be examined. Transits and progressions to these planets are very important in timing career crises. These are the planets that are most likely to "rule" the profession in the conventional sense used by astrologers or to indicate the action of the life in the sense that I have been using it in this paper.

The 6th House—This is the traditional house of work and health. Actually, in the old works on astrology, it is the house of *slavery* and *sickness*. Modern astrology likes to put things politely! For this discussion, we can ignore the health (or sickness) attribute of the House and concentrate on the work (or slavery) attribute. The ancient term, slavery, while unpleasant to the modern ear (and not all that pleasant to the ancient one either) does denote a real quality of the house. It is a place in the chart that denotes *necessity*. It is that which must be done. But by this I do not mean that which must be done according to destiny, but rather that which must be done in order to succeed at doing something else.

I like to define work as any activity that must be pursued for the sake of some other activity. Work is not by nature something that someone does for its own sake. The 6th House holds that kind of activity. The 6th House is trine by house (*in mundo trine†*) to the 10th. Its success assists the success of the affairs of the 10th House. The 6th House is also especially useful to determine what kind of daily activity an individual should actually pursue in the course of the work.

---

* In fact, in two German schools of astrology, the Ebertin School of Cosmobiology and the Hamburg or Uranian School of Alfred Witte and his followers, the Midheaven is regarded as more important than the Ascendant because it describes the basic Ego. I am reluctant to ascribe the Ego to any single astrological point, but I do believe that they have hit upon something quite important. The basic structure of the Ego and the nature of life direction and action are all very strongly connected. One is almost, though not completely, what one does.

† *In mundo* means "in the world" and refers to the spatial coordinates by which a House system is constructed. In these coordinates, the 6th House is *always* trine to the 10th, even though the ecliptical relationship or aspect is not a trine.

The Timing of Crises in Life Direction

The Saturn Cycle of Career and Life Direction—This is one of three Saturn cycle patterns first described by Grant Lewi in his book, *Astrology for the Millions.** These were the cycles of Saturn transiting with respect to its own natal position, Saturn transiting with respect to the natal Sun, and Saturn transiting through the Houses with special emphasis on Saturn transiting with respect to the 10th House. It is this last one that concerns us here.

It operates in four distinct phases and begins with the transit of Saturn over the IC or 4th House cusp. The diagram on page 123 shows the basic pattern. What follows is a description of the major features of each of the four phases.

Phase I – Laying the Foundation—This is the transit of Saturn through Houses 4, 5, and 6. Beginning with the transit of Saturn over the 4th House cusp, this is a time in which the individual takes actions that will later prove to have laid the foundations for the *action* that will culminate when Saturn transits the Midheaven. The work done at this time does *not* necessarily have any *obvious* connection with what will take place 14 years later, when the cycle culminates. It is quite seldom that there is an obvious connection. There is most likely to be a clear connection only when the individual's life action has a particularly well-defined direction, a condition not characteristic of most people's lives.

The most important need of this period is the need to pursue one's action with complete integrity. Whatever one does in this time must be done as competently and carefully as possible. This is the laying of a foundation and, like all foundations, if weak, the structure built upon it will not survive the stress placed upon it in future crises. It is not necessary that the individual completely understand what the foundation is for or what he or she may be doing, only that whatever *is* done, is done as well as the individual can. No corners may be cut. No rules that the individual holds sacred may be broken.†

---

* Published by Llewellyn. See bibliography.

† It is not clear whether rules that others hold sacred are as important for the individual to observe. It depends upon the fundamental rightness of those principles with respect to the path that the individual is on.

Phase II – Manifesting the Purpose—This is normally the transit of Saturn through Houses 7, 8, and 9. However, the period may also begin when Saturn transits in square to the Midheaven. There is no clear way of telling in advance which way the cycle is going to work. The reason for this is that both the transit of Saturn over the 7th House cusp and the transit of Saturn in square to the natal Midheaven are kinds of squares, the first being a square by house or *in mundo* square, the second a square in the zodiac. The first square in a transit cycle after the conjunction always represents a crisis in a cycle of manifestation.

Whichever transit it may be that begins it, the second phase begins to manifest the purpose or direction of the current cycle of life direction. Gradually during this period it becomes clear to the individual where he or she is going. This is in contrast to the previous phase in which action usually takes place without a clear understanding of overall direction. However, one can not assume that such purpose or direction will become clear right at the beginning of the second phase. This varies from individual to individual.

Phase III — Manifesting Consequences—This is the most critical part of the cycle. It is the time when and where the consequences of the life path, the life action, become completely manifest (except in one type of individual that will be discussed later). If the foundation of Phase I has been properly laid, then one should experience considerable success during this period. If it has not been properly laid, then one may well experience failure at this time. Failure can come not only through cutting corners and violating one's principles in Phase I. It can also come from having gotten onto the wrong path!

This brings up an interesting point. Given what has already been said about life action, can one really go onto the "wrong" path? Are not all paths actually taken correct ones for an individual from a higher point of view? Can one really go off the proper path? The answer largely depends upon one's point of view.

From the highest point of view, as I put forth earlier, the answer is probably that one can not go onto the wrong path. However, there are paths which are more or less in accord with our nature, and we will do better or worse accordingly to follow these paths. What I mean here is failure from a practical point of view, from a short-term perspective, not from the highest meta-physical point of view. Let's put it another way which may appear to be more neutral and less judgmental: failure from our point of view means that a great divergence between what the individual intends and what is achieved results in creating pain and suffer-ing for the individual, regardless of what longer-term gain the individual may get from the experience.

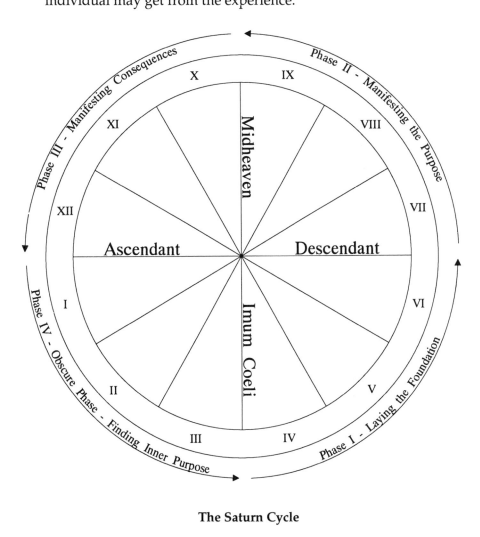

The Saturn Cycle

The transit through the 10th House is the most difficult part of Phase III. If failure is going to occur, it will occur in this time period. This is why the transit of Saturn through the 10th has such a bad reputation according to some authors. And even with success in the conventional sense of the word, it is a time of very hard work and responsibility. One seems to have the weight of the world upon one's shoulders. And one must bear this weight to the full extent of one's abilities in order to reap the maximum benefit from this period. Avoiding either the work or the responsibility can still result in failure at this time, even if one has laid the proper foundation in the past fourteen years. However, it must also be said that laying the foundations properly is one of the best ways to ensure that one will be able to hold up under the strain and even prosper under it.

The transit through the 11th is usually easier. Here one is able to share both the work and the responsibility with others in a team effort. In fact the purpose of this period is to begin to hand over the effort to others and to share the positive results of one's work as well.

The transit through the 12th can be difficult if one has not made the changes called for during the 11th House part of the cycle. At the most extreme, the 12th House transit is a time in which the individual may seem to be deprived of all the gains and rewards gotten through the 10th House transit.

The key to this transit is detachment. During the 12th House period, the individual should turn within and find out what he or she has learned or gotten from the cycle so far. The burden and responsibility of Phase III should be left to others as much as possible. If one cannot let go, then this time may be quite difficult.

Phase IV – Obscure Phase – Finding Inner Purpose – This usually corresponds to the transit of Saturn through Houses 1, 2, and 3 and represents the closing of a cycle of life action. However, the comments that were made earlier about the Saturn transit over the 7th House cusp versus the zodiacal transit square to the Midheaven also apply here. The last phase can begin with either the Saturn transit over the Ascendant or the Saturn square to the Midheaven. However, it is more common for the Saturn transit over the Ascendant to be the timing factor, because this is such an important transit in its own right.

The goal of this period should be to take whatever has been gained or learned from the preceding parts of the cycle and to incorporate them into one's inner being. It is a clear continuation of a process that began with Saturn transiting the 12th. But now the individual should not only try to understand the inner dimension of the current cycle of action but actually incorporate knowledge into one's inner self. This phase of the cycle is actually the culmination of the cycle. The 10th House transit may appear to be because it so often coincides with external achievement, but this fourth phase involves the entire purpose of the cycle, which is to grow!

In many people, the transit of Saturn through the 1st House appears to be similar to the better side of Saturn's transit through the 10th House, i.e., increased opportunities for social success, responsibility and achievement. However, when this happens it is really another opportunity to learn more about the nature of one's life action. It should not be looked at as another chance to make a large impact on the outside world. The Obscure Phase has not been canceled. It is only starting a bit late.

The Obscure Phase itself, therefore, may start with either Saturn's entry into the 1st or 2nd House. In fact for some it may have already started in the 12th House!

In Grant Lewi's original description of this period, the reader gets the impression that this is a negative period characterized by failure and defeat. However, from what I know of Grant Lewi as an astrologer, I suspect that this was an intentional oversimplification for the purposes of a popular book. Remember that *Heaven Knows What* was written before Dane Rudhyar and Humanistic Astrology had really made an impact.*

In fact, while the Obscure Phase is obscure in many ways, it is not an unmitigated disaster by any means. Indeed, it can be a period of tremendous external success that even the outer world can easily see. It is one's intentions for the period that make the difference! If one devotes the time to inner work and finding one's true needs as well as incorporating within oneself the experience of the previous three phases, then the period can be very successful from every point of view. But if one is completely outer-directed, paying

---

* Rudhyar was already a well-known author and had written several of his more important books. But the real impact of his ideas on the mass of astrologers was not to take place until the 60s and 70s.

little attention to the inner world, directing one's energies entirely toward outer world achievements, then one is likely to experience genuine defeat. It is this phase that most illustrates the difference between the idea of this cycle as a cycle of career in the conventional sense, as opposed to its being a cycle of life action in the sense defined in this article. For most people, the obscure phase is not especially notable for a career, but it is the absolute culmination of a cycle of action, a completion of a dialogue between oneself and the outer world.

A signal is sent out into the world from the inner self as Saturn transits the 4th House. It is answered by the outer world as Saturn transits the 10th. The individual takes the answer back within and understands it in the Obscure Phase.

Limitations to be Observed in Practice—At some level, it is probable that this grand cycle works in the manner described above for just about every individual. But it is most clearly observable in persons who have a definite external career that provides a focus for their lives. This is because it is in these individuals that there is the closest identity between life action and career. Persons whose lives revolve around the search for inner truth, or persons whose lives are lived out through their involvements with family or friends will not show the pattern as clearly—women who have played the traditional role of wife and mother fall into the latter category. Persons in the first category have so little connection between life action, what their own lives are about, and normal career, that the cycle can only be detected through an exploration of the life that focuses on inner development. Putting this in simple terms, before the counselor speaks in learned terms about career peaks and Obscure Phases, he or she should make sure that the individual *has a conventional career*, and has exposure to the outside world.

Another factor that should be observed is the age of the individual. A classic Saturn in the 10th House career peak is not likely to make much of a showing in a fifteen-year-old.

A final note for this section, politicians seem to show the classic cycle more clearly than any other career category. For this reason a number of examples in this article are drawn from politics.

Case Study #1 — Jung and the Break with Freud

One of the most important career crises to affect Twentieth Century intellectual history was the encounter and subsequent break between Carl Gustav Jung and Sigmund Freud. The break resulted from the beginnings of Jung's evolution of the theory of archetypes which has been so important in modern astrology. The break is an excellent study for our purposes, because both Jung and his biographers have documented not only the external circumstances of the break, but also the inward psychological and spiritual aspects of it.

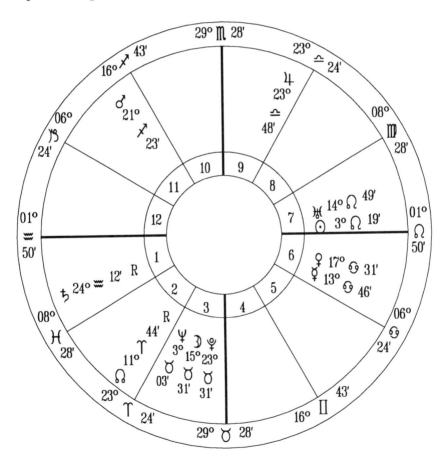

C. G. Jung
(See footnote overleaf for birth data.)

For the purposes of this study, I am using the same chart of Jung that I used in my book, *Planets in Composite*. It seems to work with events in his life very well and is close enough to the other variants of his birth data to be useful for our purposes.*

Let us first look at Jung's natal chart to see what indications there are that might determine the life action. This is one of those charts in which any error in the time of the chart may make major changes in the symbolism. The Midheaven is the very last degree of Scorpio! However, assuming that we do have the accurate Midheaven for this chart, Scorpio is an excellent sign for both the career and style of pursuing the career that Jung demonstrated. It is the sign of "depth" psychology par excellence! Beyond that, however, things are not as clear as some might wish. But there are some features in the chart that do have bearing on life action.

First of all there is Pluto. Pluto is located in the 3rd House according to most systems of house division, but the usual method of placing planets in houses is somewhat dangerous with Pluto. I have shown elsewhere† that Pluto is often so far off the ecliptic that its zodiacal position may not show its house position accurately. This is the case with Jung's Pluto.

As the more technically minded readers may be aware, the Midheaven and I.C. of a horoscope are actually based on right ascension (abb. R.A.), the measure of positions along the equator, rather than in longitude which uses the zodiac. When one checks the R.A. of Pluto, one discovers that it is almost exactly on the I.C. of Jung's horoscope. This makes Pluto one of the strongest planets in the chart, aspecting the Midheaven. Pluto becomes a major determinant of life action. However, being on the I.C. rather than at the Midheaven, Pluto points inward. Therefore Jung should be

---

* *Planets in Composite*, p. 63, where it is given as 18:55:32 U.T. or 19:32:48 for the time zone then in use throughout Switzerland. For additional material on Jung's birthdata I quote from the biographical material of the Blackwell Data Base, an IBM PC based database of birthcharts created by Astrolabe Software.

  1875, July 26 at about 7:30 p.m. LMT (18:52:40 UT) in Kesswil, Switzerland (47N35, 9E20). Birth data of the psychotherapist has been given by him. Time of birth given by Jung as "7:20," "7:30," and for other times near sunset and dusk. A good discussion of the data was given by Lois Rodden in the *Journal of the Seasons*, vol. 19 for Autumn 1980, published by the Astrological Society of New Zealand. Carl Jung's daughter, Gret Baumann-Jung, was cited for a "7:32 p.m." time of birth in the *Journal of Geocosmic Research* for Autumn 1975.

† See *Essays on Astrology*, the article "Astrology's Second Dimension: Declination and Latitude", pp. 95-97.

an individual who would have a Plutonian effect on the inner rather than the outer world.

Before we move on, we must note two zodiacal aspects to the Midheaven. Saturn widely squares the Midheaven and closely squares the aforementioned Pluto. The astrological study of Jung's life shows that this is an extremely important aspect in Jung's life and career. However, for our purposes here, it is mainly interesting to note it in connection with the difficulties that Jung might have with father figures. Freud comes to mind, as we shall see.

Mercury also aspects the Midheaven by 135° or sesquiquadrate from the 6th House, a location that also affects work and career. Of course, this could suggest work that has to do with writing, which is appropriate. But even more, it indicates his working not only with his own mind, but also with Mind in the abstract.

Let's now turn to the break with Freud. Although the break itself, insofar as it can be dated precisely, occurred in early January 1913, Jung believed that the beginnings of the break could be seen several years earlier, the so-called "bookcase incident." The following is a description given by Jung in his autobiography, *Memories, Dreams and Reflections.* They were discussing occult phenomena.

> While Freud was going on this way, I had a curious sensation. It was as if my diaphragm were made of iron and were becoming red-hot—a glowing vault. And at that moment there was such a loud report in the bookcase, which stood right next to us, that we both started up in alarm, fearing that the thing was going to topple over on us. I said to Freud: "There that is an example of a so-called catalytic exteriorization phenomenon."*
>
> "Oh come," he exclaimed. "That is sheer bosh."
>
> "It is not," I replied. "You are mistaken Herr Professor, and to prove my point I now predict that in a moment there will be another such loud report!" Sure enough, no sooner had I said this than the same detonation went off in the bookcase.†

---

* For those who are not familiar with the jargon of Nineteenth century psychic research, a "catalytic exteriorization phenomenon," is an event in the outer world triggered by psychic stress within an individual.

† Jung, *Memories, Dreams and Reflections,* p. 155.

Freud, despite the strangeness of his own research in many ways, tried to be a devout mechanist-materialist while Jung was already beginning to depart from that tradition. Freud obviously found this disconcerting! Jung believed that Freud never quite trusted Jung again after this incident.

The incident occurred in the evening of March 29, 1909. The transits for 8:00 p.m. GMT are located in the outer wheel within Jung's natal chart in the inner wheel.

Transiting Saturn is in Jung's 2nd House. He was in the middle of his "Obscure Phase." This is quite significant because of what was happening between the two men at the time. Jung was considered to be the most significant of Freud's "followers." I use the quotation marks because it is not clear that Jung ever considered *himself* to be a follower of Freud; junior colleague would be a more accurate characterization.

Freud had decided that Jung would succeed him as the leader of the Psychoanalytic Movement. Thus Jung was being propelled in the direction of outward success and achievement at precisely the time when he should have been concerned with inward evolution. The *action* of Jung's life gave no energy to material plane success, especially if it had to come at the price of his own authenticity. In the 6th House, transiting Neptune is very close to conjoining Jung's natal Mercury and making a 135° aspect to his Midheaven. Their conversation was at every level a Mercury-Neptune communication, which had the short-term affect of weakening Jung's career!

The actual break took several years to develop. There was a gradual widening of the gap between the two men, especially after a joint trip by the two of them to the United States in late 1909. On January 6, 1913, Jung wrote to Freud agreeing to discontinue their personal relationship. Saturn at this time was at about 27–28 of Taurus, almost exactly on his I.C. This was the time to lay a new foundation for the next cycle of *action* and to let go of the previous cycle. At the same time, Uranus was transiting conjunct his Ascendant with Neptune transiting square the natal Jupiter in the 9th (Koch) from the natal 6th, a conflict over worldviews (Jupiter in the 9th) caused by disagreements over actual therapeutic practices (Neptune in the 6th). Transiting Saturn was also not far from a square to natal Saturn in the 1st. As mentioned above, Jung's natal 1st House Saturn in a wide square to the natal Midheaven could be read as difficulties with authority figures posing as father-figures. Freud tried to be a father-figure to Jung, while Jung, with Saturn in the 1st, did not feel that he needed one.*

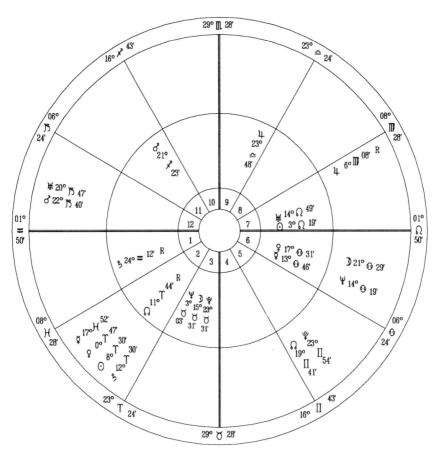

Jung and the Bookcase Incident

The years that followed were very difficult for Jung. His entire professional world was connected to his involvement with the Psychoanalytic movement. Severing those ties caused him to become an isolated figure. It is significant to note that Jung's biographer, Gerhard Wehr, entitles the chapter on the period directly after the break with Freud, "Transformation Begins Within!"

---

* His relationship with his actual father was rather cool although not hostile. His actual father did not function as an especially close guide figure.

Ideally, if one were managing the Saturn cycle of action according to the scheme laid out previously in this chapter, the passage of Saturn through the natal 4th should have been a period of laying the foundation for external achievement based on the inner work done in the previous obscure phase. However, in Jung's case, the inner work had been the laying of that foundation.

Case Study #2 — The Surrender of a Throne

This is a study of King Edward VIII who in 1936 abdicated the throne rather than give up his relationship to Wallace Warfield Simpson.* This is perhaps one of the outstandingly dramatic career crises of the twentieth century. And it was much more than mere drama as the publicity of the day would make it seem. King Edward, or the Prince of Wales as he was usually called, could have dramatically changed the immediate future had he stayed on the throne. Recent research has suggested that King Edward VIII was more than a little bit of a fascist sympathizer. Would a Britain ruled by him have put up quite the battle that it eventually did against Hitler? This is clearly one of the great "ifs" of history.

The entire year of 1936 was critical for the Prince. On January 20, 1936 his father, King George V, died, and Edward ascended the throne.† Prior to this, it had been rumored that the Prince had a special relationship with Wallace Warfield Simpson, but it was widely assumed that some kind of accommodation short of marriage could be made for the relationship. After all, in the not so distant past, kings had had proper marriages with properly Protestant, un-divorced women and had additional relationships with other women on the side.

Edward's namesake as king, King Edward VII, had had a succession of mistresses of more or less official status. Unfortunately for Edward VIII, Edward VII (see footnote below) had been

---

* From the Blackwell Data Base we have the following data:

    1894, June 23 at 9:55 p.m. GMT in Richmond, England (51N27, 0W18). Birth data from official announcement recorded in the "Annual Register"; it reads " . . . The Duchess of York was safely delivered of a son at White Lodge, Richmond, at five minutes to ten o'clock on Saturday night, June 23, 1894 . . ." See "Spica" for Oct. 1967.

† Although he ascended the throne, he never was officially crowned. The controversy over his marriage delayed the coronation ceremony. He abdicated before it took place.

followed by George V who was married quite faithfully to his wife, Queen Mary. Apparently between the two Edwards the rules of the game had been changed. Also Edward VIII, himself, was not Edward VII. Edward VIII had something of his father's sense of morality. He did not want Wallace Simpson as a mistress. He wanted her as full queen with him on the throne. Since she was divorced, a state that the Anglican Church, like the Roman Catholic Church, did not recognize, she could not be married to a King of Great Britain who was, in theory at least, the head of the Anglican Church!

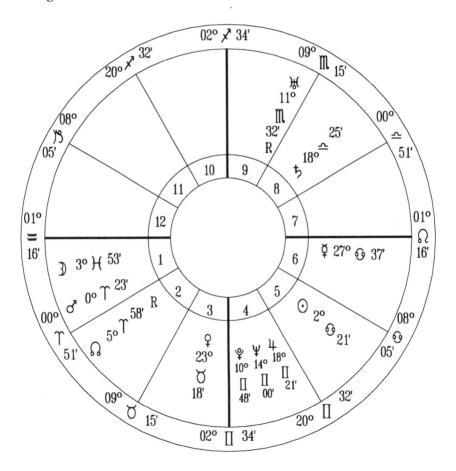

Edward VIII

Thus the whole year of 1936 was fraught with tension and controversy over the King's desire to marry Wallace Simpson. We would expect something to show up astrologically throughout the entire year. A table of outer planetary positions for every fifteen days of 1936 follows for the reader's convenience.

0:00 et Tropical Geocentric Longitudes for 1936					
mm/dd	Jupiter	Saturn	Uranus	Neptune	Pluto
1/ 1	1Sg40	5Pi56	1Ta35R	16Vi44R	26Cn39R
1/16	14 43	7 20	1 33D	16 34	26 19
1/31	17 31	8 57	1 44	16 18	26 00
2/15	19 58	10 41	2 05	15 57	25 42
3/ 1	21 58	12 31	2 37	15 32	25 26
3/16	23 25	14 21	3 16	15 07	25 16
3/31	24 15	16 07	4 02	14 44	25 10
4/15	24 24R	17 47	4 52	14 24	25 10D
4/30	23 51	19 17	5 44	14 09	25 16
5/15	22 41	20 33	6 35	14 01	25 26
5/30	21 02	21 33	7 23	13 59D	25 42
6/14	19 08	22 13	8 06	14 05	26 02
6/29	17 18	22 31	8 43	14 18	26 24
7/14	15 49	22 27R	9 10	14 37	26 48
7/29	14 52	22 01	9 28	15 02	27 13
8/13	14 36D	21 15	9 35	15 31	27 36
8/28	15 00	20 15	9 31R	16 03	27 58
9/12	16 05	19 07	9 16	16 37	28 17
9/27	17 44	17 59	8 52	17 10	28 32
10/12	19 55	17 00	8 21	17 41	28 41
10/27	22 30	16 15	7 45	18 08	28 45
11/11	25 26	15 51	7 08	18 31	28 44R
11/26	28 36	15 49D	6 34	18 47	28 36
12/11	1Cp57	16 12	6 06	18 56	28 24
12/26	5 23	16 57	5 46	18 57R	28 08

At the beginning of 1936, Jupiter had just crossed his Midheaven and entered his 10th House. This could be read as a call to fulfill his life's direction. Clearly it was not an indicator of success! Jupiter is not in fact a malefic, but it does not always make things easy either. Saturn transited his 1st House (Koch) and had both

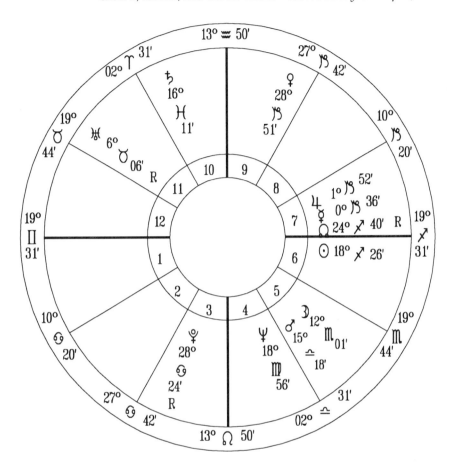

Edward VIII Abdication
Dec. 10, 1936, London, England, 00W10, 51N30, 3:51 p.m. GMT

conjoined his Moon and squared his Midheaven. Saturn places stress on whatever point it transits, not for the sake of destruction, however much it may feel that way sometimes, but as a *test of the validity of the functioning of that energy.* Here, the Saturn-Moon-Midheaven complex suggests the tension between personal emotional needs and what was at least supposed to have been his life's destiny.* In addition, Uranus was squaring his Ascendant-

---

* Note that the Moon in his chart would have been in the 2nd House in Placidus. I think that the symbolism makes much more sense as a 1st House—10th House conflict than as a 2nd House—10th House one. However, such debates rage on endlessly!

Descendant Axis from the 2nd House. This would have significantly increased his sense of insecurity about the survival of the relationship. Pluto transited his 6th conjunct his natal Mercury close enough to his Descendant to begin to affect the house of marriage as well as the house of service! A decision had to be made that could not be put off.

Here we have an excellent setup for one of the most common crises of life-action: the conflict between important relationships and life-action. And with transiting Saturn in the 1st House moving into the obscure phase, there is no energy for him to make a decision in favor of life direction. He was moving into the retreat period of the Saturn cycle.

On December 10, 1936 at 3:51 p.m., he abdicated the throne (see chart). The day is itself interesting in several ways. For example, there is a very close transiting Venus-Pluto opposition,with this Pluto still very close to Edward's natal Mercury and even closer than it was to his natal Descendant. This was the symbolism for a fateful decision about a relationship. Saturn was now transiting in square to his Jupiter and Neptune in the 4th House. In fact, the transit was almost exactly square to the Jupiter-Neptune midpoint. Ebertin in his *Combinations of Stellar Influences*, states the following about Saturn square to Jupiter-Neptune:

> Pessimism, a lack of self-confidence, the feeling to be abandoned by one's luck—the experiencing of the consequences issuing from false hopes, plans which come to nothing, disappointments, losses.*

Transiting Neptune repeated the theme by closely squaring his Jupiter from the 7th.

The group of planets in Edward's 4th House and the absence of planets in his 10th helped to reinforce his decision to abandon what seemed, at least to the outside world, to be his proper life action in the public eye and pursue one that was more purely personal.

---

* *Combinations of Stellar Influences*, p. 165.

Case Study #3 — Ulysses S. Grant

The life of Ulysses S. Grant is an excellent example of the 29 year rhythm of Saturn in the life action of an individual. His career went from total failure to Civil War general to president of the United States.

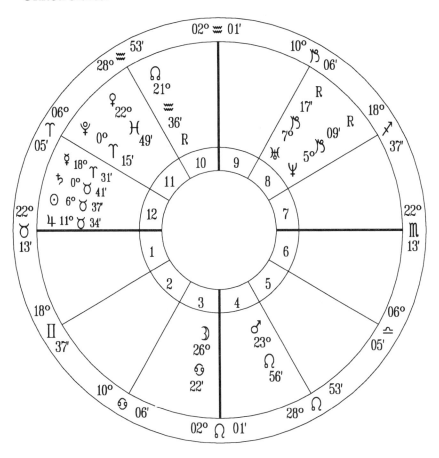

Ulysses S. Grant*

---

* From the Blackwell Data Base we have the following material on his birth data.

1822, April 27 at 6 a.m. LAT (11:34:27 UT) in Point Pleasant, OH (38N54, 84W13). Birth data of "about 6 a.m." from Grant's father to Thomas Lister in 1872 is cited in W. H. Chaney in his *Primer of Astrology*, p. 71. See "CO" for Summer/Fall 1977. Dr. L. D. Broughton's *Elements of Astrology* (p. 343), a less reliable source, gives "5 a.m. - Galena, Illinois," and states that Grant's father gave that data.

His natal 10th House has Aquarius on the cusp but nothing in it except the North Node. This is not, by itself, a particularly strong indication of anything about life action. However, the planet Mars is on the South Node in the 4th. While there is considerable disagreement as to exactly what the Nodes mean, I believe that the conjunction of Mars-Node in the 4th suggests that martial activity was an area in which Grant was intrinsically skilled.* It was not a talent that he had to acquire in this life. He already had it. Both the contact of Mars with the S. Node and its presence in the 4th House suggest that military ability was not actually part of what Grant had to accomplish in his life.

We could get more about Grant's true life direction if we had a precise Midheaven. However, the birthdata are not sufficiently precise. We do get an indication from how his life actually went, however, which we shall look at further on.

He was an average student at West Point and gave little indication of the military ability that he was to display later. At graduation from West Point, Saturn was not well-poised for an early, instant success in his career.

After a few years as army officer, on April 11, 1854 with Saturn at 29Ta38 in his 1st House, he resigned his commission, because of heavy drinking and neglect of duty, according to some authorities. After his resignation in 1854, he began a period of civilian existence that was largely characterized by failure. Most obscure phases are not so obscure as his. However, the obscure phase was over by 1861, when after failing in business he rejoined the army, answering Lincoln's call for volunteers at the beginning of the Civil War. Saturn was by now in early Virgo in his 5th House, quite close to squaring the position it had when he left the army in 1854.

He first distinguished himself in the battle of Belmont in Missouri on November 11, 1861. At this time Jupiter, and Saturn were conjoined in his 5th House at 20–21 Virgo, trine his Ascendant. From here on, his career was on the rise until he became the gener-

---

* Many astrologers believe that S. Node contacts have to do with previous incarnations. I am not comfortable with this idea. I do not necessarily disbelieve in past lives. It is that I find the use of past lives to explain current conditions unfruitful. Since there is no way of definitely checking past lives, there is no way of testing the hypothesis. However, it does seem plausible to me that the S. Node has to do with skills that are to be found in the individual at birth and challenges that have already been met. I leave it to the reader to figure out how this may have come about.

al of all Union armies in 1864. During the entire period of the war, Grant was in Phase I of the Saturn Cycle, "laying the foundation."

It was not until 1867 that Saturn entered his 7th House. The war was over, and Grant had no clear direction to follow. However, in 1867 he was appointed to replace Stanton as Secretary of War during the battle between President Johnson and the Congress.* This was his first foray into politics and represented a change of course from purely military to political. It was an entirely appropriate change to happen at a Saturn transit over the 7th House cusp. This transit is often a redefinition of life direction, not in such a way as to invalidate what had gone before, but rather to fulfill it and establish a truer course.

The following year, Grant was nominated for and elected to the presidency. He served for two terms, from 1869 to 1877. During the second term, Saturn transited his Midheaven and moved all the way to the middle of his 11th House by the time he had left the presidency. In 1880, he was considered seriously for a third term in office, a move which would have violated a long standing tradition in American politics. By this time, however, Saturn was in Grant's 12th house, and the move to nominate him failed.

In 1881, he moved to New York and formed a partnership in a banking firm. In 1884, the firm went bankrupt due to the dishonest transactions of his partner. Grant was exonerated of any wrongdoing, but he was financially ruined as a result. Saturn was now in his 1st House where it had been in 1854! But at this time, Grant was persuaded to write his memoirs for a magazine. He agreed to do so as a way of raising money for his family—and thus he spent the last year of his life examining the entirety of his life and writing it down, a perfect activity for the obscure phase. Almost as soon as he had finished, he died, but the book sold very well and made enough money to take care of his family after his death.

The implications of this are quite interesting. To most people, Grant was pre-eminently a general. Historians regard his presidency as a somewhat unsuccessful anticlimax. His terms in

---

* President Andrew Johnson had originally been Lincoln's Vice-President. When Lincoln died, Johnson became president. Johnson was from Tennessee but had been pro-Union through the War and had retained his seat in the Senate. After the war, Johnson favored a policy of reconciliation with the former Southern states. Congress was dominated by the so-called radicals who favored a much harsher treatment of the Southern states. In the subsequent power struggle, the Senate tried to impeach Johnson on a largely trumped up charge. The impeachment failed.

office were characterized with spectacular corruption and scandal by officials in his administration. Yet none of this affected his popularity, as witness the third-term movement after he had been out of office for a term. It appears that, from the point of view of Grant's life action, his being president had actually much more to do with his popularity than his having been a general in the Civil War.

Case Study #4 — Saturn Cycles in the Ford-Carter Election

In early 1973, Gerald Ford was the minority leader of the House of Representatives.* He had hoped earlier in his career that he might become Speaker of the House, if the Republican party ever became the majority party in the House. Unfortunately, the Republican party had had no majority in the House since Eisenhower's presidency. By 1973, Ford was about ready to give up. In frustration, he seriously considered not running for reelection at the end of the then current term and retiring from politics. These were plans that were entirely in accord with obscure phase symbolism. As it later turned out, his wife, Betty Ford, was also ready to leave politics. As it is for many political wives, her husband's career was quite hard on her.

Then the unexpected happened. The vice-president, Spiro T. Agnew, who was under indictment, was forced to resign under pressure. Nixon had to appoint a new vice-president. He appointed Ford. At the time, Saturn was transiting in early Cancer on Ford's 3rd House cusp. He was deep into his obscure phase. Why would someone, especially someone in politics, a career in which the Saturn cycle is so strong, be catapulted so high in the obscure phase and then move on to the presidency itself?

This is a *classic* example of the Obscure Phase affect: Ford had no ambitions for further advancement. In fact, it was rumored at the

---

* From the Blackwell Data Base we have the following data for Gerald Ford:

1913, July 14 at 00:43 a.m. CST in Omaha, NE (41N15, 95W57). Birth data from President Ford's "baby book" according to "FC." Same data obtained from the first lady's press office by S. Erlewine and reported in "AAM" for January 1975. A birth time of 00:35 a.m. was, according to astrologer Carroll Righter, given by President Ford to Julie Nixon.

time that Nixon chose Ford for the vice-presidency precisely *because* Ford had given up all further ambitions and was ready to retire. His appointment would offend no one, it was reasoned. Ford was doing exactly what he should have been doing at the time, turning away from politics to pursue his own personal development.

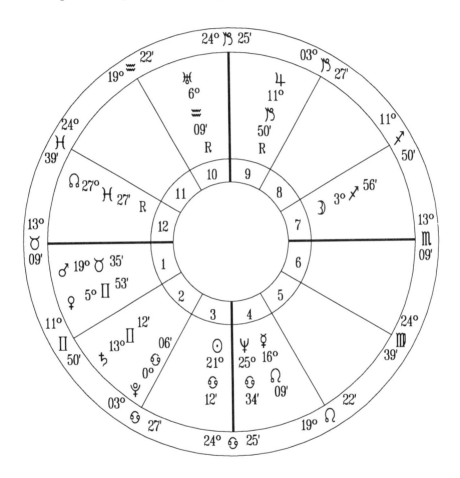

Gerald Ford
(See footnote on preceding page.)

Ford has natal Uranus in his 10th House. This could imply a Uranian type of profession. But Ford is a conservative from the slightly right side of the middle of the road. His whole style of doing politics showed nothing of Uranus. Uranus is closely trined by Venus in the 1st House, ruling the 1st House. And Uranus is in Aquarius which is generally regarded as its own sign.* This symbolizes the possibility that something might happen of a Uranian nature that would affect Ford's life action.

And so it was: Ford was appointed completely "out of the blue" to replace the first vice-president ever forced to resign while in office, and Ford would eventually replace the first president ever to be forced to resign while in office, two unprecedented events occurring in rapid succession!

It is my contention, however, that if Ford had been *trying* to gain the appointment he would *never* have gotten it. Ford was moving with, not against, the flow of the Saturn cycle and that flow did not prevent him from gaining success. This is a clear example of the principle that the obscure phase does not necessarily doom one to failure as long as one is fulfilling the purposes of the phase.

By 1976, Saturn had moved from Ford's 3rd House well into his 4th. All things being equal, he could have sought the presidency on his own at this time without completely going against the flow of his Saturn cycle. However, it was not an ideal time to do so.

Franklin Delano Roosevelt had made a major move in his political career when Saturn entered his 4th House. He began his run for the governorship of the state of New York. However, FDR had an unusually powerful call: he was not merely president but president during two of the worst crises that the United States ever had to face, the Great Depression and World War II. Also FDR was striving to attain a governorship, not a presidency.

What Ford should have been doing was quietly and somewhat privately building the foundations on which to lay a major cycle of life action *later on*, not trying for a peak attainment right away. And he might have gotten away with it, if he had not come up against Jimmy Carter.

In the year 1976, Saturn transited from early Leo back into late Cancer and forward again to about 16 Leo by November. Meanwhile, Uranus was located between 3 and 8 of Scorpio. As Uranus transited late in the 6th House, it spent quite a bit of time making squares to Ford's 10th House natal Uranus. This was not a good indication that events would go according to one's expectations.

---

* I am not entirely convinced of this myself. But the symbolism of a 1st House, 10th House trine regardless of sign and house rulerships is quite good by itself,

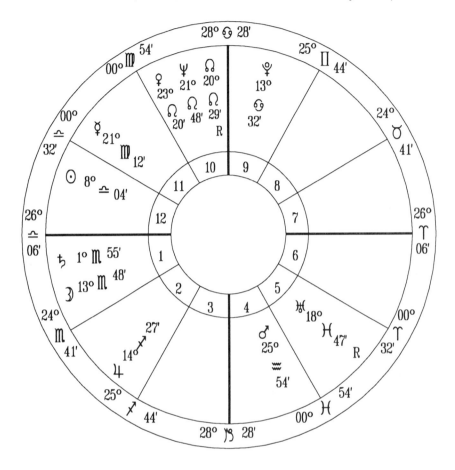

Jimmy Carter*

Saturn in transit also squared the transiting Uranus from Ford's 4th and opposed his natal 10th House Uranus. This was also not a good indication.

And to top it off, Carter's Midheaven is almost exactly opposite Ford's: *while Saturn transited Ford's 4th, it was transiting Carter's*

---

* The Blackwell Data Base gives the following data for Jimmy Carter:

1924, October 1 at 7 a.m. CST in Plains, GA (32N02, 84W24). Birth data of the U.S. president from birth certificate according to astrologer Zip Dobyns in the "MH" for April 1977, p. 49; Carter's mother said that he was born at ". . . 7 a.m. just before sunrise" in a letter to J. Kahila. Sunrise occurred at about 5 a.m. CST. Rodden's "AD III" has "7 a.m. EST" from birth certificate. It has been asserted that the stores in Plains, Georgia used EST rather than CST. Shanks' *American Atlas* (4th edition, 1987) puts Plains on CST.

10th! Carter was at the peak of his life action cycle. Therefore Carter was well set up to win the election simply on the basis of being more in tune with his own Saturn cycle.

So why did Carter's presidency turn out so badly? Fourteen years before, Carter had laid the foundations for his Saturn cycle. He took those actions which would enable him to make his bid for the presidency later on. How did he do this? Instead of following a career as an apprentice politician in some way, he was a nuclear engineer, a very good and respectable career but not one that would suit him for politics. When Carter should have been learning the ABC's of politics, he was involved in something utterly unrelated to politics. Engineering teaches one that there is a right way and a wrong way to do things. But in politics there is no such clear distinction. It is generally agreed that Carter's tragic flaw as a politician was that he did not know how to maneuver in practical politics. He was *unprepared* for the peak of action that came with his Saturn cycle.

Anyone who has followed Carter's career since then must be aware of how much more distinguished in its own way his work has become. He is a man deeply committed to practical action to cure social ills. His real career, the one subsequent to politics, is much more in keeping with his idealistic Venus-Neptune conjunction in the 10th.

It is also interesting to wonder, in view of some of the allegations that have been made with regard to the Iranian hostage taking, how much of his difficulty as president came from his Mars opposing his 10th House conjunction. Could it symbolize forces in the military or intelligence communities that opposed his efforts to curb their power? Certainly this Mars was no friend to his success in politics!

Bibilography

Ebertin, Reinhold. *The Combination of Stellar Influences.* Translated by Alfred Roosedale. Aalen, Germany: Ebertin Verlag, 1960.

Hand, Robert. *Essays on Astrology.* Gloucester, MA: Para Research, 1982.

Jung, C. G. *Memories, Dreams and Reflections.* Recorded and Edited by Aniela Jaffé. Translated by Richard and Clara Winston. New York, NY: Vintage Books, 1963.

Lewi, Grant. *Astrology for the Millions.* St. Paul, Mn: Llewellyn, 1969.

Ptolemy. *Tetrabiblos.* Edited and translated into English by F. E. Robbins. In Manetho; Ptolemy volume of the Loeb Classical Library. Cambridge, MA: Harvard University Press, 1940.

Wehr, Gerhard. *Jung, A Biography.* Boston, MA: Shambala, 1988

General Note

The Blackwell Data Base is available from Astrolabe Software and is available for both the IBM PC and the Macintosh.

The illustrations for this article were prepared using Astrolabe Software's Printwheels Desktop Publishing Module and Corel Draw. Printwheels is available from Astrolabe Software at 350 Underpass Rd. Brewster, MA 02631 Tel 1-800-THE-NOVA.

Timothy Lee Bost

Reading Chaucer's description of the Wife of Bath's horoscope in the *Canterbury Tales* inspired Timothy Lee Bost to begin learning astrology in 1967. A 1970 graduate of Lenoir-Rhyne College with postgraduate studies at Union Theological Seminary and the Liberal Catholic Institute of Studies, Tim Bost has worked as an actor, newspaper editor, arts administrator, and college professor. An ordained clergyman, he also served as the national advertising director for a chemical company and as vice-president of a motion picture production company before starting his own marketing and public relations firm and then turning to astrology as a career.

Tim Bost's work as a financial astrologer has been featured in *Business North Carolina* magazine. He is the author of several astrological monographs, including *How To Find The Money In Your Horoscope*. His articles on astrology have appeared in *Horoscope Guide* and *Horary Practitioner*. Since 1988 he has published *Financial Cycles*, a monthly newsletter on financial astrology.

Tim lives in Greenville, South Carolina, where he teaches astrology classes and workshops, conducts research, and provides astrological services to businesses and individuals.

Person-Centered Financial Astrology: What We Know About Financial Crisis

Timothy Lee Bost

Negative financial news has become a routine part of daily life. Unemployment figures continue to climb. Persistent inflation causes deep concerns in all sectors of the economy. Bankruptcies are on the rise, and financial institutions as well as industries close their doors with increasing frequency.

Behind every grim headline there are hundreds of human faces. Real people confront intense challenges as they struggle with the personal impact of hard times. Many find themselves experiencing financial crisis. Some bring their problems to astrologers, seeking help as they fight off desperation.

The past few years have seen some extremely exciting developments in financial astrology. It's a field filled with creative possibilities. But there's still a gap when it comes to using modern financial astrology to benefit clients in financial crisis. In a time in which national economies move toward depression, and in which millions of people find themselves unemployed, it's increasingly important to narrow that gap.

The recent advances in financial astrology can potentially give significant help to clients in financial crisis. But before that can happen, counseling astrologers need to become more aware of the techniques used in financial astrology. They must also be ready to explore new ways of working with clients in counseling sessions. The ultimate result will be a person-centered approach to financial astrology, which offers clients the hope of achieving economic health in their own lives, as well as providing them with tools that can be used to enhance their financial well-being.

The Changing Face of Financial Astrology

Even though few of today's astrologers have any knowledge of financial astrology as a specialized discipline, financial astrology itself is not something new. It's been around for thousands of years. The *Brihat Samhita*, an ancient Indian text, advised its readers that "If one stores up gold and silver when the Sun enters Simha [the sign of Leo] and sells them in the 5th month, he will get profit." King Ashurbanipal of Assyria (699–635 B.C.) got advice from his astrologer-priests about the planetary prospects for his kingdom's economy.

Financial astrology also played a role in ancient Greece. Aristotle told how Thales of Miletus (636–546 B.C.) was able to make a fortune by putting his knowledge of the stars to practical use. Thanks to his understanding of heavenly cycles, Thales realized one winter that the following summer would bring a larger than usual olive crop. So he rented all of the olive presses he could find in the towns of Miletus and Chios at very advantageous rates. The next summer, when the olive growers all needed oil presses for their bumper crop, Thales turned around and rented out the presses himself at high prices, making a comfortable profit in the process.

By the time of the Renaissance, financial questions had become a regular part of the professional astrologer's practice. William Lilly (1602–1681) wrote in *Christian Astrology* about clients with concerns about the success of voyages made by merchant vessels, about the profitability of buying and selling real estate and commodities, and about the best ways of getting rich. Lilly even used horary astrology to determine the likelihood of discovering buried treasure.

During the past two or three centuries, there has been a growing understanding of business activity as a cyclic phenomenon. This understanding has not always come from astrology *per se*, but nevertheless it has been an important factor in the development of financial astrology as we know it today. Among the most important contributors to this understanding were the English businessman John Mills, who theorized in 1867 that the mental mood of people involved in business tends to run in cycles, creating a corresponding cyclic fluctuation in business activity; and University of Kansas psychologist Raymond Wheeler, who did an exhaustive study of long-range cyclic patterns in the development of cultures, nations, and empires. Because such non-astrologers of the past have studied and defined business cycles, today's astrologers have been increasingly able to find a sympathetic and supportive clientele in certain sectors of the business community.

There have also been important contributions made by individuals who saw direct relationships between celestial phenomena and economic trends. In 1801, for example, the English astronomer Sir William Herschel, discoverer of the planet Uranus, suggested that agricultural and business cycles may be related in some way to the cycle of sunspots. In 1875, the economist Stanley Jevons studied agricultural prices over a 140-year period, and discovered a clear correlation with solar cycles. Jevons noted that if these speculations should prove to have any validity, we get back to something which might be mistaken for the astrology of the Middle Ages.

As more and more researchers explored planetary phenomena, the relationships between cosmic cycles and market events became clearer and clearer. It's little wonder then that J. Pierpont Morgan (1837–1913), one of the richest men of his day, regularly sought the advice of the astrologer Evangeline Adams, who kept him informed of the planetary cycles that could be expected to be reflected in business trends. Adams remarked that "J. Pierpont Morgan, the world's biggest financier, drove the world before him because he had astrology behind him."

By the early years of the twentieth century, astrological techniques were being used by some of the most successful men on Wall Street. W. D. Gann (1878–1955), the genius who developed his own system of technical analysis for price trends in the stock and commodity markets, used not only astrology but also numerology and biblical interpretation to become one of the most successful speculators of his day. Over a 50-year period, Gann earned more than $50 million in the stock and commodity markets. His market forecasts proved accurate more than 85 percent of the time.

In the 1930s, Louise McWhirter wrote about ways of applying traditional astrological methods to the analysis of the stocks offered by corporations. But she also observed an empirical correlation between the cycle of the Lunar Nodes and cycles in business activity. Since McWhirter's time, the nodal cycle has repeatedly been confirmed as a reliable astrological indicator of business trends.

In recent decades, other individuals have continued to use financial astrology to enhance investment profits. Lieutenant Commander David Williams, for example, who for many years was the head of purchasing for Consolidated Edison in New York, made over $1 million in the stock market between 1982 and 1987, using financial astrology to get into the market at the beginning of a major rally and to get out of the market just before the 1987 crash.

Also by the 1980s, thanks to the advent of personal computers and to the work of astrological computer programmers like Robert Hand and Michael Erlewine, financial astrology was able to move far beyond the limits of traditional astrology. It became possible for a desktop computer to generate an ephemeris of planetary motion, and then to correlate that ephemeris with a database of stock or commodity prices, or with data from any other type of business activity that is quantifiably measurable at regular time intervals. Thanks to the computer, new correlations have been found between market activity and planetary cycles.

Today's financial astrology has thus become a hotbed of empirical research, in which hypotheses about planetary correlations are generated by the astrologer or market analyst, refined through computer simulation, and then tested against actual market behavior by actively trading the stocks or commodities in question. Jeanne Long, Bill Meridian, and Larry Pesavento have been some of the leaders in this exciting work in recent years.

Because of the rapid advances being made in financial astrology, however, it has become an extremely specialized field. Its techniques are a far cry from traditional natal astrology and have even less to do with the oversimplified generalizations presented in popular Sun-sign astrology.

Many astrologers who are otherwise competent make the mistake of assuming that they can take their knowledge of traditional astrology and transfer it comfortably to the world of business and finance. They often become frustrated when they discover that they are working *with a different set of rules*, and that traditional astrology doesn't always work as well as they would like it to in the financial arena. They typically encounter major roadblocks when they try to use only the methods of traditional astrology to understand market cycles, or even to fathom the financial behavior of an individual.

At the other end of the spectrum, the ranks of the most successful financial astrologers, as well as the most successful speculators and investors, have consistently included those individuals who started with an empirical approach, who combined a thorough knowledge of business with astute observations of market behavior, and who then later looked at astrological patterns to help make sense of their observations. This is not to say that a traditional astrologer can't also become a successful financial astrologer, or even a successful speculator. But if that's going to happen, the astrologer needs to understand that a basic knowledge of business and investments is an absolute prerequisite.

Where Financial Astrology Falls Short

Financial astrology is rapidly evolving into a highly sophisticated tool for identifying financial opportunities, which can bring profits to investors and speculators who have the courage, the capital, and the clarity of consciousness required to take advantage of them. But even though the tools of financial astrology can be used with some degree of certainty to identify market rhythms and the opportunities provided by turning points in business cycles, the empirical approach to market-oriented financial astrology seems to have some real shortcomings when it comes to identifying financial crisis and to helping clients who are in the midst of it.

These apparent shortcomings may be due to the fact that a crisis for one person is often an opportunity for another. During every financial panic, during every recession or depression, there are still some individuals who are making a great deal of money. During a period of financial panic, property typically becomes cheap, so people with capital are able to acquire more property and thus become richer. Labor typically becomes cheap, so people with the money to hire labor become even richer. But even for people without money, a time of financial panic for others can be a time of major financial opportunity. The most important difference is one of *attitude:* individuals who see the glass as half-full are quick to identify chances to increase their wealth, while those who see the glass as half-empty anticipate financial calamity around every corner.

The potential for converting crisis to opportunity is especially present in the world of financial markets. When the modern empirical approach to financial astrology is employed in speculative markets, it is used to identify potential turning points in price trends: the times at which a market that is in an upward trend will reverse direction and go down, or at which a market in a downward trend will reverse direction and begin to move up. Active market traders can use this information to make money, if they also have reliable non-astrological tools which will help them identify the prevalent trend. Such tools are provided by the methods of technical analysis, the market charting techniques that examine market price movements at regular intervals and look at the overall patterns those price fluctuations make as a way of determining current and future market trends. But such tools and astrological techniques are completely useless to anyone who is psychologically unprepared to view a negative turn in market trend as a positive financial opportunity, and it is just such an individual who is most likely to experience financial crisis.

The Nature of Financial Crisis

A crisis is a turning point, a line of demarcation. It's always an opportunity for learning, for growing, and for redirecting our lives in significant ways. When we're in the midst of a crisis, it's often difficult to see those opportunities, but the opportunities exist nevertheless.

Financial crisis is an acute condition, *but a chronic condition often underlies it.* Our typical response to crisis is to attach a great deal of urgency to it, but financial crisis usually results from long-term patterns of financial behavior. That behavior needs to change if there's to be any long-term resolution of the crisis.

If, for example, a client has gone through two or three years of irresponsible spending and has managed to squander the family fortune, he or she may not feel any sense of crisis until the present, when suddenly there's not enough money to pay this month's bills. The question that client needs to address is not how to get through the current month, but rather how to change his or her long-range patterns of money management.

In working with clients in financial crisis, I like to think in terms of helping them achieve a state of *economic health*. Economic health has nothing to do with having a certain amount of money in the bank, or with having a job that pays well. Instead, economic health is the experience of a dynamic flow of abundance, coupled with the awareness that all wealth ultimately results from the creative energy of the human mind. The emphasis in economic health is on circulation of resources and on the knowledge that an infinite supply of potential wealth is available in bad times as well as in good times.

This state of economic health is a prerequisite for anyone who hopes to be successful in financial markets. An experienced speculator or trader who has both a knowledge of the current market trend and a knowledge of the potential turning points in that trend can use such information to make a profit, *regardless of whether the market is moving up or down.*

The ability to make a profit in either a rising or a falling market is a basic skill of the professional trader, who remains emotionally unattached to the market. The professional trader may make mistakes, but uses precise trading strategies to avoid incurring big losses as a result of those mistakes. But to an individual who is emotionally as well as financially invested in a market, an unexpected trend reversal can be a complete calamity. The same market event can be a profit-making opportunity for the trader and simultaneously the start of a financial crisis for someone else. In other words, the former individual exhibits a state of economic health and well-being, while the latter individual shows symptoms of economic illness.

Financial crisis is thus an internal event rather than an external one. It actually has very little to do with gaining or losing money, changes in job situation, or indebtedness. But it has everything to do with the client's attitude toward financial patterns and circumstances. It's not what happens to a client that creates a financial crisis; the client's reaction to events is the determining factor.

Astrological Triggers of Financial Crisis

There are a number of possible ways that financial crisis can be triggered in the natal chart of an individual. Sometimes it's Saturn entering the 2nd House, but that particular transit does not invariably produce a financial crisis. Some individuals with Saturn transiting the 2nd House will simply reevaluate their finances and get serious about gaining control of expenditures and learning to manage money effectively.

Pluto going through the 2nd House can make its effect felt in various ways. Pluto transiting the 2nd House represents a transformation of the native's finances and personal values, which can be either positive or negative. It's not uncommon for Pluto to enter the 2nd House destructively, bringing with it an immediate financial loss. But after this initial period of disintegration, there's also a longer-term transformation, allowing the individual to begin working with a new paradigm about what it means to be financially secure.

Sometimes a financial crisis can be triggered by what would seem to be a rather benign aspect. The transiting Sun opposing natal Jupiter, for example, may be accompanied by a spurt of extravagance, with the native going on a credit card spending spree, and then winding up in financial hot water. But this particular transit will not uniformly produce a financial crisis: everyone experiences a Sun-Jupiter opposition once a year, but not everyone goes through a financial crisis on an annual basis.

In short, there are planetary configurations that may act as triggers for financial crisis in the charts of some individuals, while failing to have the same effect in the charts of others. There are no hard and fast signatures of financial crisis in an astrological chart that can be consistently recognized whenever they occur. It thus becomes the responsibility of the astrologer *to move beyond* simplistic, cookbook thinking, and to search for astrological triggers on an individualized, case-by-case basis.

In the case of country singer-songwriter Willie Nelson, for example, Mercury, the ruler of the 5th and 8th Houses, is conjunct the *Pars Fortuna* in the 2nd House, presenting a picture of strong financial potential. But Mercury is in mutual reception with Mars, suggesting possible confusion of thought and action, and Neptune, as co-ruler of the 2nd House, adds to the potential for financial disarray. In 1990, when the Internal Revenue Service hit Willie Nelson with a $32 million bill for income taxes, his progressed Mars had just entered his 8th House of taxes and indebtedness, while transiting Saturn had just moved into his 12th House, squaring his natal Mercury.

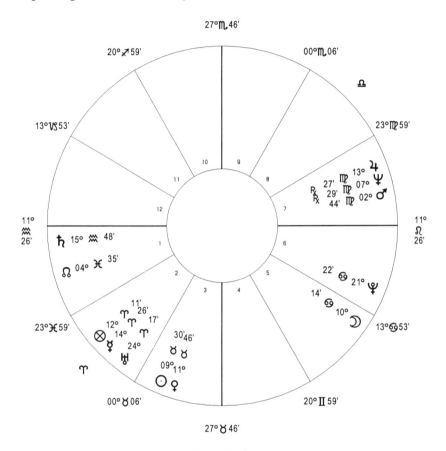

Willie Nelson
Apr. 30, 1933, Fort Worth, Texas, 1:40 a.m. CST
97W18 32N45

At times, the triggers of financial crisis may seem to jump out of the horoscope, grabbing the astrologer's attention in no uncertain terms. In other cases, however, it takes a little bit of digging to uncover the roots of financial crisis in a particular chart. Planetary patterns may occur which seem to indicate financial distress, but no crisis may take place. On the other hand, the client may be feeling acute financial pressure, without any obvious astrological indicators of financial crisis. That's why it's important for the astrologer to do a systematic analysis of the horoscope prior to meeting with the client.

Preparing to Meet a Client in Financial Crisis

First of all, it's useful to examine the longer-range planetary cycles to get a wide view of the general background against which the client is experiencing the current state of crisis. The most important of these is the Saturn cycle, which was described so effectively by Grant Lewi in his book *Astrology For The Millions* [and by Robert Hand, in this volume's preceding chapter.–Ed.]. When transiting Saturn hits the Midheaven of a natal chart, it brings the potential for maximum power and prominence in the career. A second potential peak occurs when Saturn crosses the natal Ascendant. When Saturn returns to its natal position, the client may experience a wiping-out of the past, and go through a crisis that provides an opportunity to start life afresh in some way. Other climaxes occur when transiting Saturn is in square or opposition to its natal position, or when it forms a hard aspect to the natal Sun. All of these points in the Saturn cycle may set the stage for financial crisis.

Second in importance only to the Saturn cycle is the cycle of the progressed Moon. A client who is experiencing financial crisis while going through a progressed New Moon phase, for example, is likely to be trying to create new structures in his or her life. Yet such clients may also be finding it difficult to get a clear idea of what they are doing and why, a fact that is likely to exacerbate the sense of immediate crisis.

Clients who are going through the waxing square of the First Quarter progressed Moon typically experience a strong push toward decisive action, while struggling with a tendency to get pulled back into their old ways of doing things. In such a case, any financial crisis is likely to bring with it a compelling sense of urgency, which can reduce these clients' willingness to consider slow, systematic change.

When the waning square of the Last Quarter progressed Moon is in effect, the financial crisis is much more likely to be characterized by doubt. The client may have been following a methodical plan of savings and investment, for example, but in the midst of the crisis may suddenly be questioning the wisdom of that long-range strategy.

The Pluto cycle also has a direct bearing on finance, especially when large amounts of money are concerned. Its transits through the houses of the client's natal horoscope provide a slow-moving background against which short-range financial crises can be seen as figures in the foreground. Transits of Pluto move excruciatingly slowly, taking from 13 to 33 years to move through each sign of the zodiac. For this reason, Pluto will rarely be involved in any short-range strategies for ameliorating financial difficulties, unless it is currently hitting a house cusp or forming an exact aspect to a natal planet. Even so, an awareness of transiting Pluto can prove a considerable aid to the astrologer in understanding the client's willingness or ability to make significant changes in financial behavior.

Pluto transiting the 6th House, for example, emphasizes the client's need for persistent hard work in regaining a sense of financial security. In such a case, new ways of handling finances must become part of a daily routine, and the client can be expected to make slow, steady progress towards financial goals. If Pluto is transiting the 7th House, it hints at the desirability of the client's working to transform relationships, with a possible financial benefit through the agency of a marriage or business partner.

Once the underlying cyclic patterns have been examined, it's time to take a comprehensive look at the client's natal horoscope itself, with an eye toward understanding how money functions in the life of this particular individual. By examining the 2nd, 5th, 8th, and 11th Houses in the natal horoscope, along with their planetary rulers and the planets that occupy these Houses, the astrologer can gain valuable insights into the client's basic potential for experiencing financial crisis.

The 2nd House, as the house of money and possessions, has obvious implications for the client's state of economic well-being and reactions to financial events. But the three other Succedent Houses need to be considered as well. The 5th House relates to the client's ability to take risks, with a direct bearing on the client's aptitude for financial gain or loss, especially through investments and speculation. As the house associated with other people's money, the 8th House may reveal the likelihood of financial gain or loss through inheritance, indebtedness, or taxes. The 11th House, although it seems to have the weakest impact of any Succedent House on financial affairs, is directly related to the client's ability to receive. A great deal of money may flow through the client's life, but if conditions associated with the 11th House indicate difficulty with being a good receiver, the client may not get to keep any of the money that comes through, setting the stage for financial crisis.

In analyzing the Succedent Houses in a horoscope, the astrologer should do more than just study the planets posited in those houses. The planetary rulers of those Houses also need to be examined, along with the aspects they make to other planets in the chart. Are any of these planets involved in major aspect patterns within the chart? Are any of them being triggered by current transits? Are any of them being triggered by Secondary Progression or Solar Arc direction?

It's also important for the astrologer to examine the 12th House in the client's natal chart, along with the planets it contains and its planetary ruler. The 12th House is concerned with hidden fears and the client's ability to be self-destructive, so it often contains important clues about possible triggers for challenging life situations, including financial crisis.

After exploring the structure of the relevant houses in the natal horoscope, the astrologer should examine the role of specific planets in the chart. Although Jupiter and Venus, as the greater and lesser benefics, have traditionally been associated with money in the horoscope, my personal experience has been that their roles are often insignificant at times of financial crisis, unless they are connected to the aforementioned houses, either by position or by rulership.

When preparing to meet with a client in financial crisis, experience has shown the great value of examining the role of the Moon in the natal horoscope. The Moon serves to identify the emotional hot spots for the client, both by its position within a particular house and by its rulership of the house that has Cancer on the cusp. The house position of the Moon will identify the activity or life concern that is most likely to generate a state of emotional crisis for the client, while the sign of the zodiac that the Moon occupies gives an indication of the manner in which the client will try to resolve emotional crisis. The Moon typically has a role to play in any kind of crisis that a client experiences, financial or otherwise, so it's a useful starting point for the astrologer examining the role of planets in the natal horoscope of a client who is going through a financial crisis.

Once the role of the Moon has been understood, it's helpful to take a look at the action of Saturn and Neptune in the natal chart. Saturn rules greed and Neptune rules fear, which are the two emotional motivators of most financial catastrophes. An understanding of these two basic emotions can be a key factor in turning financial crisis into financial opportunity. The specific ways that greed and fear are likely to manifest for the client are suggested by the action of Saturn and Neptune in the natal chart.

Actually, the client's potential for greed will be reflected by both Jupiter and Saturn in the natal chart. Jupiter, as the planet of growth and expansion, is naturally associated with acquisition. But I think it's more important to examine Saturn's role in the natal horoscope when trying to understand what motivates greed for the client. Saturn has to do with self-containment, security, and survival. Saturn creates sense of limits. Everyone has a natural need to grow, but people only become greedy when they have a sense of being overly limited, of not having enough, either now or in the future.

Neptune is the planet ruling fear because it is associated with the power of the imagination. It's when the imagination runs wild, picturing vague yet disastrous uncertainties, that fear can become rampant. An individual who is under the Neptunian spell of fear is virtually incapable of making prudent financial decisions, and is easy prey for the terrors of financial crisis.

In examining Saturn and Neptune in the natal chart, it's important to consider the houses ruled by Saturn and Neptune as well as the houses in which these planets are located. Even though Saturn or Neptune may be associated with a house in the horoscope that's not traditionally linked with money, the fear and greed symbolized by these planets can nevertheless make a powerful impact on the client's state of financial well-being. If they should happen to fall in a Succedent House, the effect can be extraordinarily strong.

With Saturn posited in or ruling the 2nd House, for example, the client may try to compensate for low self-esteem by acquiring possessions or by accumulating money. A sense of never having enough money may become the motivator for greediness. With Neptune posited in or ruling the 2nd House, the client is often confused about financial affairs, turning money into something unreal or intangible and making money issues a basis of fear. Fears about losing sources of income seem to be especially common with Neptune in the 2nd House.

Chiron, the comet which was discovered in 1977, is still basically an experimental factor in natal astrology. Even so, I've found that an examination of Chiron in a natal horoscope can often provide valuable insights into a client's psychological makeup, especially when Chiron is involved in close aspects to other planets. Chiron seems to function as an *inconvenient* benefic, indicating areas of concern that are likely to be experienced as major difficulties by the client, but which offer vast potential for individual benefit. The benefit that comes through Chiron, however, typically manifests in totally unexpected ways, and usually has very little to do with what the client *thinks* is going on.

If Chiron is connected in any way with indicators of financial crisis in a horoscope, it serves as an important clue that the financial crisis is *ultimately for the client's benefit*. Every crisis is a potential turning point, for good or for ill. A careful examination of Chiron can help the astrologer understand the latent benefits that may lie hidden in the crisis.

The astrologer's primary aim in examining all of these factors in the natal chart should be to gain some awareness of the client's basic psychological structure, especially as it relates to giving and receiving, the emotions of fear and greed, and the sense of self-worth. When examining the natal chart, the astrologer should remember that aspects to the Sun, Mars, Jupiter or Pluto may increase the likelihood of large amounts of money flowing into the client's life, but that they also tend to make it easy for money to flow *out* of the client's life, creating the possibility of an easy come, easy go type of financial crisis. This possibility is even stronger when Saturn or Neptune is involved in aspects to the Sun, Mars, Jupiter, or Pluto. Saturn tends to bring such gains and losses into actual manifestation, while illusory Neptune promises the vague potential of gains or losses, stimulating irrational, emotion-driven behavior on the part of the client.

Once the astrologer has examined the underlying cyclic patterns, and has come to an understanding of the financial dynamics in the natal chart through a consideration of the Succedent Houses, the 12th House, and the role of the Moon, Pluto, Chiron, Saturn, and Neptune in the horoscope, it's essential to look at transits to the natal and progressed charts, especially those transits involving the natal Moon, Saturn, and Neptune. If the financial crisis is being triggered by a particular transit, the astrologer can gain valuable information about the probable *duration* of the crisis.

In examining the influence of transiting planets as possible triggers of financial crisis, it's also useful to look for transits to selected planetary midpoints in the natal chart. Among the most important are the Saturn/Neptune midpoint, the Jupiter/Saturn midpoint, the Jupiter/Neptune midpoint, and the Neptune/Midheaven midpoint. The Saturn/Neptune midpoint encapsulates the entire spectrum of fear and greed, bringing it into focus in a single sensitive point in the horoscope. When it gets hit by transiting planets, it can trigger a debilitating internal conflict between materialistic tendencies and idealistic fantasies, leading to the experience of financial crisis. The Jupiter/Saturn midpoint, because of its association with perseverance and persistence, can reveal much about the client's willingness to stick with long-range plans for financial management. The Jupiter/Neptune midpoint is strongly linked to speculative behavior and the client's tendency towards self-deception, both critical factors in financial crisis. The Neptune/Midheaven midpoint is a point of confusion and uncertainty, which is connected with the client's gullibility and tendency to be deceived by others.

After looking at current and forthcoming transits, the astrologer may wish to go into a more detailed examination of secondary progressions and solar arc directions, as well as current solar and lunar returns. In most cases, however, studying the natal chart, the major planetary cycles, and the planetary transits to key points in the natal chart will give the astrologer enough to go on.

A good illustration of the way that natal factors and cyclic influences combine at a time of financial crisis is provided by the horoscope of Nikola Tesla (1856–1943), the eccentric Serbian genius who was the originator of alternating current, fluorescent lighting, and a host of other inventions. Neptune in the 12th House of Tesla's natal chart sows hidden seeds of fear and confusion, with Jupiter, the ruler of the 8th House of borrowed money, also confined in the 12th House, where it squares Saturn, suggesting a tendency toward tension due to shortages of funds. The Moon-Mars conjunction in the 6th House adds to Tesla's tendency to act precipitously in times of crisis, while their square to the Sun in the 4th House sets the stage for an "easy come, easy go" attitude toward money. Tesla himself once remarked that "The only way I shall ever have a cent is when I have enough money to throw it out of the window in handfuls." Perhaps most telling of all is the fact that Mercury, the ruler of the 2nd House, is unaspected in the 3rd House, indicating a tendency to think about financial matters a great deal, but to leave them somewhat unconnected to all of life's other concerns.

Shortly after the turn of the century, Nikola Tesla began one of the most ambitious projects of his career. He raised money for an experimental laboratory in Wardencliff, a Suffolk County real estate development on Long Island, about 60 miles from New York City. Tesla's plan was to erect a tower over 150 feet high, topped with a giant copper electrode, 100 feet in diameter. It was to be powered by its own electric generating station. Tesla's scheme was to broadcast worldwide over all known radio frequencies from this single station, giving him a total monopoly on the radio broadcasting business. He also envisioned his Wardencliff laboratory becoming the hub of a power-generating system that would supply wireless electricity to the entire globe.

In March 1903, with transiting Mars moving retrograde over his natal Moon, Tesla began to feel such a severe financial pinch that he returned to New York to try to raise additional money for his project on Long Island. On April 8, he asked for money in the first of a series of letters to J. P. Morgan, who had already loaned him $150,000 for the construction of his Wardencliff laboratory. Tesla's repeated appeals to Morgan went unanswered until mid-July, when Mars, now in direct motion, was once again conjunct Tesla's natal Moon. Morgan's disappointing response to Tesla's pleas for funds was simply that "I should not feel disposed at present to make any further advances."

In the fall of 1903, the Rich Man's Panic hit the financial markets, and Tesla continued to come up empty-handed in his search for funds. Solar Arc Neptune conjoined his natal Pluto in early September, making matters even worse by intensifying his preoccupation with his schemes for new inventions, while he left practical financial matters unattended. In early November, Solar Arc

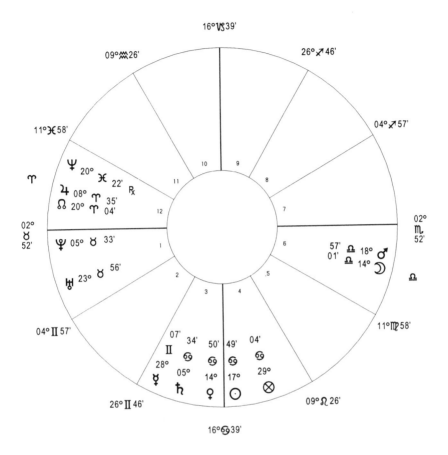

Nikola Tesla
July 10, 1856, Smiljan, Yugoslavia, 12:00 a.m. LMT
15E19 44N35

Jupiter, the ruler of his 8th House of indebtedness, conjoined his natal Uranus, and Tesla became embroiled in a frenzy of begging from banks, trying to get loans from friends and acquaintances, and dodging bill collectors. He repeatedly had to lay off his workmen because there wasn't any money to pay them, and he found himself unable to buy coal to fuel the steam generator for his laboratory. He was also sued for nonpayment of the power and water bills he had run up during his experiments in Colorado several years earlier.

In January 1904 transiting Saturn moved into Tesla's 11th House, where it was to remain for the next three years. This transit apparently had the effect of further inhibiting his ability to receive benefit from others. As Saturn moved through his 11th House in 1904, it formed a quincunx to the money planet Venus, the ruler of the Ascendant and the dispositor of Pluto. Later in the same year, transiting Saturn turned retrograde, making its direct station in October in exact quincunx to Venus once again. Tesla's finances continued to deteriorate, and in 1905 he was forced to shut down his laboratory at Wardencliff for lack of funds.

Strategies for Counseling Clients in Financial Crisis

In most cases, an individual's ability to handle money is a direct outgrowth of his or her self-esteem. Although there are many potential triggers for financial crisis, every individual who is confronted with a time of financial stress ultimately has to deal with questions of self worth. An important role of financial astrology is to help individuals understand themselves as dynamic individuals, capable of both giving and receiving.

Every financial crisis is essentially a crisis of self-worth, providing a clear opportunity for potentially therapeutic interaction with the astrologer. Whether the client is looking for a new job, or is struggling to get out of debt, or is simply overdrawn at the bank, his or her efficacy will be seriously diminished without a strong self-image. Competent astrologers can aid their clients in seeing what makes them unique as individuals, and therefore what empowers them to make valuable societal and interpersonal contributions deserving financial remuneration.

The first step in counseling a client in financial crisis is to recognize the client's frame of mind. Consulting an astrologer is often a frightening experience, especially for clients who have had little prior experience with astrology. The client may feel that the astrologer has access to supernatural sources of information, or that the astrologer will reveal things that are embarrassing or distressing to learn.

This sense of apprehension may be amplified when the client is experiencing financial crisis. Financial crisis itself is often accompanied by genuine feelings of panic, a state of mind that may lead some clients to hope the astrologer can work miracles, revealing secret or magical ways of setting their lives straight and reversing their financial misfortunes in the twinkling of an eye.

Both the overly-fearful extreme and the overly-hopeful extreme are obviously rooted in client misunderstandings about the true nature of astrology and its capabilities. Nevertheless, the competent astrologer must take these extremes into consideration when sitting down to meet with a client for the first time. Regardless of how unrealistic they may be, such distorted perspectives are by no means uncommon, particularly among clients who come to see an astrologer as a last resort. It's incumbent upon the astrologer to clear up such distortions early in the consultation, so that the remaining time with the client can be spent in productive, professional, and potentially therapeutic interaction.

At the outset of a consultation, it's often helpful for the client to discuss financial arrangements up front with the astrologer. This helps clear the client's mind of at least one source of worry— paying for the services the astrologer provides. The specific payment arrangements are up to the astrologer, but they should be openly and clearly discussed with the client. The astrologer may wish to make special payment arrangements for clients in financial crisis. One possibility is to offer alternative payment plans for astrological services or to encourage clients to consider bartering arrangements. In every case, however, the idea is to make it clear to the client that the astrologer has a commitment to providing a service, and while the astrologer certainly deserves to be compensated for those services, that the astrologer views the client as a person rather than as a dollar sign.

Just as a medical astrologer needs to be clear about the limitations of medical expertise, so too must financial astrologers be careful to inform their clients about the limits of their own competence. Unless the astrologer also happens to be a certified financial planner or another sort of financial professional, it's only ethical for the astrologer to offer financial advice if it's accompanied by a clear statement that the advice being offered is based solely on astrology, and not on any sort of financial training or expertise. If a client discusses financial difficulties with the astrologer, it's usually also wise for the astrologer to suggest that the client see an accountant, attorney, or financial planner as well. Every financial crisis has an important role to play in the client's life, and a part of that role may be in stimulating the client to take on greater levels of financial responsibility. Bringing in the help of a financial expert can help the client go a long way toward acknowledging and accepting such responsibility.

It's always important for the astrologer to get a clear picture of what the client is actually experiencing, and to get an accurate idea of what kind of help the client is seeking. Sometimes a client may describe financial problems, while the horoscope suggests dynamic stress in relationships, communications, or some other area that may not seem astrologically related to money. This provides an opportunity for the astrologer to explore with leading questions a way of encouraging the client to re-examine basic assumptions and see his or her problems from a broader perspective. In some cases, clients look to the stars to rescue them from circumstances they're unwilling to address by themselves. The astrologer's role is to help them face their difficulties and to explore ways of taking responsibility for their own lives in a creative, positive manner.

Sometimes the astrologer needs to question the client simply to clarify details about the client's attitudes and current circumstances. For example, if a client inquires about the advisability of changing jobs, it's always helpful for the astrologer to ask if the client has indeed already been offered a new job. The client's response will make a great deal of difference in the discussion that follows.

What the client presents as a financial difficulty may in fact be something else altogether. It's the astrologer's responsibility to find out what's *really* going on. The client who has just taken heavy losses in the stock market is different than the client who is experiencing financial difficulties because his free-loading brother-in-law has just moved in with him and he's having trouble making ends meet. They are both cases of financial crisis, but one client needs to talk about issues of risk and security, while the other could use a discussion of ways to make family relationships more functional.

Early in my career as a professional astrologer, an earnest young man came to my office for a consultation. We discussed a variety of concerns, and then he asked me if I saw anything in his chart that would indicate the possibility of significant income through investments during the coming year. I noticed that he had some favorable transits to the ruler of his 5th House, but fortunately a flash of inspiration led me to ask him what kind of investments he had.

"I don't have any investments at all," was his reply.

"And do you have any money now that you're planning to invest?" I asked.

"No," he said. "I just wanted to know if you saw any money coming into my life that way. I figured that if there was any chance of my getting any income from investments, I might be able to quit my job and spend more time doing the things I really like to do."

It was clear that he had very little understanding of what investments actually are, or of how they can be expected to produce a financial return. If I had answered his original question without getting some clarification, I would have run the risk of compounding his confusion and doing him a real disservice. But as it turned out, my willingness to probe soon got us to my client's real issue—his dissatisfaction with his current employment and his desire to explore a new career.

The astrologer's ego is often the biggest obstacle to asking the kind of probing questions that can open the door to a productive session. If the astrologer feels an obligation to deduce all of the client's current circumstances from an analysis of the horoscope, if the astrologer's ego requires that the client be given a proof of astrology, then the astrologer may be reluctant to question the client. Ultimately, however, the astrologer's role is not to prove astrology, but to provide a genuine service to the client. This is especially true when the astrologer is involved in crisis counseling, which has nothing to do with demonstrating superiority to the client or with displaying some sort of paranormal ability.

By working with transits, Secondary Progressions, and Solar Arc directions,the astrologer should be able to gain some sense of the probable duration of a financial crisis, and in some cases it's useful to share that information with the client. Many clients who are experiencing financial crisis tend to have a very short-range perspective on their difficulties. Even if a client faces years of financial difficulty, the astrologer can at least help the client understand that the problem is finite. It won't last forever.

Discussing the possible duration of financial difficulties with a client accomplishes two very important things. First, it gives the astrologer a sense of how conscious the client is of his or her financial behavior. If, for example, the client says "I don't know what happened; all of a sudden there just wasn't any money to pay the bills," while the astrologer sees astrological evidence of long-term financial upheaval going on for the client, it becomes the astrologer's role to help the client understand the bigger picture, seeing the current situation from a broader perspective.

Second, a discussion of the possible duration of financial crisis can help reassure the client. Rather than feeling at the mercy of a malevolent universe, the client can gain some sense of the finite nature of the problems being experienced. Problems don't last forever, and it's important for the client to know that. By sharing an understanding of cycles with the client, the astrologer is able to mention specific time frames and say to the client, "This is when your financial troubles actually began, this is when you became aware of them, and this is when they're likely to move out of the picture, provided you take appropriate action in the meantime." With that kind of reassurance, most clients are typically willing to move into a discussion of specific ideas for solving financial problems.

One of the most valuable tools that can be used to supplement the natal chart in working with clients is the 45-degree graphic ephemeris (a year-long spreadsheet of major transits to natal positions with aspects in the fourth harmonic). It can show at a glance the kind of duration that can be expected for specific transiting influences. This is especially helpful when the client can provide some information about when a crisis began, and the astrologer can point to specific patterns on the graphic ephemeris associated with the planetary transits in that particular time frame. In many cases a client's first awareness of financial crisis will coincide quite closely with a planetary transit that will show up on the graphic ephemeris, within the context of a whole year seen at a glance

In spite of the fact that the 45-degree graphic ephemeris is still a relatively new tool that is used by a limited number of astrologers, my experience has been that most clients who are basically ignorant of astrology are nevertheless quick to grasp planetary cycles and their duration when those cycles are pointed out to them with the graphic ephemeris. The graphic ephemeris gets the conversation with the client focused on specific periods of time, which can be useful in reinforcing the need for the client to take personal responsibility in creating positive change. I point out the timing factors at work and suggest that there's a particular time frame within which the client can expect to get the greatest results if he or she uses that time to take appropriate remedial action. This helps the client visualize the *potential limits of the crisis*, while leaving the responsibility for change right where it belongs: squarely on the shoulders of the client, and not in the hands of the astrologer.

Once the dynamics of the financial crisis have been discussed with the client, it's time to focus on strategies for ameliorating the situation. In many cases, the simple process of discussing the problem is enough to inspire a client with the ideas and motivations needed to resolve the crisis. In other instances, the astrologer may wish to discuss remedial options with the client, while making it clear that the client has the ultimate responsibility for choosing among those options. This stage of the consultation also presents another good opportunity for the astrologer to refer the client to another counseling or financial professional if the nature of the difficulty warrants such action.

In working with a client who is going through financial difficulties, it's often helpful to share the concept of financial crisis as essentially a form of economic illness, rather than as an external event that impacts the client arbitrarily. Economic health is always a state of flow, a process of resources moving in and out of the operations of business or the life of an individual. When that flow is disrupted, the result is a state of economic illness. From this point of view, it's irrelevant whether this takes place against a background of wealth or of poverty. In either case, the client may experience the disruption of the flow as a state of financial crisis. Financial crisis is thus not merely a lack of money; it is a state of imbalance, an interrupted flow, which is typically exacerbated by the client's distorted sense of self-worth.

In this paradigm, the role of the astrologer who is trying to assist a client experiencing financial crisis becomes one of facilitating a process of healing. But as with any other kind of healing, it is ultimately the client who must do the real work of restoring equilibrium and harmony.

Finally, the most important role of the astrologer in counseling clients in financial crisis is to have those clients leaving their consultations feeling better about themselves than they did when they walked into the astrologer's office. As we have discussed, ultimately all financial crisis boils down to a question of self-worth. If the astrologer can't enhance that sense of self-worth in some way, the appointment time has essentially been wasted. This often means that the astrologer essentially plays the role of a cheerleader, balancing a sober discussion of financial realities with enthusiastic efforts to leave the client feeling empowered and optimistic.

A Case Example

At times, a session with a client who is experiencing financial crisis will feature very little discussion of financial matters *per se*. In the case of Rachael, it was emotional issues that were the real focus of our consultation. In fact, this was a client who was essentially trying *to use her financial problems as an excuse for failing to confront some deeply-rooted emotional concerns.* Rachael, a corporate executive, had been a regular client for a little more than a year, meeting with me to discuss business concerns as well as her personal life, and we had developed a comfortable level of rapport. It had been several months since I had seen her, and during that interim Rachael had purchased a condominium and had it remodeled. As she was moving into her condo, she discovered that she had unexpectedly run out of money. When she called to schedule an appointment with me, she was clearly in a state of panic. For her, this was obviously a traumatic financial crisis.

I began our session together by asking Rachael if she had ever experienced a financial crisis before. She remembered three or four occasions when she had been overdrawn on her checking account, which involved some financial inconvenience but not real crisis. "There was also a time, throughout most of 1987, when I had a lot of credit cards and I was pretty much in debt," she told me. "I was going overseas, so I sold my car and I sold my computer to help get myself out of debt. It took me another six months while I was overseas to get out of debt completely.

"Actually I built up that credit card mess over a period of time, throughout 1986 and 1987. Since that time, because of the mess I got myself in with the credit cards back then, I've not allowed myself to own a credit card that charges interest. I've only got an American Express, which you have to pay off imme-diately each month, and a direct debit card, which takes money directly out of my savings account. So I've never gotten myself that badly into debt, but I've also eliminated a way that I could have avoided getting myself into the mess that I'm in right now, because I haven't been able to charge any purchases that I've had to make; I've had to pay for everything in cash.

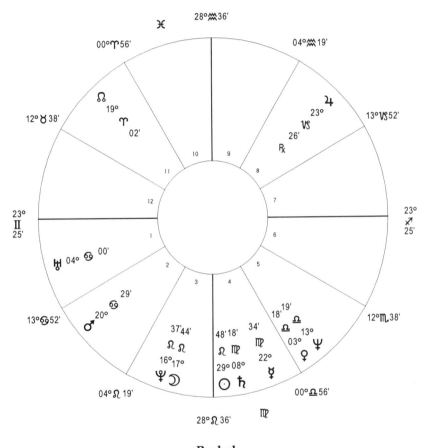

Rachel

"I've been used to living on a cash basis. But right now, because of my miscalculations, I've got about $2,000 in bills that are due and I don't have any money in my account to pay them. And I can't do anything about paying it off right now because of all the other regular bills and payments that I have. I'll only be able to chip away at it at the rate of about $200 a month, so it will take me about a year to pay it all off."

I could find no short-term transits that were obviously connected with Rachael's problem. Her current crisis seemed to be triggered by Solar Arc Uranus conjoining her natal Pluto, and moving within orb of her natal Moon, the ruler of her 2nd House. During her previous period of crisis, Solar Arc Mars had begun to oppose her natal Midheaven, shortly after Solar Arc *Jupiter* had come to her Midheaven. Since her Mars-Jupiter opposition in the 2nd and 8th Houses of the natal chart was part of a T-square pattern with the North Lunar Node, I told her that her horoscope indicated that she had some real issues with money in general, issues which remained dormant and built up energy until they happened to be triggered by various short-term factors. The fact that her Leo Moon, powerfully conjoined with Pluto, was currently involved (Solar Arc Uranus approaching natal Moon) told me that discussion of emotions and Leonine needs was in order.

"It's obvious that you have financial problems to deal with," I told her, "but I'm wondering whether this isn't more of an emotional crisis than a financial crisis. Your horoscope suggests to me that you're really dealing with questions that have to do with your self-worth, with your own level of emotional security, and with how loved you feel. Based on the astrological information I have, it seems to me that we're looking at a long-term internal situation, rather than simply a set of financial problems that have suddenly come up because of some miscalculations on your part. Does that make sense to you?"

"I think so," Rachael said. "If I hadn't spent so much last year and had saved up enough cash, then I wouldn't have gotten to this point. The money would have been there when I needed it."

"But what did your spending actually do for you?" I asked. "Well, it had to do with fixing up my new place, so that it would be livable before I moved in. I was making the changes that I felt needed to be made, to make the place suit me more. But I tried to get all of those changes made at the same time, instead of moving in and having them done gradually. And because I was always really busy with my job, I didn't keep a close enough control on the work that was being done. I didn't watch what the contractor was doing, and the whole thing ended up costing me a lot more than I had expected. Actually, I didn't try to control the cost at all. I just made my decisions based on trying to get the best quality I could find, and once I had made my mind up, I would just go with it.

"In a way, though, I know what you mean when you mention the emotional thing. When I spend like this, it's a way of taking care of myself; it's a way of making myself feel better. And if I hadn't been doing it to make myself feel better I would have sat down with the contractor and figured out the costs ahead of time. The contractor wasn't working with a specific budget. I just went with a contractor who was a friend of my brother, who promised me a good deal if I would hire him to take care of all the little renovation and remodeling jobs that I wanted done. I was paying him by the day, and he told me how many days it would take. But then when I got the bill, the number of days had doubled.

"I also didn't negotiate with the seller of the condo, who should have probably taken care of a lot of the repairs before we closed the sale. But I was too anxious to move in, I was too anxious to make the place mine, to really think about all the maintenance and repair things that I could have gotten them to pay for. Like there were no mirrors in the bathrooms, and some of the faucets needed to be replaced. The kitchen needed to be completely redone. And I just decided to get top quality stuff, without really thinking about how much it would cost.

"Once the work was done and I got ready to move in, I wrote a check to the contractor. I have overdraft protection on my checking account, and about a week after I paid the contractor I got a notice from my bank that it had kicked in. But now I'm sitting here without the phone bill paid at either location, without the movers paid, without the dry wall people paid, without any of the other subcontractors paid. I had expected the contractor to pay the dry wall people and the electricians from what I paid him, but all of that subcontractor work turned out to be separate, and I still owe money for all of it. That's in addition to all of the regular monthly bills that need to be paid. And then to top everything else off my company just changed the payroll: we used to get paid every other week, but starting this month we get paid monthly, so I'm going to have to wait almost another month before any money comes in at all. And to complicate matters evenmore, I have a cracked tooth and I've got to have a crown put on. If I need a root canal it could end up costing me $800. It's really a big mess. I've made some steps toward getting out of this problem, but it's still a long way from being solved."

"What kind of steps have you taken?" I asked.

"I wiped out my savings account at the credit union. I asked my brother if he would loan me some money, but he can't. I also asked my sister, but she said she wouldn't loan it to me. She said I have lessons to learn. A friend of mine has agreed to loan me a little bit of money, enough at least to keep me from getting my phone cut off. It's really embarrassing to have to borrow money from friends."

"I'm curious about your sister's suggestion that you have something to learn," I told Rachael. "What do you think you have to learn?"

"To handle my finances better and to budget my money. My sister's always been very tight with her money. She always budgets and she never spends too much. She's always got thousands in savings and I always have zero."

"Once again," I said, "it seems to me that there are some core emotional issues at work here. You're saying 'If I don't look at the money I'm spending, then somehow nobody will know that I don't feel completely okay about myself. In other words, *the money I have is a reflection of my self-worth.* At an emotional level, they amount to the same thing. If I have an infinite amount of money, then I have an infinite amount of self-worth. If I never keep accounts, if I never keep track of how much I spend and how much I actually have, *then I never have to examine myself in terms of what I think I'm really worth—not financially, but what I think I'm really worth as a person.'*

". . . The real question here is not whether you can get out of the hole financially and get everybody paid off. Sooner or later, that's going to happen. What you could be asking yourself right now is, 'What can I do to prevent this sort of thing from happening again, and what am I trying to prove to myself with this kind of behavior?' . . ."

"That's true," Rachael said.

"What I'm suggesting is that there's a lesson to be learned here. It's an opportunity to get clear about your own emotional process as you get things back on an even keel financially. In terms of your self-worth this could be a very challenging time as you get things paid off during the next twelve months. You can discover ways of loving yourself, of being affirmative and approving of yourself. If you create some new constructive patterns at the emotional level, you can spontaneously transform your behavior so that you naturally begin to do the appropriate thing financially. Do you have any ideas about how that might happen?"

Rachael laughed nervously. "I don't budget," she said. "I don't plan what I eat. I don't plan what I spend. I just take a *laissez faire* approach, with only a vague idea of what I'm spending until the bank lets me know I'm overdrawn. In a way I think that's a sign of what you were saying about my not doing the loving thing in taking care of myself. I'm telling myself that it doesn't matter; as long as there's some money there I don't have to think about myself.

"It feels like what I ought to do is first sit down and pay bills and put my financial life in order. It always makes me feel good when I feel like I have things under control and organized, as opposed to never actually settling down and getting into things."

"How do you really feel about getting organized financially right now?" I asked. "Are you really looking forward to sitting down with all those unpaid bills?"

Rachael chuckled. "No," she admitted.

"How do you *really* feel?"

There was a long pause. "In a way, it gives me something to do," Rachael said at last. "Which is not to say that I don't already have enough to do. But I guess sitting down with the bills would give me a detailed activity to do that would help me focus somehow"

"I'm not hearing much of a real payoff in that," I said.

Rachael laughed again. "No," she said. "It's drudgery. I don't like doing that stuff."

"But a moment ago you said you felt good about doing that kind of stuff."

"I feel good when it's *done*. It feels good when I know where to find things, when a picture of everything is within my grasp. Otherwise I feel real scattered. I can't put a finger on things, so I can't plan and I can't manage and I can't get ahead. I don't have a handle on what's there.

"When I think about it, I see this reflected in my job, too. I'm staying on the surface. I keep getting calls and I keep taking care of the flashy exterior things, instead of doing the basic, solid interior work that really needs to get done."

"So what's the payoff in staying on the surface?" I asked.

"I don't know," she said. "I guess it keeps me from looking inside, from looking at what's really going on."

"And when you look at what's really going on, what do you see?"

"I don't know. I haven't looked at it."

There was an uncomfortable pause. "Rachael," I said, "right now your body language is suggesting to me that you're feeling a lot of fear. Are you aware of being afraid of anything?"

"Not anything in particular," she said. "I've been uncovering a lot of stuff in therapy recently, so it may have something to do with that. The therapy's going well, but I guess I'll have to discontinue it now because of the financial mess I'm in. Anyway, I haven't been doing the journal work that my therapist wants me to do. I guess that's part of the avoidance thing, too. But we've been talking about a lot of childhood stuff, about family interactions having resulted in issues of self-worth. It's about how I view myself, and my role in relationships, and my role in society, that kind of thing."

"Would it be going too far out on a limb to say that there's some kind of connection between your not doing the work in therapy and the financial situation you've found yourself in?"

"Well, in both cases I haven't been doing the work. I prefer to stay on the surface and not go beyond that."

"Rachael," I said, "as I told you a few minutes ago, I think your financial questions are really self-worth questions. And what I'm hearing from you now is that you're not really willing to confront those self-worth questions in therapy, either. You're willing to deal with things on a superficial head level, but you're not willing to go beyond that."

"Maybe that's where the fear is," she said. "I'm afraid of going beyond the head level and getting into my emotions . . .

"It's the same thing with gaining weight, with not taking care of myself physically, isn't it? I can see the connection. Wow!"

"What I'm suggesting here is that the emotional stuff and the self-worth questions are what's really going on, and that the financial crisis you're experiencing is just a symptom of a much deeper pattern. You obviously have to do whatever you feel is appropriate with regard to continuing or discontinuing your therapy, but it seems to me that it would be a real shame to waste a perfectly good financial crisis without doing the emotional work behind it."

Rachael laughed.

"How you do the emotional work is up to you," I told her. "You can continue with your therapist, or you can do the journal work on your own, or do whatever else you think might be valuable. But the key question is whether or not you're actually willing to do the work. That's why this financial crisis may actually be a blessing in disguise. It's serving the function of getting your attention in a powerful way, of getting you focused on the emotional work that you really need to be doing."

"It sure got my attention," Rachael said. "You're right about that!"

"Once again, Rachael, I would discourage you from looking at this as simply the need to keep your checkbook balanced. That's obviously part of the game plan, but that's not the main point.

"You know, when I was looking over your natal chart again today in preparation for this session, a question came to mind: `When someone loves Rachael, when someone really cares about Rachael, how much does Rachael require the other party to take the initiative in expressing that love? And how much does that love need to be expressed financially?'"

"Oh, I definitely expect the other person to take the initiative," Rachael said.

"So it's hard for you to say to someone 'I know you love me, and I accept that.' Instead, you want them to prove it, you want them to show you."

"Yes."

"So how much of a financial component is there in that expectation?"

"It's a pretty big component," Rachael said. "That's how my father showed us that he loved us, by spending money on us. He didn't know any other way. We grew up with a father who showed zero emotion, except for anger."

"Say that again," I requested.

"My father didn't express any emotion except anger. The only way he showed love for us, the only way he showed positive emotion, was by buying us things."

"So you're saying 'When someone else loves me, I expect them to show that love by spending money on me?'"

"That's right."

"'And when I want to show love for myself?'"

"I do it by spending money on myself. But what's going on? Am I spending all this money as a way of showing that I love myself? Or am I making sure that I run out of money to prove that I don't love myself? "

"I think you're giving yourself contradictory information. On the one hand, 'I spend a lot of money on myself, so I must love myself.' On the other hand, 'I don't know how much money I'm spending, so I'm setting myself up to take periodic financial falls, just to prove that I'm not really worthy of love. If I weren't basically unlovable, I'd be in a satisfactory relationship right now; people would be expressing love for me.'"

"I can see that. But how do I get out of it?"

I took a moment to look at her natal chart again before I replied. Seeing Neptune in the 5th House reminded me of how much fear Rachael could attach to expressing love for others, and to allowing herself to be creative. This capacity for fear was amplified by the fact that Venus, also in the 5th House, ruled the 12th House in her natal chart.

"So far we've talked about three main areas," I told her. "The first is your own sense of self-worth. The second is your financial interaction with others, borrowing money and owing money. The third is your ability to accept love from other people. What we haven't talked about yet is your ability to express love to others. And it seems to me that's where you have the greatest potential for doing something constructive right now.

"In terms of dealing with the financial situation, you already know what has to be done. The bills eventually have to be paid, and you're already working on a plan for doing that. But in terms of getting to the root emotional questions, the idea is to explore how creative you can be, to see how many different ways you can express love for other people. Your typical way of expressing love for others is to spend money on them, but right now that simply isn't available to you. Thanks to the blessing of your being in a financial crisis, you've got to find alternatives."

"That's true. That's very interesting. "

"Rachael, there's no way you can change your father's inability to express love to you when you were a child. What you've done to your bank account has been done, and there's no way you can undo that except over a period of time, in the way that you've already planned to correct the situation. But your own sense of self-worth can be enhanced by understanding yourself as someone who is creative, who is able to create positive change in your own life. And the one big opportunity that you've got for doing that right now is by expressing love for other people."

Together, we explored ways she could indeed be more expressively loving to others.

"I think you're exactly right," Rachael said. "I've been using my spending as a way of not keeping in touch with myself. In the situation I'm in right now, I'm not only going to have to be creative about expressing love for others, I'm also going to have to be creative about furnishing my condo. After all, I don't have any more money to spend. I'm already coming up with some neat ideas about making my own curtains, instead of paying to have them made. I think I'm really going to enjoy fixing up my place."

"Are you saying you're actually going to have some fun with your financial crisis?"

"I think I probably will," Rachael said. "And I think it's about time, too. I deserve to have some fun. And I'm tired of crying."

Moving Toward Person-Centered Financial Astrology

Astrology has a great deal to offer clients in financial crisis, but there is much work that can be done to enhance its effectiveness. One of the most immediate needs is for systematic research into the astrological dynamics of individual financial crisis. Because there are no clear-cut and consistent astrological signatures of financial crisis, it's important that astrologers working with clients in financial crisis *document what they learn about the astrological triggers involved,* especially when those triggers aren't obvious or when they fail to fit traditional expectations.

In understanding the potential triggers for financial crisis, there's a need for further research into the impact on individuals of the planetary cycles that are being explored by empirical financial astrology. The cycle of the Lunar Nodes, for example, has been shown to be a planetary cycle that's fairly consistently correlated with business rhythms. It may be useful to research this cycle's impact on *individual* finances as well. It would also be interesting to investigate the reactions of individual clients to the synodic cycle of Venus and Uranus, which seems to show a consistent relationship to turning points in stock market trends.

A second major need is for more astrological education. Traditional counseling astrologers need to learn more about financial astrology, especially the empirical work that is currently contributing so much to our knowledge of financial markets. Astrologers also need to know more about the workings of financial markets themselves, and need to become conversant with the tools of technical analysis, which can be used to measure and forecast market trends.

Finally, it's important for astrologers to learn enough about money management to be able to take care of their own financial concerns. The old admonition of "Physician, heal thyself" no doubt applies to astrologers as well, especially astrologers working with financial crisis. Astrology is a powerful tool for understanding human beings. When used appropriately, it can be incredibly effective in promoting individual growth and in advancing the process of economic healing. But no client in financial crisis can realistically expect to get significant help from an astrologer if that astrologer is going through a financial crisis too.

Thanks to research advances in empirical financial astrology and to increasingly higher professional standards in counseling astrology, the time is ripe for building a bridge between the empirical approach, which uses astrology to enhance trading activity by identifying potential turning points in markets, and the person-centered approach of client counseling.

A common link between the two approaches can be found in the psychology of the individuals involved. What financial astrology has to offer is not a methodology for getting rich quickly, but rather a way of understanding that financial markets can be predictable and that they can be interacted with profitably, provided that the individual ego is kept out of the picture through some sort of psychological self-management. In fact, an underlying assumption in successful stock or commodity trading is that the trader has a level of psychological self-control. Every good trader knows that the major struggle is not one of prices going up or down; it's an internal struggle within the trader's own consciousness. That's why professional traders build safety mechanisms into their trading plans to help limit the impact of emotional fluctuations and shifting ideas of self-worth, whether those ideas be inflated or deflated. By devising a specific trading plan and sticking to it, the trader is able to keep his or her ego out of the way.

Most clients who come to see an astrologer at a time of financial crisis, however, seem to have no sense at all of the possibility of getting their egos out of the way. They exhibit very few, if any, psychological self-management skills, at least as far as their financial issues are concerned. A counseling session with a competent astrologer offers them an opportunity to start learning those skills.

On the one hand, with a person-centered approach to counseling astrology, our profession possesses some very effective tools for helping people to understand themselves better, to learn new ways of working with their emotions, and to achieve new levels of psychological health.

On the other hand, with the empirical approach to financial astrology, we are developing some good tools for analyzing and forecasting the behavior of markets.

The common ground is psychological self-management, which is so readily assisted through astrological counseling and which is such a fundamental prerequisite for anyone hoping to become profitably involved in financial markets. As astrologers, we will come closer to merging the two approaches when our clients learn that they can go to an astrologer, enhance their sense of self-worth, learn ways of managing the fluctuations in their self-esteem and emotional states, and through that process ultimately find themselves psychologically prepared to take advantage of some of the profit-making opportunities that empirical astrology can offer in financial markets.

Ironically, it is through learning to work with financial crisis more effectively that we can best discover ways of bringing about such a synthesis of astrological approaches. Clients in financial crisis present some of the biggest challenges that a professional astrologer has to face. But every client who brings a financial crisis into an astrologer's office provides another opportunity to move closer to a genuinely person-centered financial astrology.

Suggested Reading

Adams, Evangeline. *The Bowl of Heaven*. New York: Dodd, Mead & Co., 1928.

Dewey, Edward R. with Mandino, Og. *Cycles: The Mysterious Forces That Trigger Events*. New York: Hawthorn Books, 1971.

Gann, W. D. *How To Make Profits Trading in Commodities*. Miami, Florida: Lambert-Gann Publishing Co., Inc., 1951.

Gillies, Jerry. *Moneylove: How To Get the Money You Deserve for Whatever You Want*. New York: M. Evans & Co., Inc., 1978.

Laut, Phil. *Money Is My Friend*. New York: Ivy Books, 1989.

Lewi, Grant. *Astrology For The Millions*. 4th ed. St. Paul, Minnesota: Llewellyn Publications, 1971.

Lockhart, Russell A.; Hillman, James; et al. *Soul and Money*. Dallas, Texas: Spring Publications, Inc., 1982.

Long, Jeanne. *Basic Astrotech*. Fort Lauderdale, Florida: Professional Astrology Service, Inc., 1988.

McEvers, Joan, ed. *Financial Astrology for the 1990s*. St. Paul, Minnesota: Llewellyn Publications, 1989.

McWhirter, Louise. *Astrology and Stock Market Forecasting*. 2nd ed. New York: ASI Publishers, Inc., 1977.

Matlock, Clifford Charles. *Man and Cosmos: A Theory of Endeavor Rhythms*. Waynesville, North Carolina: Development Cycles Research Project, 1977.

Merriman, Raymond A. *The Gold Book: Geocosmic Correlations to Gold Price Cycles*. Birmingham, Michigan: Seek-It Publications, 1982.

Pesavento, Larry. *Astro-Cycles: The Trader's Viewpoint*. Pismo Beach, California: Astro-Cycles, 1988.

Phillips, Michael. *The Seven Laws of Money*. Menlo Park, California: Word Wheel and Random House, 1974.

Weiss Research. *Timing the Market*. Chicago: Probus Publishing, 1986.

Williams, LCdr. David. *Financial Astrology*. Tempe, Arizona: American Federation of Astrologers, 1984.

Periodicals on Financial Astrology and Related Topics

Astro-Cycles, P.O. Box 1106, Pismo Beach, CA 93448.

Astro-Investor, P.O. Box 11133, Indianapolis, IN 46201.

Astro-Market-Letter, Postfach 68, D-W-2552 Wetter-Hessen, Germany.

Astro-Trend, 1967 North Halsted Street, Chicago, IL 60614.

Crawford Perspectives, 205 East 78th Street, Suite 12-R, New York, NY 10021.

Cycles Research, Box 43910, Abu Dhabi, United Arab Emirates.

Cycles, 2600 Michelson Drive, Suite 1570, Irvine, CA 92715.

Financial Cycles, P.O. Box 9211, Greenville, SC 29604-9211.

Global Research Forum Journal, 757 SE 17th Street, Suite 272, Ft. Lauderdale, FL 33316.

Investor's Fortucast, P.O. Box 2066, Fairfield, IA 52556.

Market AstroPhysics, Box 33071, Northglenn, CO 80233.

Market Systems, 2761 Mansfield Drive, Burbank, CA 91504.

Traders Astrological Almanac, 757 SE 17th Street, Suite 272, Ft. Lauderdale, FL 33316.

Trader's World, 2508 Grayrock Street, Springfield, MO 65810.

Joan Negus

Joan Negus is a teacher, consultant, lecturer, and writer. In connection with her teaching, she is Director of Education for the National Council for Geocosmic Research. Her writings include three books: *Basic Astrology, Cosmic Combinations, Astroalchemy,* a computer text on relationships entitled *Contact Astro Report,* a booklet on *Interpreting Composite and Relationship Charts,* and numerous articles.

Her educational background includes a BA in sociology from Douglass College, with a minor in psychology. Both subjects have had an impact on her astrology, and continue to be useful in her practice.

She is married to Ken Negus, Professor Emeritus of German, Rutgers University. Ken was her teacher in astrology and now is her partner in that field.

Averting the
Relationship Crisis

Joan Negus

If you are in a relationship crisis, you know how complex your situation is. Even if your partner, and not you, seems to be experiencing difficulties, the problems will have an impact on both of you. The one who believes that he or she is *relatively* happy still has to deal in some way with the one who is not.

In a personal crisis you must cope only with yourself. You can make your own decisions as to how you want to handle your circumstances and then take measures to improve conditions. When another person is in the picture, your actions will be limited because you have to consider the needs and desires of that individual along with your own—unless you choose to leave the relationship. And that is not always the best solution, at least immediately.

Before you can determine the most effective course of action, you should examine what is wrong with the relationship. You might ultimately decide to terminate it, but if you do this without investigation you could then make the *same* mistakes in relationship after relationship. The couple should investigate together, but unfortunately, this is not always possible because there are two separate people involved and one may not want to cooperate with the other. I frequently say to clients that, before a couple marries, while they are still learning about each other, they should either spend six months with a marriage counselor, or have one or two consultations with an astrologer!

Astrologers have a certain advantage over ordinary marriage counselors. A marriage counselor has to rely on listening to the partners to gather information. An astrologer, on the other hand, can look at the natal charts of the two people as well as a

185

composite chart or a relationship chart, and obtain a great deal of information without even talking to the couple.

But there is one potentially serious disadvantage as well. The astrologer may tend to predict the course and outcome of a relationship based only on narrowly-interpreted information provided in the horoscopes. For example, an astrologer might tell a client that a relationship is doomed because of certain factors in the natal chart or a composite chart. When this happens, the astrologer is "playing the odds." Perhaps the motivation is merely to try to help the client avoid pain, or maybe the astrologer truly thinks the relationship must end. Personally, I believe that astrology describes potential conditions, not results.

Trying to avoid situations that might be problematical is understandable, but if the client follows the advice of the astrologer and breaks off the relationship, an important (and perhaps even positive) experience might be missed. Furthermore, it is highly likely that what is indicated in the natal chart will be manifested *in some other way* if you intentionally deprive yourself of the relationship. Rather than ignoring the energies, it is better to attempt to express them in a manner acceptable to you.

What an astrologer should do is present a number of possibilities so that the client knows that there are alternatives. For example, an interaspect between the Sun in one horsocope and Saturn in another is sometimes considered "the kiss of death" for a relationship. If, however, you know that, yes, Saturn can limit the vital flow of energy of the Sun, you should also be made aware that the Saturn can help *structure* and *focus* that Sun's energy. Knowing both the negative and positive possibilities can help you to be prepared for the negative but also to be aware that you can work to accentuate the positive.

Let me share the experience of one client to illustrate my point. This client came to me for the first time after he had fallen deeply in love. Several years before, he had seen another astrologer who had told him that he could never have a successful marriage and that he should avoid close ties. From that time on, the client had consciously kept his distance from women. He dated, but if he felt someone was getting too close he would stop seeing that person.

Yet, just prior to his session with me, in spite of his controls, he had met a young woman to whom he was so attracted that he could not force himself to end the relationship. He did not know what to do. Admittedly, there were some difficult aspects in his chart, but there also were seemingly contradictory factors that suggested he might not feel fulfillment without an intimate relationship. When he came for his reading, he was experiencing the wonder of love, but he was also fearful because of the admonition he had received about his inability to have a happy marriage.

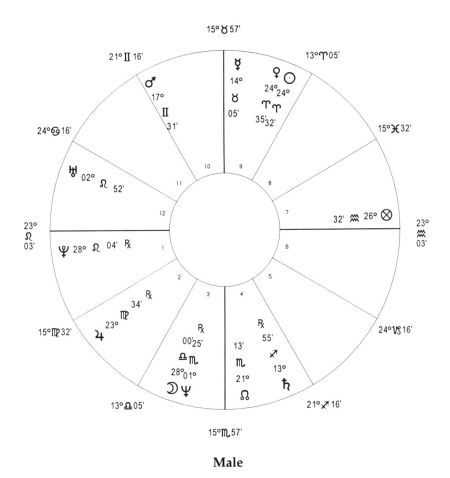

Male

It is clear from the horoscope that maintaining a relationship could require effort: the Sun in the "me-first" sign of Aries, conjunct Venus within 3 minutes of arc, indicates that personal pleasure and gratification could be more important than the needs of others. Neptune conjunct Moon might mean that there is not a clear understanding of women, possibly stemming from a relationship with an inconsistent mother.

This opposition of conjunctions compounds the possibility of not seeing women realistically. Females may be expected to be perfect and be placed on a pedestal. Then, when their flaws become evident, they fall out of favor, and my client could abruptly end the relationship. In further support of this, Uranus squares the opposition axis, accentuating the word "abruptly."

The signs of Aquarius and Pisces in the 7th House can add credence to these assumptions. Aquarius states a need for independence and possibly detachment, and Pisces restates the desire for the perfect partner (repeating the message of Neptune conjuncting the Moon and opposing Venus).

What has been ignored, however, is that the Part of Fortune is in the 7th House indicating a need for a partner in order to have personal fulfillment. The Part of Fortune *softens* the opposition by sextiling the Sun-Venus conjunction on one side and trining the Moon-Neptune conjunction on the other.

Pluto in the 1st House does oppose the Part of Fortune in the 7th House and adds the warning that power could possibly be an issue in relationships. However, it also alleviates Venus-Sun opposite Moon-Neptune by trining the Venus-Sun and sextiling the Moon-Neptune. Pluto not only represents power, but also depth, and connected harmoniously with both the Moon *and* Venus indicates tremendously deep feelings and emotional needs that should be expressed and met in order to make this person feel complete.

It is understandable why an astrologer might advise the man to avoid serious romantic involvements. The complexity of the relationship requirements does indicate that it will probably take a great deal of effort to maintain an intimate relationship. And because of the seemingly conflicting information it would be simpler and safer to remain detached. But by avoiding close one-to-one relationships something will definitely be missing in his life. My client confirmed this when he said that the new romance opened him to feelings he had never experienced and added a wonderful dimension to his existence.

Being aware of potential problems is important. In fact, along with the neutral or positive relationship requirements, the possible difficulties can provide the foundation for the formation of satisfactory partnerships. There are a few messages that are clearly spelled out in his horoscope, both against and *for* partnerships.

On the one hand, he needs a degree of independence (Venus in Aries, square Uranus and quincunx Jupiter; the Moon conjunct Neptune square Uranus; Aquarius on the 7th House). He also may not have a realistic view of women (Venus opposite Neptune; Moon conjunct Neptune) or any partner (much Pisces in the 7th House). And, because he is looking for the ideal in relationships, with the Neptune and Pisces observation, he could often be disappointed in the women with whom he becomes closely associated. One added issue which has not yet been mentioned is that because of the Neptune and Pisces there could also be concern about being victimized. This is further substantiated by Pluto in the 1st House which states that he does not want anyone to control him.

The Pluto, however, as we have seen, is trine Venus and sextile the Moon. He has a deep capacity for love and a strong need to express his feelings. The Moon is also in the partner-oriented sign of Libra. Then, the Part of Fortune in the 7th House again shows the importance of relationships in his life.

Understanding and accepting *all* the messages in the chart is an important first step. The problems do not automatically disappear because they are acknowledged, but once you know what they are you can begin to work on them. Explaining to his partner his need for a degree of independence and possibly some time alone would help to make her feel less threatened or neglected. And working out schedules together to accommodate these requirements could strengthen the relationship indeed.

His high expectations of women, or lack of clarity about them, may never totally disappear, but at least intellectually he knows that perfection is impossible. He is also aware that when such feelings occur, he can talk about them with his partner. He can also use Neptune and Pisces to instill some romance into the relationship and temporarily alleviate the difficulties. Yes, it may take effort to maintain the partnership, but it can work, and work well. All that is necessary is that both parties *understand the relationship requirements in each horoscope,* and cooperate in satisfying them.

Had the other astrologer's advice to avoid close relationships been helpful to the client? I think not. Fear had been instilled. And because of this fear the client may even have missed other opportunities that could have brought him satisfaction. Of course, I believe this because I am of the opinion that any relationship can last if two people want it to, and are willing to work at it. Let me add, however, that I also believe that no relationship is totally self-sustaining, nor can one person hold a relationship together single-handedly for an extended period of time. It takes two people to make and sustain a relationship.

Astrological Maxims

As an individual, you have to project certain personal qualities that are an undeniable part of your character, and in partnerships you also have some basic requirements that must be met. You therefore cannot become a person who is not described by your horoscope, nor can you be happy in a relationship that does not satisfy any of your needs. There is, however, a great deal of latitude in the ways in which you may choose to express the personal qualities *and* to meet your relationship requirements.

♌ You may find that different people with whom you come into contact seem to evoke different sides of your character. Yet you will always be living in a manner indicated in your natal chart. To give a simple illustration—let us say that the sign of Leo is strongly emphasized in your chart. Leos can be warm, generous and outgoing. Or they may be dictatorial braggarts. An important issue for a Leo is to be liked. So if you are involved with someone who is fond of you and always tells others how wonderful you are, you will display the warm side of your nature when you are with that person. This is because that individual makes you feel good about yourself. Another person may be very cool toward you. This attitude may elicit your more boastful, dogmatic side because you are trying to convince that individual that you *are* wonderful. So whether you are involved in a serious relationship or not, it is always important to understand yourself first, and then evaluate any relationship you have in light of who you are. Astrology offers ways to do this.

In a way, this essay, especially in light of its title, should be thought of partly as preventive medicine: how to establish a relationship from its onset in such a way as to help avert crises. The first suggestion is a simple task that requires no knowledge of astrology at all. The suggestion is that, when you meet someone to whom you are instantaneously drawn, or even a person who is mildly attractive to you, begin to a make a list of the qualities you admire in this individual. You can make use of this list when the "glow" begins to wear off. Everyone tends to see new romantic involvements as perfect. Intellectually you may know that no one is perfect, but your new partner is always the exception. However, eventually, reality sets in and you begin to see the flaws.

As you view the imperfections, you could become more and more disenchanted with the individual. In fact, it is possible to become so obsessed with a single flaw that it is all you can see in that person, and you end the relationship. Then a few days or weeks later you might question your actions. You remember the fine qualities the person possesses and you think about how nice it would be to be back together. But it might be too late to renew the relationship. Whereas, if you had had a list of attributes from the beginning, you could look at it to balance out the flaws and perhaps avoid prematurely ending the relationship. Of course, if your con list becomes longer than your pro list, it may be time to look elsewhere.

Sometimes those involved in serious relationships try to convince the partner to work on eliminating the annoying characteristics. This is not always possible, however, because, as is evident in the horoscope, certain qualities must be expressed. And if the demands of the one partner on the other mean that crucial factors have to be removed, the changes will only be temporary. No matter how much you want to please your partner, or how hard you try, you cannot maintain a demeanor that is alien to you. For instance, if your partner thinks you are sloppy and is bothered by this, you might be told to become neater. You may make a serious attempt to comply, but if you have no Virgo accentuation in your chart, for example, you will probably soon fall back into old patterns.

In some cases, however, it may be possible to redirect the energies in a manner that is satisfactory to both parties. This is where astrology can be of assistance. Since the signs of the zodiac have both positive and negative definitions, you can concentrate on manifesting the most admirable qualities connected with the signs that are strongly represented in your own horoscope. And by knowing the signs most emphasized in your partner's chart, you can support the positive traits and work on helping to redirect those that are most irritating to you. An example was given above with the description of Leo. If this sign is emphasized in your partner's chart he or she may be bossy, loud, and boastful. If this annoys you, you can tell everyone how great your partner is, and see if that roaring lion does not turn into a purring pussycat. Now let's look at each of the other signs in an orderly fashion.

♈ Among the annoying qualities associated with Aries are impatience, lack of persistence, arrogance and self-centeredness. Aries people seem to be so self-assured that others often take pleasure in criticizing them. This treatment, however, tends to make them less dependable and more overbearing. But if you praise their efforts, you will see that they become more enthusiastic. This enthusiasm leads to further accomplishment and you will be amazed at how much the Aries can achieve. Your partner will also become so busy that there will be neither time nor the inclination for arrogance.

An Aries quality that you will probably want to encourage is *joie de vivre*. You may not be asked to join in the fun because Arians are spontaneous and also may rarely consider your needs. But participate anyway! You will find that the enjoyment is contagious. By sharing in the pleasure, you will not even have to think about your partner's self-centeredness.

♉ If your partner has Taurus emphasized, pleasure will still be a characteristic that is important. But in this case the pleasures are almost always sensual. Anything that can be tasted, smelled, heard, seen, or felt will be enjoyed. As with Aries, you should join in, even if you believe that your partner is being overly self-indulgent. Criticism will do little good. In fact, it may produce the exact opposite of what you want.

The symbol of Taurus is the bull, and criticism or giving orders is like waving a red flag in the face of the bull. If Taureans are told what they *must* do, you can count on them doing the opposite whether they had originally intended to or not. The best way to handle such situations is never to say "don't do that," but rather to offer alternatives—all of which are desirable to you. In that way, Taureans can choose the route, but it will be acceptable to you as well.

Taureans are also creatures of habit, repeating patterns again and again, which can be boring. And they can also display an obstinacy that can be very irritating. If, however, you convince yourself that your partner is "predictable" rather than "lacking in originality," and "steadfast" instead of "stubborn," you will surely see the advantages of these qualities! In terms of predictability, it is easier to plan your own strategy when you know how your partner will behave. And loyalty and trust go hand-in-hand with steadfastness. So Taureans may stay with individuals to whom they have made a commitment for long periods of time, perhaps sometimes longer than they should.

Ⅱ Predictability is not a quality associated with Geminis. They are changeable, and that could make you feel insecure. But if you look at it from a different perspective it might be easier to cope with. If you do not like what they are doing or if you do not agree with their opinions, you need not be upset nor immediately confront them. You can relax and be assured that they will probably soon change their behavior and thinking.

In spite of the changeability, Geminis—or people with obvious Gemini emphasis in the horoscope—always seem to be busy. Yet their attention span is usually not very long, and if you check too frequently on their progress, you might feel that they are accomplishing little. This, however, is not necessarily true. The wider the variety of activities, the more likely that something *will* be achieved. If Geminis are forced to stay with one activity, or even the same mode of activity, their minds may shut down and they look off into space and do nothing. By encouraging Geminis to alternate a number of tasks, some of which are physical and some mental, they can accomplish a great deal.

Another Gemini quality that might annoy you is the lack of depth. Geminis learn quickly, but often superficially. Their motto seems to be "If you can't learn it fast, it isn't worth knowing!" Do not frustrate yourself trying to have profound, intellectual conversations. Instead, take your Gemini to a party. Geminis have the ability to fit in with anyone. Their quickness allows them to pick up important terms and phrases and make them appear knowl-edgeable to experts with whom they are conversing. You can be proud of the impression your partner makes in the social world. The trick is to leave the gathering before your partner runs out of applicable vocabulary. Since the Gemini is in constant motion, however, getting him or her to walk out the door should not be too difficult.

♋ Cancerians tend to be nurturing, and this can be a sooth-ing quality if you are the recipient. But they can also be doting, and make their partners feel smothered. If you are that partner, you may have the urge to run away from home, but there is an easier way to escape this treatment. Try mothering your partner back! Not only will Cancerians stop the over protec-tion, they will also enjoy being taken care of.

An admirable quality common to Cancerians is the ability to make a house homey. Once accomplished, however, the Cancer-ian may never want to leave the house. One way to solve this problem is to pack a special suitcase with the Cancerian's favorite possessions, which you then place around any strange room in which you and your partner stay. It may make you both feel more at home.

Since Leo is discussed earlier, on page 190, we will go on to Virgo.

♍ One extremely bothersome trait sometimes displayed by Virgos is criticism. Although constructive criticism may be a virtue, Virgo grievances more often stem *from* being "nitpicky." It may be some consolation to know that Virgos fre-quently will be most faultfinding when they are unhappy with themselves, but this information will probably still not make your anger disappear. The best way to handle situations in which criti-cism is an issue is to allow the Virgo to take over whatever task you have been told *you* did poorly. Not only will it be done better, but it will be one less responsibility for you!

Virgos need to be of service, and a redeeming quality they possess is the ability to work hard. Unfortunately this can lead to being a workaholic. "Fun" can become a dirty word. The trick to dealing with this problem is to restrain yourself from using the word "fun" or "pleasure" or "enjoyment." However, if you attach some chore to each pleasurable activity, or infer that it will take effort to complete the activity, you may be surprised at the cooperation you receive.

♎ Librans profess to want harmony and will rarely overtly start a controversy. They are so sweet-tempered that, if anything goes wrong between you, you will believe it is all your fault. If, however, battles always break out in the vicinity of your peaceful Libran, you might begin to get a little suspicious. If this occurs a number of times, observe your partner's behavior. You will then see that the innocent Libran has the quiet ability to manipulate. This could cause you to view yourself differently in the relationship and even possibly help you to learn a few subtle tricks to try on your partner.

Another irritating characteristic common to many Librans is indecisiveness. For example, if you allow your Libran partner to select the restaurant for dinner, you may never eat because by the time the decision is made, the restaurant will probably be closed. Either offer only two alternatives or, better yet, make the choice yourself. Your partner will probably keep mulling over which is the right restaurant, but just keep smiling and driving to the spot you have selected. This approach is applicable to any type of situation in which decisions must be made.

♏ A Scorpio asset is the ability to keep secrets, so you can be assured that it is safe to confide in your Scorpio partner. However, the problem is that your Scorpio can keep secrets from you as well as everyone else. And the harder you try to pry out the information, the more close-mouthed the Scorpio becomes. Therefore, when Scorpio is strongly accentuated in the horoscope, the direct approach is not the correct one. There are two ways to induce a Scorpio to divulge information: one is to ask your partner to play detective (Scorpios love to ferret out the facts); the other is to play psychiatrist. Somehow baring your soul to a therapist is not as threatening as giving crucial information to your partner!

Other unpleasant qualities that Scorpios can manifest are jealousy and possessiveness. There are not always logical reasons for these characteristics to be displayed, but the more secure your partner feels, the less frequently they will be exhibited. One way you might try to instill a sense of security in your partner is to provide a list of everything you plan to do and every place you expect to go when you are not together. Probably your partner will check on you the first few times to make sure you are where you said you would be, but once trust is established this will most likely not happen. Then you need not be so thorough in accounting for your time and whereabouts.

♐ Sagittarians, on the other hand, do not want to be weighted down with such extraneous information. There is the desire for freedom for oneself, the spouse and the world, because freedom enables you to explore and grow, unencumbered by responsibilities. Carried to extremes, however, this quality can degenerate into irresponsibility which is not a characteristic that fosters stability in a relationship. The way to combat this is the opposite of the suggestion made for the Virgo: with a Sagittarian you should make life fun instead of work. This is an approach that can be successful for all the fire signs. Remove the words "work" and "responsibility" from your vocabulary and replace them with "fun," "pleasure" and "enjoyment." Even the most menial task becomes a challenge if you consider it a game.

For example, if you say to a Sagittarian, "I wonder how long it would take to dig a ditch, 2' X 3' X 6'?" before you know it, the Sagittarian will not only be at the digging site with a shovel and a stop watch, but the hole will probably be dug in record time! You may also be successful in getting your partner to assume responsibilities if you couch this word with the term "growth experience."

Sagittarians are also noted for their candor, and such honesty can be admirable. But there is a fine line between candor and tactlessness, and if you live with a Sagittarian for long you will probably regard the ability to communicate openly as "foot in mouth disease." It may be impossible to stop this tendency. Besides, if your Sagittarian stopped talking, you would undoubtedly miss the sense of humor that is also an integral part of your partner's communications. The best way to deal with this problem is not to be too sensitive. Know that if your feelings are hurt by thoughtless words, an opposite statement will undoubtedly be made within a few minutes. And it may also be a good idea to keep any information you do not want spread throughout the world to yourself.

♑ Capricorns are ambitious and status-oriented, and seem to be so self-sufficient that you could sometimes feel unneeded. However, if you do your share in achieving material goals, even without being asked, you can become an indispensable asset. You may not be praised for what you have done, and it can be annoying not to be appreciated. Because Capricorns are anything but lavish in their verbal praise, you may feel taken for granted. But even though nothing is said you will notice that the more you achieve, the more you will be included in the plans.

Another bothersome quality often seen in Capricorns is the attitude that there are two ways to do things: their way and the wrong way. Each task you take on is accompanied by a lecture on how it should be accomplished. Do not argue, because you cannot win. Just nod your head, and then do it as you please.

♒ Aquarians tend to be objective and non-judgmental. These are attractive qualities if you want a mediator, but can be difficult to deal with in an intimate relationship. If you try to discuss emotional issues, the Aquarian can become annoyingly detached. The harder you push, the more remote your partner becomes. With this approach, there may come a point at which you feel that an impenetrable screen has come down between you. To avoid this, do not try to arouse your partner emotionally. It is better not to accuse. Appeal to the Aquarian's sense of fairness and justice. Use hypothetical situations that describe points you want to make. The response will be based on logic and not feelings, but, because the Aquarian will not feel attacked, you will reach your partner and probably get the results you wish.

When it comes to expressing opinions on almost any subject, Aquarians always seem to take the opposite point of view from yours. Because of this, you and those who are exposed to this side of Aquarius, may consider your partner argumentative. This could arouse anger. Then you begin to show your hostility. And while you are becoming more and more upset, your partner seems to be getting calmer and more in control. This of course will upset you even more.

What you should do is try to think of your conversations as debates rather than as confrontations. You can then take such situations more in stride and feel more in control. To help you to develop this attitude, listen to your partner's next discussion on the same subject. You may hear your views being expressed as your partner's views. This means that you are either an excellent debater, or your partner enjoys playing Devil's Advocate. But whichever is the case, you should feel better about the communications between the two of you.

)(Pisceans have the ability to identify themselves so closely with people with whom they are intimate, that they seem to be an extension of the other. They not only sympathize with their partners, they empathize. You may enjoy this quality, but if so much bonding causes you to feel restricted or to question your own identity, assist your Piscean partner in finding a person other than you to help. This will give your partner someone else to identify with, and permit you a little more freedom.

Since people with Pisces emphasize the need to be needed, they can be subject to the victim-savior syndrome. They may give to the point of personal deprivation, which can make you feel guilty because you are not giving enough. Or, the complete opposite—they tend only to take from others without giving anything in return. The attitude seems to be "I'll get you before you get me." The best way to combat either tendency is to keep restoring balance in the relationship. If you see that your partner is giving too much, give something back; or if your partner is not giving you anything, *ask for a favor.*

The foregoing presentation of irritating qualities associated with each of the signs is by no means exhaustive. Think of them as your "starter list"of astrological maxims. As you try the suggestions for redirecting the energies and notice that they often work, you may be stimulated to combat other flaws in your partner. Do not be upset, however, if periodically the same problems recur. You are treating the symptoms, not eliminating the cause. But when old patterns emerge, the same treatment will probably work time and again.

Another measure that might help to prevent a relationship crisis is to understand your own relationship potential. Astrologically, this can be quite complex. Components include the 5th House for courtship and romance, the 7th House for close one-to-one relationships, the Moon for emotions, Venus for affection, and Mars for sexual needs. To cover each of these topics fully would require more space than is available here, but we can briefly discuss the essentials of each and a method of approach.

Working with the Houses

In interpreting any house you can look at the sign(s) in the house, planets within the house in terms of sign and aspect and house placement of the house ruler. If there is more than one sign in the house (because of interception or greatly expanded area), the requirements are naturally more complex than if there were only one. The definitions ascribed to the signs must be combined. In regard to the planets in the house, they add intricacy and make your requirement list a little longer. The house placement of the ruler then provides even more information.

The 5th House is the house of courtship, and describes the process of becoming acquainted. The element of the sign on the cusp denotes how you interact with others when you first meet them. If it is a fire sign you become actively involved immediately. With earth you look at the other person from a practical perspective, evaluating the physical appearance, possibly standing in the community, and what he or she can do for you. Air on the cusp of the 5th House indicates that communication is the way through which you determine what the other person is like. You may seem to be actively involved because of your friendly conversation but you maintain your objectivity and your distance until you form an opinion. If you have a water sign on the cusp of the 5th House your intuition and instincts are the main way through which you judge others.

As already stated, by looking at the signs in the house, the planets in the house and the house placement of the house ruler, you can form a coherent picture of your needs in courtship. Although a relationship crisis can occur during the courtship period, it is usually not until the relationship moves into the 7th House, when an emotional commitment has been made, that serious crises are most likely to arise.

The first opportunity for a grave crisis could be the period of transition—the movement of the relationship from the 5th House to the 7th House. A crisis will most likely occur *if your intimate relationship needs differ markedly from your courtship requirements.* Signs and/or planets can describe possible inconsistencies.

For example, if you have the planet Neptune in the 5th House, you might tend to use your imagination and not view the object of your romantic attachment realistically. This may be satisfying during the courtship period, but as you become more intimate and you shift into the 7th House, you may have to change your attitude *because of the signs and planets in the 7th House.* Otherwise, problems can arise.

In the case just mentioned, the person with Neptune in the 5th House has Capricorn in the 7th House. She was aware that she was a romantic. She described herself as being in love with love, but complained that every time one of her romances became serious she began to see that this prince in shining armor was really a frog. She wanted very much to be married and had no problem finding attractive men, but was frustrated because she could not find the right man.

I met this woman many years ago, and she was the first person to whom I suggested making lists of attributes. It may have helped because she has been married (relatively happily) for about 14 years now. But, I must admit that she also had a relationship reading with her present husband before she accepted his proposal of marriage. However, since the time of my first discussion with this client about making lists of attributes, I have discovered that these lists help whether you have Neptune in the 5th House or not. But if you do have Neptune or Pisces in that area the list-making realism can be doubly beneficial.

There are, of course, many possibilities in terms of adjustments that might have to be made when you move from courtship to marriage, aside from the one just mentioned. A few other themes are dependency-independence, initiating-responding, and togetherness-solitude. Some requirements may not change. For example, you could have Saturn in the 5th House and Capricorn in the 7th. Therefore you would want your responsible lover to become a responsible partner; or the themes should shift in either direction. In dating, for instance, you might look for someone you can count on—an individual who will be responsible and make you feel secure. This would probably be indicated by Saturn or Virgo or Capricorn in the 5th House. Then the relationship becomes more intimate, and in the 7th House you may have Aquarius, Uranus, Jupiter, or Sagittarius, so new requirements emerge. You begin to feel restricted instead of secure. You need more independence.

Without astrology, you might wonder what is wrong with you, but with it you can see the possible contradictions in your horoscope. Once you know this and accept that both sets of needs are part of you, you can deal more rationally with the concepts, and make the most of them. You might stretch your boundaries slowly, and help your partner to do the same. Or together, you might become involved in activities that are unusual, creative or challenging. These would also be manifestations of the definitions ascribed to planets and/or signs indicated above. Conversely, if independence is an issue in the 5th House, and dependability or responsibility is important in the 7th House, you would want a great deal of freedom in dating, and then need security in marriage.

The initiating-responding and the togetherness-solitude motifs can also be seen through the signs and the planets, and can go in either direction. With initiating-responding, you might be attracted to someone who is aggressive, but in partnership you do not want to be ordered about. Or you might be looking for romance with someone who is gentle and responsive to your needs, but expect this individual to become more assertive when you move into the 7th House. The planets and signs most likely connected with initiating are Aries and Mars. The responding or receptive principles are often connected with Venus, the Moon, Cancer, and Libra. Although Cancer and Libra are cardinal signs, they usually initiate in response to familial needs (Cancer) and those of the significant other (Libra).

The togetherness-aloneness theme can show up in a variety of ways. The Sun, Mercury and Venus usually are the planets, and

202 / How to Manage the Astrology of Crisis

Leo, Gemini, and Libra the signs that indicate the need for other people. The Sun wants appreciation and Leo wants an audience. Mercury represents communications and this infers that there must be another person with whom you converse, and Gemini is considered a gregarious sign. Venus is, among other things, the planet of sociability and Libra is the partnership sign. Neptune, as already stated, can be looked to as the planet which creates illusion, but it is also connected with escape—possibly a need to meditate or daydream alone. And Uranus, the planet of freedom, also could denote a desire sometimes to be by yourself. The signs that would signify time alone are Scorpio and Aquarius. With both these signs there is periodically a strong desire to temporarily separate yourself from others.

With knowledge of the signs and planets, you can make your own lists of themes relevant to your own chart and that of your partner. The important message here is to be aware that there can be *different requirements in courtship than in marriage,* and if they seem to conflict, you should acknowledge this fact and try to find ways to make the transition and possibly avert crises that might occur.

Once you establish a definite partnership, the emphasis in the relationship shifts from the 5th House to the 7th House, as we have seen. After you have made the transition from courtship to marriage, you can be less concerned with 5th House matters and concentrate on the 7th House. The 7th House describes both what you need in a close one-to-one relationship and *what you have to give*. Problems arise in this area if you expect your partner to take care of all the relationship needs, or if you try to satisfy all the requirements yourself. Instead, you should recognize that you *as a couple must share in the demands of the house.*

If you try either to fulfill all your relationship requirements yourself, or expect your partner to handle them, you will ultimately discover that neither course is satisfactory. Should you manifest either extreme and decide to change the pattern because you are disenchanted with it, there is a tendency to move to the other extreme. And the movement from one extreme to the other often continues until the pattern is consciously broken. One example that comes immediately to mind is a client with a Sun-Saturn conjunction in the 7th House. In this woman's own words she said, "I left my strict father and married a man who became my strict father." Over the years, she felt more and more controlled by her husband, and finally left the home and the relationship. She then met a man who was looking for parenting, and she became *his* father figure. After they had lived together for a few months, she began to experience the same feelings of restriction she had felt in her marriage. She came to the realization that it was as dissatisfying *being* the authority figure in a relationship as it was to be dominated by the partner. On an intellectual level, she now understands her need to share responsibility. This is a crucial step. Actually curing the problem, however, may take time. This pattern was part of her life for about fifty years, and it cannot be expected to disappear immediately.

Studying relationship patterns can be a complex process, but by simply looking at the signs and planets in the 7th House you can obtain a great deal of information. If you have only one sign in your 7th House, you should study the keywords connected with it thoroughly and try, in as many ways as possible, to express them yourself in your partnership, and also work on assisting your partner to use them.

If you have two signs indicated in your 7th House, the principles are the same. You both should be manifesting the characteristics of each sign. It is more complicated with two signs than with one. Frequently, what happens is that one partner will manifest one sign and the other the second sign. You may express one sign in a particular relationship, then end that relationship and manifest the other sign in the next relationship. It is even possible to keep making the shift within the *same* relationship!

This was the case with a client who has the signs of Capricorn and Aquarius in his 7th House. He told me that when he got married he thought he needed a wife who would stay at home, take care of the children, etc. (in other words the Capricorn qualities) so that he could operate freely (Aquarius) out in the world. Then, his wife began to complain. She announced her feelings loudly and clearly, and with the help of a marriage counselor, he began to understand her needs. Gradually he allowed her more freedom. However, the more liberated she became, the more insecure and restricted *he* felt. With the assistance of astrology, he and his wife are now working on maintaining a balance in terms of freedom and responsibility. They are becoming more and more aware of the symptoms of imbalance and are trying to correct them as soon as they appear.

7th House Signs

By looking at the signs in each partner's 7th House you can become cognizant of the relationship requirements of both parties. You can make lists of these requirements and determine ways to share in their expression. Examining the signs in the 7th House can also provide information about the types of issues that can arise between the partners. As we go through the signs, we will discuss the two extremes, and ways of balancing them.

With Aries in the 7th House you do not want a passive partner. If you become involved with someone who is forceful and aggressive, and does not allow you to make any decisions, you could fight back. Or, if you choose an inactive partner you could become bored and dissatisfied with your relationship. Then you may begin to nag and become argumentative in order, perhaps subconsciously, to make your partner assertive. If your strategy fails, you will undoubtedly become unhappier in the relationship and have no respect for your partner. If you succeed, you will probably become more contentious and your relationship could be just as stormy as it would be with the partner who begins the aggression.

If both partners are supposed to be active, initiating, and assertive, the best way to deal with these requirements is to find areas in your shared life in which each of you can take charge. You will probably still argue sometimes over who is the leader, but disagreements are not always bad and they can instill life or add to the excitement in the relationship, which is definitely a requirement if you have Aries in the 7th House.

Since Taurus is a fixed-earth sign, if it is in the 7th House, dependability and practicality are what you are looking for, and also could be issues in your partnerships. You would undoubtedly mention loyalty as an important requirement in marriage, but loyalty can become possessiveness if carried to an extreme. And there might be the tendency for you or your partner to treat the other as a possession. In terms of practicality, it is reassuring to have reasons for actions, but if feelings are totally ignored, this can create problems.

Although emotions *per se* are not connected with the sign of Taurus, sensual pleasures are. In fact, if either of you is unhappy in the relationship, the dissatisfied partner might turn to someone else for personal gratification, and as a means of escaping from a possessive, and/or boring, predictable partner. One way to avoid or resist such occurrences is to indulge yourselves as a couple. Arguing about qualities that cannot be eradicated is a waste of time, but if you buy beautiful items, eat tasty food, or visit interesting places, together, the negative characteristics may fade into the background. If this does not occur, at least you will have stored up some wonderful memories, and possibly some fine belongings.

♊ Gemini in the 7th House indicates that communications between you and your partner and sociability are essential matters in your relationship. Charm and wit are very possibly characteristics that attracted you to your partner or vice versa. But on a long term basis they might seem superficial. There could be indications in your horoscope that you want to analyze and talk in depth and at length on various subjects, but with Gemini in the 7th House this may not be an easy task.

This does not mean, however, that serious topics must be avoided, nor that crucial issues which arise between you must be suppressed. Just do not expect to cover the entire subject or problem in a single discussion. Break it up into segments. Talk seriously for short periods and intersperse the conversations with other forms of activity. You might escape from each other for a brief period of time and then speak again. Or you could take time out and go to a party or engage in some physical activity such as jogging. These latter two activities could be done together. In fact, socializing should be a joint activity, as it can be an asset in a Gemini relationship. And by joining in the fun, your partner may never discover that parties can be successful without your presence.

♋ Mothering is the most essential requirement of a Cancerian relationship. With Cancer in the 7th House, you can attain pleasure by taking care of your partner and feel secure with a partner who nurtures you. But, as with all of the signs, imbalance can cause problems. It may be comforting for a time to be involved with someone who takes care of your every need. But you could eventually begin to consider yourself inadequate because you are not allowed to tend to any of your own needs. Or you might feel smothered by all the attention.

If one partner is doing all the nurturing, the other partner will undoubtedly play the child. And the person taking on the role of the child has several courses of action. It is difficult to play the obedient child if you are feeling inadequate or smothered. You might, therefore, have tantrums, even though afterward you might feel guilty because you should not be nasty to the "mom" who takes care of your every need. Or you might look for someone else whom you can nurture, and perhaps escape from the nest. All of this can be avoided by *sharing* the nurturing. If you are feeling angry or suffocated in your relationship, do something to mother your partner. Or, if you see these symptoms in your partner, ask for a little tender, loving care.

♌ Leo in the 7th House indicates that you need a relationship with someone who is warm, outgoing and a performer on the stage of life. It is easy to promote someone with these qualities, but if you feel upstaged or neglected you might then search for someone who will let you be the star. However, that too can be dissatisfying because that individual lacks the spark that is essential in your partnerships.

If, from the onset of the intimate phase of a relationship, you consciously work on sharing the spotlight, you could avoid the painful learning process found in the extremes. One way in which you can do this is to look for places where you can be seen by and interact with the public—you need a stage on which to perform. You should also search for and cultivate friends who appreciate you as a couple, because if the two of you are performing, you need an audience to applaud.

♍ There is a perfectionist quality associated with Virgo and with this sign in the 7th House one or both partners could have extremely high expectations of the other. If perfection is not forthcoming, and it rarely is, the disappointed partner could become critical. Then two of the possible scenarios could be that the supposedly imperfect partner feels inadequate and makes more and more mistakes. Or possibly that person stops trying to do anything. In either case, the critical partner will probably become even more critical and the relationship can begin to disintegrate.

Instead of dwelling on what is wrong with your partnership, look for some service-oriented project that you can share. Work hard together and concentrate on helping others. If your partner continues to complain about you, point out how hard you have been working together and what you are accomplishing. This will give you a common goal and help to make your relationship seem more worthwhile.

Libra in the 7th House indicates that sharing and equality are essential ingredients in intimate relationships. If there seems to be imbalance, such as one partner taking charge without consultation (which can happen often because the Libra 7th House person will have Aries on the Ascendant), conflicts can arise. This certainly will interfere with the Libran need for peace and harmony. Then the discontented partner can begin to undermine or manipulate the other. And rather than restoring the balance, the scales become more lopsided. Because of the subtlety of the approach, the manipulation may continue undetected for some time, but once discovered it can do serious damage to the relationship.

It is better from the onset of a problem to use the charm and diplomacy you possess as a couple. Openly, but objectively, discuss the problems, with emphasis on compromise and maintaining the peace. Discussing issues together in a calm manner with the focus on fairness can only strengthen the relationship.

If you have Scorpio in the 7th House, your close one-to-one relationships are undoubtedly intense. You will not be attracted to superficial people. Devotion and emotional support may also be important to you as a couple, and if either of you is not providing these qualities for the other, certain unpleasant side effects may result. The partner who feels abused may become suspicious of the other. This can lead to possessiveness and, if the situation does not improve, it can change to vindictiveness. Once this stage is reached, it is difficult to recapture the positive qualities in the relationship.

Discussing and analyzing your feelings together from the very beginning of the intimate phase of your relationship can help to avert the potential crisis just mentioned. Talk about negative thoughts as soon as they arise, because the longer you wait the more difficult it becomes to bring them out, and possibly the more obsessed you can become with them. Remember that Scorpio is the sign of transformation, and by examining potential problems and working on them as a couple, you will find that it is not so difficult to make the necessary changes.

Sagittarius in the 7th House indicates that the relationship requirements include expanding and developing as a couple and a strong need for a degree of freedom. A problem that can arise is that both partners may be so intent on freedom that they can grow in different directions and ultimately find that they have little in common. Or only one partner concentrates on self-development and views the other as stagnating. So again, they ultimately find that they share little or nothing.

The best way to avoid the possibility of your mate becoming a stranger, is to have a number of activities which you do separately, but make sure that there are some that you share. Pursuing separate interests allows each of you some freedom as well as providing information to be shared in order for each of you to enrich the life of the other. The common interests insure that in certain areas you are growing together. Some activities you might enjoy together are travel, religion or taking formal classes.

With Capricorn in the 7th House, you are looking for a partner with whom you can shoulder responsibility, and succeed in the material world. You may tend to evaluate partners in terms of their mundane accomplishments. And you might feel that it is easier to succeed if you are involved with someone who is already established. Therefore, you could find yourself attracted to those who are older because they have already made their mark on the world. If your partners are mature and already successful, chances are that they will be responsible as well. However, you may not be allowed to participate in either the success or the responsibility. This could make you feel frustrated or inadequate and might lead to estrangement even if you remain together because you are not contributing to the relationship.

You might then find someone for whom you can be the successful, responsible partner, but that too is not satisfying. One couple who have experienced both extremes within the same relationship are now learning to travel the middle road. The wife has Capricorn on her 7th House cusp. She married a man 20 years her senior who was established in his career. She discovered before long, however, that he was not reliable in many ways. He was the breadwinner in the family but she took care of all the other responsibilities. In a way, they were sharing the Capricorn qualities, but then he lost his job and she became the working person as well as the one tending to all the other family needs. She became increasingly unhappy and finally gave him an ultimatum. He would either have to assume some of the burdens or their relationship was over. They are now consciously working on a very tangible plan to share the responsibilities.

Wherever Aquarius is in your horoscope is where you will most likely break with tradition. If it is in the 7th House you will probably form intimate relationships and possibly marry someone who is from a very different background than your own. This could add excitement and creativity to the relationship. But whether you do this or not, it is essential that anyone with Aquarius in the 7th House maintain a strong sense of self in any intimate relationship as well as respecting the partner as a individual.

Problems can arise if mutual respect is lost or if either partner feels too confined or restricted by the other. Aquarius is a fixed sign, however, so there must be a purpose for the relationship—possibly a joint goal to work toward. It is also important for people with Aquarius in the 7th House to define the framework of the relationship. Although freedom may be important to the individuals involved, freedom is best expressed if you are aware of your boundaries. By knowing your limits, you can either stretch them or decide that you have a great deal of latitude within them. Without a frame of reference, against which to measure it, the limitless possibilities can become chaos rather than freedom.

)-(If you have Pisces in the 7th House the ideal script might be that the handsome prince and the beautiful princess marry and live happily ever after. Unfortunately, human beings can not live in Never-Never Land forever. It may be possible to create the illusion of a perfect union for short periods of time, but reality eventually creeps in. Then you realize that your wonderful mate has flaws. Along with other shortcomings, there may be insensitivity to your needs. In fact, you might feel that your partner takes advantage of you. (Remember, Virgo would be on the Ascendant.)

Once the imperfections become evident, there are choices as to how you can proceed. You can end the relationship and vow that you will never let anyone deceive you nor take advantage of you again. Another possibility is that you might grumble about how miserable you are and consider it your lot to suffer. (I have one client who has been doing the latter for twelve years.) And finally, a third choice is periodically to instill a little glamour and romance in the relationship. Have a candlelight dinner or go away for a romantic weekend. You may not be able totally to eradicate the negative qualities, but you can surely get some relief and release from them.

Each sign has been discussed above individually. If there is more than one sign in the 7th House, the reader must combine the meanings of the appropriate signs. Even if you have only one sign in the 7th House, you will probably be able to add more specifics from your personal experience to the definitions provided. By analyzing the condition of your own partnership, you can make use of the material given and make some creative additions.

7th House Planets

Planets in the 7th House signify energies that, like the signs, are meaningful for close one-to-one relationships. The planets, in certain ways, repeat the messages of the signs, and therefore may reinforce and accentuate certain qualities indicated by the signs, or may *modify* them. For example, you might have Capricorn as well as Saturn in Capricorn in the 7th House. This would be three indications of the importance of responsibility and security in your close relationships. Or you might have the sign of Libra as well as Uranus in Libra in the 7th House. In this case, you want an equal partner (Libra) but you would need a degree of freedom (Uranus) as well—thus modifying the sharing theme. More diversity would be implied by the second illustration, but both examples help to build a fuller picture of relationship needs.

The Sun in the 7th House has similarities to the sign of Leo there. What might be added is that wherever the Sun appears in your horoscope is where you need to shine. So even without the sign of Leo being in the 7th House, the Sun would signify that you need to share the limelight with a partner. If you had your Sun in Leo in the 7th House, you would have a repeated theme, and therefore it would be doubly strong.

The Moon in the 7th House is very much like the sign of Cancer being placed in that house. Nurturing is important and can become an issue. It also states that partnership is an area in which there can be fluctuation and emotionalism. The rest of your chart might indicate that your demeanor is cool and calm, but with the Moon in the 7th House, emotions could come spilling out in close one-to-one relationships.

Both the Sun and Moon have a further implication in a horoscope. Aside from representing your ego, the Sun may also describe your experience of your father or the father figure in your life, and the house in which it is posited is probably where your father has had a strong and direct impact on you. The same is valid of the Moon and the mother. With either of these planets in your 7th House, that parent probably has a definite influence on your intimate relationships. You might consciously or unconsciously look for a partner like or unlike the appropriate parent (depending on whether your childhood experience of that parent was positive or negative). It is possible that the mother or father is not the *role model* for the partner but is important in some other way in your close relationships. An example of this is a man with the Moon in the 7th House who told me that he was not looking for someone like his mother, but would never marry anyone his mother did not approve of!

☿ Mercury in the 7th House bears a strong resemblance to Gemini being there. A partner with whom you can share the social scene is probably high on your list of requirements for a partner. You will also want someone with whom the lines of communication are kept open. If they seem to be blocked, it is a symptom of problems in the relationship that need attention.

♀ Venus in the 7th House shares the love of pleasure shown by Taurus, and the strong desire for peace, harmony, and diplomacy indicated by Libra. However, Venus, more than either of these signs, also signifies the desire for an attractive partner. It may be physical appearance or it could be inner beauty, but some form of beauty will be important to you. Difficulties may begin to arise if you feel that your partner is becoming less attractive, or if your partner complains that you are ignoring your appearance.

♂ Mars or Aries in the 7th House have a great deal in common. Both indicate the need for an active relationship in which *leadership plays an important role*. The house in which Mars is posited is where you can initiate most directly, and, in the 7th House, if your partner becomes too placid or just doesn't move quickly enough, you could tend to push or nag. Or you might put yourself in a position where your partner will take on the role of directing you. Either way, of course, could lead to disagreements. Anger could arise. If arguments take place frequently, you might consider walking while you have your discussions. Expending physical energy as you talk could keep the situation under control.

♃ There is little difference with Sagittarius in the 7th House and Jupiter placed there. One thing that might be added here, however, is that the strong desire to grow and to be challenged might make other people look more appealing than your partner, especially if you have been together for a long period of time without much challenge or excitement. Several people with this placement have told me from their personal experience that a shift of partners can lead to establishing a pattern of changing partners frequently. The new partner, with time and continuous interaction, can become just as boring as the old and, therefore, you move on to someone else. So, before you change partners, try to develop in some way with your present partner. As mentioned as a possibility with Sagittarius, take a trip together. Look upon this journey, not for the purpose of solving all your marital problems, but rather as a pleasurable experience to broaden you as a couple. If you can enjoy some activities together, the dissatisfaction with the relationship might begin to fade.

♄ In traditional astrology, Saturn in the 7th House is said to mean that there will be no marriage, a late marriage, or a burdensome one. Any of these alternatives is possible, but not inevitable. As with Capricorn, shared responsibility is one way of dealing positively with this placement. Another key word associated with the planet Saturn is "clarification." Therefore, defining your intimate relationships and working to keep them clear and honest may relieve some of the limitations and frustration.

♅ Uranus in the 7th House states, as does Aquarius in the 7th House, that independence and freedom are important requirements for close relationships, and you will probably break with tradition in selecting a partner. A couple who have been married for many years are a good example of how both Uranus and Aquarius can be manifested. He has Uranus in the 7th House and she has Aquarius there, and only Aquarius in that house. Their family backgrounds are very different, which fulfills the requirement of both the sign and the planet. Then, a few years after they married, both became astrologers, which is another way to use either Uranus or Aquarius. They work together to some extent in their chosen field, yet they have their own specialities and maintain a degree of independence and individuality within the relationship.

Ψ Neptune in the 7th House repeats the Piscean desire for the perfect union. If you can create the illusion of a flawless relationship and sustain that image, as well as believing in it yourself, by all means do it. However, should a less-than-perfect reality enter the scene, be prepared to view your partner accordingly, and also be aware of some the other negative alternatives that might develop. A number of these alternatives hinges on the victim-victimizer theme. There is the strong desire to help others, but this does not have to be to your detriment. Needy people will probably be drawn to you, and you will likely be attracted to them. You might easily establish the pattern of being the savior because it is a way to assure yourself that your partner will be faithful to you.

A person who is extremely dependent on the partner is not apt to leave that relationship. But the dependent partner may go to such extremes as deception and further dependency *to maintain* the partnership. Neither of these alternatives can be satisfying in the long run. If your partner begins to show signs of strong dependency, ask your partner *to do something for you.* Or if you recognize such symptoms in yourself, do something special for your partner. Another possibility is that the two of you might find a third person whom you can help together. This can remove the dependency issue from your relationship. And finally, you can always escape occasionally from any negative scenarios by instilling a little romance into the partnership.

P Three definitions ascribed to Pluto are power, deep-probing analysis and transformation, and any or all of these can be part of your relationship picture if Pluto is in the 7th House of your horoscope. The power issue is common with this placement because you are drawn to powerful people and yet you do not want to be controlled. This may lead to competitiveness to see who is strongest, or confrontations to prove who is most powerful. Some people may take a more subtle route. They try to manipulate their partners. This can work sometimes, but if you have a powerful partner who is also adept at the art of manipulation, this route could still lead to competitiveness or confrontations.

The partners can become so obsessed with one-upmanship that they do not realize that there are other possibilities. The most obvious course of action is to share the power, and to assign together who is in charge of what. But the other definitions (deep-probing analysis and transformation) inform you that there is another choice. You can analyze your problems together and transform the relationship.

The meaning ascribed to the planets can be modified or accentuated by the signs in which the planets are located and the aspects they form with other planets and points in the horoscope. But planets, whether they are in the 7th House or not, may have an impact on close relationships. The significance of planets in partnerships may vary according to their interconnections in the natal chart, but Mars, Venus and the Moon are *always* meaningful.

Mars by sign, house and aspect can provide insights into sexual needs, and also possible problems. For example, Mars in Pisces could indicate that you are looking for the perfect sexual union. One person with this placement found herself sexually attracted to guru types, or men who are inaccessible. This was a pattern that she repeated several times, but once she recognized the pattern, she began to avoid such relationships before they became an integral part of her life. Now she is involved with a man who is spiritually-oriented, but they share this quality, rather than his being the spiritual leader.

Venus by sign, house, and aspect offers clues into your needs in terms of affection. It indicates how you are likely to express affection, and what you expect from others in regard to love. If your Venus is in Aries, you are probably aggressive and demonstrative in expressing affection, and you could feel dissatisfied or insecure with a partner who is very reserved.

The Moon represents our emotions in a more general sense than Venus and includes feelings other than affection. You can combine the signs of the two planets in discussing the love nature. So that if with your Venus is in Aries, and you have the Moon in Taurus, you would probably want your partner not only to be demonstrative, but also to offer tangible proof of feelings.

The Moon, however, besides being broader in scope than Venus, also adds another dimension. Since the Moon represents the mother as well as the emotions, it can inform you of the impact of your mother or a mother figure on your feelings in childhood, which will be part of your interaction on an emotional level as an adult.

Although the astrologer cannot know with absolute certainty if the impact of the mother were positive or negative, *simply being aware* of the possibilities can help to open the door to diaglogue and more successful handling of some relationship problems. Let us say, for example, that a man has the Moon in Aquarius. Perhaps as a child, he had the experience of walking into the house with a black eye. His mother may have looked at him and, instead of showing sympathy, asked for all the details of the situation in order to determine objectively what happened. If this type of response from his mother recurred again and again, the child might have begun to wonder whether his mother was on his side. So he could have started to conceal his feelings. He developed an air of detachment and avoided being hurt. Perhaps this strategy worked so well that his pattern of behavior became an integral part of the way he related to others. Then a problem arose in marriage because his inability to show his feelings made his wife feel that he did not care.

Other possibilities in his childhood experiences with his mother could have been that he was told not to show his emotions, or his mother might have been too affectionate and this embarrassed him. In either case, his adult response, as well as his wife's reaction, might have been the same as the one mentioned above. Once you discover the source of the problem, you can begin to work on ways to express the Aquarius Moon satisfactorily. An initial step might be to discuss the details of the childhood experiences, and then, in true Aquarian fashion figure out *logical* alternatives that could be tried. The husband might start by occasionally taking the time to tell his wife that he loves her. This could lead to other forms of expression, although both parties have to accept the fact that he probably will never be extremely demonstrative.

So far we have concentrated on how to avert a crisis in a relationship, and in so doing have assumed that you are the person in control. This, of course, is not always the case. It is possible that you thought you were relatively secure and happy with your partner. You might even have felt that you were working diligently on your relationship, and then one day you are told or find out that your partner has found someone else. It is difficult enough to deal with two separate entities. Now you must cope with three. No matter how wonderful you thought your relationship was, nor how much effort you put forth, you are now in a relationship crisis. Astrology may still be helpful in such cases.

You can use the material just covered, but from a slightly different vantage point. We have discussed manipulating the signs in order to bring out the finer qualities of your partner in order to make your relationship more satisfactory to you. But you can do exactly those same things in order to make your partner happier and more secure.

When someone who is married or has a serious commitment to a relationship becomes involved with a third person, this can be as traumatic for the perpetrator as for the seemingly innocent partner. Even if one verbally blames the partner for one's transgressions, inwardly there is often the feeling of personal inadequacy—somehow sensing that something is wrong inside oneself. Frequently, clients in such a situation will say something like, "I wasn't looking for an affair," or ask "What's wrong with me that this happened?" If you are the "wronged" one, you may not see that your partner is also in need of support.

You may be too hurt or angry at this point to care, but should you want your partner to return to you, you can make use of the astrological information you have *to make your partner feel better.* If the third party does *not* have this information, he or she might not give the proper stroking, and your partner could return to you! Once this happens, you can continue to work on the relationship by adding astrological techniques such as interaspects and composite charts which combine the two partners in various ways.

The intent of this essay was to view a relationship from the perspective of the individuals involved. The justification for this is that it may help you to avert crises in your intimate relationships. But there is another purpose: if a crisis, such as your partner leaving you, has occurred, and you do *not* want that person back, you will still have valuable information. You will be aware of the mistakes you made so that you can consciously try to avoid them in future relationships. And you will have a clearer concept of your relationship needs; so that, when you meet a new potential partner, you can work on establishing acceptable patterns before crises arise.

Tim Lyons

Born in Boston, Massachusetts in 1949, Tim Lyons holds a B.A. degree in English from Occidental College in Los Angeles and an M.A. in Creative Writing from the Johns Hopkins University. He has practiced meditation according to the teachings of the Kagyu Lineage of Tibetan Buddhism since 1978, and began his study of astrology about the same time. He has also done formal study of stage acting and t'ai chi chuan. Author of *Astrology Beyond Ego* (Quest Books, 1986) and a columnist for *American Astrology* magazine, he teaches composition in the state college system of Colorado and maintains an active astrological counseling and teaching practice. His writings, astrological or otherwise, have appeared in *The Mountain Astrologer, Welcome to Planet Earth, Chrysalis, East-West, The Vajradhatu Sun, American Astrology,* and others.

The End of the Beginning—Astrology's Midlife Crisis

Tim Lyons

> In the middle of the journey of our life
> I came to my senses in a dark forest,
> For I had lost the straight path.
>
> *Dante Alighieri: Inferno**

Dante began *The Divine Comedy* at age forty-three. The "middle of the journey of our life" in the first canto of the *Inferno* refers to Dante's thirty-fifth year. That interval approximately spans the period we now call "the midlife crisis," and Dante, having lost his way, ended up in the underworld, which we might call the unconscious mind, the source of collective trends and personal transformation, the ambiguous world of the outer planets that bears the message of midlife.

Just as Dante descended into the earth, so at midlife we have to dig into the earth to plant new seeds. If we've not prepared the soil, if we've been swept along by collective ideas and values, we may need to uproot old plants and turn over a lot of hard soil to make way for new growth. Much that happens at midlife is under that soil, in unconscious assumptions or fears that may be embedded in collective trends, or even potentials heretofore untapped.

Midlife often brings increased awareness of impermanence, and therefore a need for new values. Materialistic values, empha-

---

* "Dante Alighieri, Inferno," trans. H. R. Huse in *Literature of the Western World*, eds. Wilkie and Hurt (New York: MacMillan, 1984), 1243.

sizing youth, beauty, vitality and socially-defined prosperity, often blind us to death and encourage a pervasive attachment to objects and attitudes that keep us entertained or imprisoned. The midlife crisis transits can free us from these personal prison-houses, but in doing so they expose us, often without much support, to a wider, often more chaotic world. They also ask us to be responsible for something beyond ourselves by being more conscious of the chaos within, the demand for change.

Personal identity is developed, to a large extent, through constant reference to *external* attachments. These attachments are supported by an *inner* value system, much of which is left unexamined. What we value is therefore reflected in our attachments or unexamined attitudes, and these are usually linked to collective (or transpersonal) factors. Collective attitudes and demands are symbolized by the movements of Uranus, Neptune, and Pluto, the three planets whose movements presently describe the very personal need for change that we feel around the age of forty.

In their more positive manifestations, these planets symbolize insight (Uranus), which in turn engenders compassion and a dissolving of self (Neptune), and consequent rebirth into transformative power (Pluto). In their more problematic manifestation as collective projections, they appear as sophisticated technologies (Uranus) that deceive people (Neptune) and so take from them the transformative power (Pluto) that is their birthright. The manifestation can seem so personally negative because these planetary energies have been *collectively* "negativized." Having been negativized, they generally arise as problems to be dealt with.

While we shouldn't minimize the seriousness of these crises, we should also realize that they are rooted in the devaluation of energies (Uranus, Neptune, and Pluto) intrinsic to human life. Having sold our birthright, so to speak, we struggle to retrieve it from the world, thereby giving birth to insight (Uranus), visionary compassion (Neptune), and transformative power (Pluto). We do this by seeing through fear and the external situations that arise from and reflect it (Saturn). Because fear has become cemented into the structure of our world (Saturn as projection), these transits, when fully accepted, can have a shattering effect on a wide variety of social attachments and the values that underlie them.

For most generations, the midlife challenge consists of two transits: the opposition from transiting Uranus to natal Uranus and the square from transiting Neptune to natal Neptune. For those born between roughly 1940 and 1970, the square from transiting Pluto to natal Pluto approximately coincides with the other two transits. The occurrence of the Pluto square so early in life suggests not only that the midlife period is more complex at this time, but also that people are now asked to make a more definite contribution to collective life, the collective situation being, as we can see around us, a good deal more threatening.

The Uranus Opposition:
The Midlife Crisis of Creative Space

> And just from this it began, that in my entirety a "something" arose which in respect of any kind of so to say "aping," that is to say, imitating the ordinary automatized manifestations of those around me, always and in everything engendered what I should now call an "irresistible urge" to do things not as others do them.

Beelzebub's Tales to His Grandson
(First Book) G. I. Gurdjieff: *

Uranus takes 84 years to orbit the Sun, so the Uranus-Uranus opposition, the approximate midpoint of that cycle, occurs around our 42nd year. Oppositions often bring a split or division, and people often experience this particular one as a split between their innate capacity for freedom and their present inability to act freely.

The transiting planet is the one more likely to be unintegrated, and it may therefore emerge through psychological projection when we will see in others our own potential for free, insightful action; i.e., they have it and we don't.

Optimally, oppositions bring objective awareness, and as a symbol of youthful rebellion, Uranus can make us aware that we are moving inexorably away from the iconoclasm of youth and into the demands of insightful maturity. The transit demands and engenders mature independence in the midst of legitimate responsibilities.

But for what will we be responsible? Insightful social change, certainly, but also for creative breakthrough, what Dane Rudhyar called "individual genius" (which we may experience as

---

* G. I. Gurdjieff, *Beelzebub's Tales to His Grandson* (New York: E. P. Dutton, 1973), 30.

glimpses of irrefutable truth or genuineness). Genius always involves stepping beyond the known or the generally accepted, and we also find that genius is moved from within, not by external coercion. These two qualities—the need to apply our glimpses of truth and to heed inner conviction—both so necessary during Uranus' midlife opposition, easily lead us to a discussion of Saturn, the symbol of worldly structure and therefore the *target of much Uranian rebellion.*

Our need for freedom often seems to arise from personal burdens or the apparent restrictions of the social order. In astrological terms, we *tend to experience Uranus in reaction to Saturn.* The midlife Uranus opposition can therefore arise simply as a desire to rebel against responsibility and order. This rebellion is often healthy, the prevailing order seeming unduly restrictive, stifling human inspiration at every turn.

However, Uranus' mythic background tells us that he should *not* be merely a reaction to Saturn. Uranus is the creative sky god and, through the earth-goddess Ge, Uranus is Saturn's father: This tells us that insight and freedom (Uranus) exist *prior to* any social ordering (Saturn). The myth shows not Uranus rebelling against Saturn but Saturn plotting to castrate Uranus: fear works to take away the life-giving power of insight. That Uranus is Saturn's father suggests that spacious insight should *create* the social order, not merely react to it!

In the myth, Uranus refuses to accept this responsibility, trying instead to bury Saturn and his siblings in the earth. Each of us probably recreates this pattern at one time or other, fearing that our freedom will be coerced, co-opted or captured by the external demand. However, it is Uranus' refusal to accept the natural consequences of his creative urge—his attempt to bury his children—that drives Saturn to his revenge. So Uranus' sudden flashes of insight, his sudden glimpses of absolute truth, will be lost if not applied to the "fallen" world represented by Saturn.

Because Saturn also rules the fear and anxiety that underlie that world, Uranus' insight must penetrate those attitudes, shattering our rigidity and opening us to new possibilities, the creative space of true open-mindedness. *The challenge of the Uranus opposition is therefore to link individual genius to the responsibilities of life without allowing that genius to be coerced or co-opted by blindness or fear.*

This transit asks us to break from old routine, but not by simply reacting *against* that routine. The break should come as a result of each person's natural impulse to express insight and personal truth. The question is not what we do, but whether our actions express personal genius, which we may define as that part of us that creates freely and is not defined by social code or form.

The Uranus opposition ushers in the second half of the Uranus cycle, and the second half of any cycle should be characterized not by external achievement, but by the harvesting of meaning. Jung wrote that for the aging person "it is a duty and a necessity to give serious attention to himself."* This may seem to contradict what was said above about applying insight to the structures of our world. However, applying insight does not mean building *more* structures or achieving *more* social distinction. We must instead understand these structures and responsibilities *in a new way*, seeing through any deceptions or self-doubts that drew us into them originally.

If we have habitually allowed Saturn to co-opt our freedom, we should pay particular attention to the Saturn-Saturn opposition that so closely coincides with the midlife Uranus opposition. The opposition, the first after the Saturn return, suggests that we are bringing many projects to fruition and that these projects reflect, not the family or karmic background (the first Saturn cycle), but our legitimate urge to make a mark on the world. Our responsibilities have a ring of authenticity to them and should not be lightly discarded. They must be met as long as they allow and empower legitimate self-expression, and if they indeed allow us to participate in freedom. If our responsibilities feel more onerous than that, we should seriously look at what role they play in our lives.

Many other astrologers have noted that this aspect often brings a renewed quest for youth. We may want to spend more time around younger people, who seem to represent the vitality and freedom we think we've lost. This reflects the nature of oppositions, which often manifest through psychological projection.† Here, we may project transiting Uranus (active freedom) onto the young, while we play the role of natal Uranus (the "lost" freedom of youth).

---

* C. G. Jung, *Modern Man in Search of a Soul*. New York: Harcourt Brace Jovanovich, 1933, 109.

† See Robert Hand's *Horoscope Symbols* and Bil Tierney's *Dynamics of Aspect Analysis*.

However, instead of experiencing Uranus vicariously, we need to recall the projections and uncover latent freedom and insight in ourselves. If we don't do this, we'll end up chasing Uranus' fleeting form hither and yon. In addition, if we've devalued Uranus within ourselves, we'll meet *his* devalued form in the world: our relationships with youth will leave us unsatisfied and ill-at-ease.

We should, however, recognize the "path quality" of such projections. They arise to bring us into a new relationship with Uranus' energy. First we see it through others, then we discover it within, then we act. We might remember Jung's admonition that projections are not harmful until they disturb our relationship with the world.

Those with natal Uranus in Cancer (c. 1948–1955) revolted against patterns of family blindness and misguided security-orientations, seeing these against the background of a destructive social order (Capricorn, Cancer's polar opposite). As these people come to their midlife Uranus opposition, we find many of them raising their own families, much involved in career and responsibility within a similar social order. Transiting Uranus in Capricorn suggests a revolt against authority, responsibility, and the established order in general. We see this trend quite clearly now in Europe (though Neptune is also participating, as we will see). On an individual level, people are struggling to make their work more meaningful, their insight more practical and their inspiration more grounded. (Because Saturn rules Capricorn, this Cancer-Capricorn opposition reiterates the mythic patterns already discussed.)

The danger is that the entrenched order will co-opt Uranus' demand for freedom, forcing people to apply their brilliance to destructive agencies. The potential is that the social order might be reformed through a revolution (Uranus) in mass-consciousness (Cancer). But only if we apply Uranus consciously and willfully to our lives will we experience personal, social and professional renewal.

Cancer emphasizes feeling, bonding and nurturing. Cancer is often called "the mother of forms," symbolizing the entrance into physical incarnation. Optimally, Uranus-in-Cancer revolts only against Cancer's excesses; for example, security bought at the earth's expense.

The midlife opposition from Capricorn may impel many people to re-discover Cancer's importance because a revolt (transiting Uranus) against some elements of "the former revolt" (natal Uranus) can enable us to see that former revolt in a new way. We therefore see many with this position marrying late, seeking a more insightful security. They need to find creative space within the twin confines of emotional closeness and social responsibility. As the Uranus-in-Cancer generation becomes "the establishment," they will find that revolution begins within—within the individual and within the social order. The external order will certainly not open up until the internal order is opened up; and to open up one's orderly, inner security is, after all, Uranus-in-Cancer's primary imperative.

Those with Uranus in Leo (c. 1955–1962) revolt against pride, arrogance and, curiously, self-identity. This group seeks new ideas about self-identity or personal creativity. Uranus in Leo often produces dramatic, unusual, socially concerned creativity. The danger is that insight (Uranus) may be subverted by assumptions of personal importance (Leo). Swallowed by the lion of self-pride, Uranus may emerge later as a union of pride, technology, and personal gain as ego extends its territory through technology. Significant social change arises, here, only from a new view of personal dignity, one free of pride or arrogance.

Leo is known as the most barren sign of the zodiac, telling us that too much emphasis on self-identity leads to isolation. Uranus in Aquarius may attempt to overcome this barrenness by *re-connecting the individual to the group*. We can certainly expect transiting Uranus-in-Aquarius to emphasize social principles and group-creativity. Individual creativity may often emerge through groups. The problem is that neither Leo nor Aquarius is oriented toward the emotions: Leo seeks creation, Aquarius seeks relationship created by shared ideas. One challenge of Uranus-in-Leo's midlife opposition will be to discover the emotional roots of all group-associations, friendships, and social-causes.

Finally, it often seems that Uranus' energy is easier for men to handle than women. (It's not clear whether this is biologically or socio-culturally based. Most likely it's a combination of the two.) Uranus is clearly a masculine figure in myth, and our society certainly encourages men more than women to emphasize Uranus' iconoclastic demand for freedom, revolutionary intellect and insight. The same behavior that might be called pro-gressive in a man will often be castigated in a woman. In any case, women may be particularly prone to experience Uranus through projection.

Projection is the "calling card" of opposition aspects, so this transit may be particularly challenging to women as they attempt to see through their strong tendencies to project Uranian freedom onto men in casual, intimate, or professional relationships. The point is not that women need to become more career-oriented (Uranus, after all, is no lover of ambition), but simply that women can see more clearly (opposition) how they've hidden or denied their insight and natural brilliance, and their potential for insight-ful contribution through new social forms.

The Uranus-in-Cancer group of women may be concerned with re-connecting to their biological birthright as the basis for creative emergence. They will seek to find freedom *within* biolog-ically-determined roles, not merely in spite of them. The Uranus-in-Leo group will be more extroverted (more concerned with creative fruits than biological roots). Both groups will insist that revolutionary changes must arise not merely through ideas, but from the innermost feelings, convictions and instincts. The realm of emotion is archetypally feminine, as is the unconscious, so it seems the particular task of women during this transit to give birth to revolutionary insight that includes a strong feeling-tone, stays connected with unconscious predispositions, and doesn't divorce genius from emotion or ideas from intimacy.

Neptune square Neptune: the Midlife Crisis of Idealism

> Form of the sea, unbreakable, and fresh,
> All that we know of spirit comes from flesh.
>
> *One Hundred Poems*, Elliott Coleman*

Neptune symbolizes our yearning for the absolute, for what by its very nature cannot be had or grasped. This yearning reflects an awakening of the spiritual instinct. Because the waxing square indicates a need for external structure-building, this is a time to

---

* Elliott Coleman, *One Hundred Poems* (Chapel Hill: Tinker Hill Press, 1972), 53.

find new life-structures to "house" that spiritual instinct—or our ideals generally. We need reliable disciplines to weave our ideals into the greater fabric of our lives.

In youth, ideals seem unattainable. The familiar image of cloud-castles comes to mind. Maturity doesn't make our ideals easy to reach, but it demands that we see more clearly what role they play in our lives. By forty, most people have seen their ideals besmirched by a world that seems increasingly mundane. Ideals may therefore lose their appeal, and because new ideals haven't yet appeared, many people experience a pervasive uncertainty or depression at this time. While external situations may remain stable, our connection to them seems hazy, incomplete, propped up or unreal.

The midlife square indicates a tension between the *generational* pattern of idealism and the possibility of attaining or realizing those ideals in the present. There is a struggle, but struggle at this time may yield only a pervasive life-fog, so we may proceed blindly. Just as fog arises where solid land meets vast ocean, so the confusion of the midlife Neptune square arises where our heretofore reliable world confronts our spiritual needs.

If the fog is thick enough, we may wander from the seashore toward the nearby swamp, which stands as an apt image for our lost ideals. While swamps eventually end up as coal, ultimately producing diamonds, in their present state they contain a lot of quicksand. Unfortunately, we may not see it because the midlife Neptune square seems to fit us with idealistic glasses that allow us to see only the lovely plumage of the local birds. To navigate with these glasses requires constant inner questioning, self-discipline and an appropriate sense of life's tangible limitations.

Neptune may also bring a sense of personal poverty, especially if we measure ourselves against an unreachable ideal. When various paths open at this time, we should question their reliability, but if we set out feeling personally impoverished or worthless (feelings reflecting the disillusionment of sullied ideals), we'll certainly be fascinated by those birds of special plumage. In such cases, the laurel wreath usually goes to the quicksand.

At the same time, we should not reject the swamp altogether. It lies between sea and land, so all paths to inspiration lead through it: Neptune's message is that disillusionment *is* the path to spiritual wisdom; to become personally disillusioned *is* to see more clearly. The Neptune square asks us to create inner and outer life-structures that will enable us to be at home with the disillusionment intrinsic to human life. The swamp demands patience of us if we're to go away with its diamonds.

Neptune's traditional rulership and dignity reiterate the need for imminent spirituality. Both Pisces and Cancer are water signs, symbols of immersion and dissolving. Water symbolizes emotion and feeling, and makes organic life possible. Neptune's exaltation in Cancer suggests that our ideals must be deeply felt, and must give birth to more enlightened life in the body. Pisces tells us that when fish leave the water, they die gasping on the sand. The fish who swim in Neptune's ocean find that most efforts to escape the water end up in the various fishing nets of ego. Cancer adds that we generally do know, on a very personal level, whether a path is the right one for us.

Though Neptune is felt as yearning, its process involves dissolving. More particularly, Neptune dissolves the solid walls (psychological, social, relational, vocational) that protect our illusion of separate identity. We often solidify this illusion through a wide variety of socially-validated structures (e.g. job, reputation, marriage), many of which are built upon our ideals. As these ideals are undermined, the life we've built upon them begins to feel shaky. It is precisely because the Neptune square *increases* the Neptune-energy in our lives that we must develop structures to discipline or house it. We must allow ourselves to feel disillusionment and to let go of old attachments or values, but this process must be disciplined to open us to vastness and inspiration. Several avenues suggest themselves.

Meditation is "disciplined dissolving" *par excellence*. Counseling can be helpful if the counselor recognizes the hollowness of the ego's defense system, and if both avoid getting stuck in problem-orientation that is often Neptune's signature. Many people also find dream-analysis helpful during this transit, probably because dreams speak Neptune's cryptic language with elegance and precision.

Training in creative self-expression is also recommended, the square suggesting structure or discipline and Neptune the yearning for the absolute that expresses itself as art. Neptune rules the fine arts and the projective arts like music, dance, and theater, as well as artistic inspiration in general; so engaging ourselves with these can enable us to dissolve self-identity *energetically*. Neptune dissolves the barriers that prevent us from connecting to the inspiration that, while always present, is experienced as confusion if we lack discipline.

Finally, many people respond to the midlife square by working with people who have been defeated by the world in some respect. This, too, is in keeping with the nature of the transit. The square again suggests order or structure; natal Neptune represents our natural impulse to help others; transiting Neptune symbolizes present obstacles and needs. With appropriate structure (e.g. scheduling), we can work openly with others yet not deplete our own energy. (Without that structure, however, the quicksand wins again as Neptune dissolves the coherence of our energy, allowing our vitality to leak out bit by bit.)

On the cautionary side, we must demand that situations or people prove their worth before receiving our commitment. We need to scrutinize all tendencies to martyr ourselves in relationships; learn how to speak our own truth (Uranus), be open and vulnerable (Neptune), yet have faith in our own basic dignity. It's also probably wise to be wary of psychic work unless we are working with a teacher of impeccable rectitude and acute intelligence (and even then proceed slowly).

A final guideline comes from Neptune's glyph, which suggests activity. In Buddhist iconography, the trident symbolizes active compassion that pierces through the three poisons: passion, aggression and ignorance. This places Neptune, our yearning for a better world, in a more active focus. The trident can be directed inward, toward our inner poisons, or outward, toward their projected forms; but its use is necessarily energetic, and only useful when ego is "refined out" of our actions. This energy can be applied to any of the activities mentioned above, or to pierce through self-deception generally.

Ironically, considering all this practical advice about integrating Neptune with daily experience, the midlife Neptune square may demonstrate that ideals are never attained, though they are often sought. What we seek during the midlife square is a reliable way to seek. Because Neptune asks us to let go of attachment, we must also let go of our attachment to "spiritual reality" and focus our attention on the here-and-now. When Neptune is active, we generally don't get what we want until we give up wanting it. "Giving up" and simply living in the moment may momentarily reveal more than we anticipate, but *to live* this way demands that we wield Neptune's trident to pierce the passion, aggression, and ignorance that draw us away from the present and into self-delusion.

This may seem like disappointing news, and even under the best of circumstances this period may leave us with a broken heart. (Neptune's exaltation in Cancer suggests the very personal nature of the transit.) Most of us would prefer to retain comforting notions of other-worldliness, but one boundary Neptune dissolves is the one between real and ideal (or real and unreal). The "other world" is all around us. The forty years between birth and the midlife Neptune square provide the experiential grounding on which we can build the structures needed to revitalize the old idealism (natal Neptune) amidst, or even because of, present disappointments. We may even see that disappointment reveals truth if we allow it to do so.

Neptune's sign-position describes the shape of one's ideals. With Neptune in Libra, those ideals often appear through or within relationship, aesthetics, or ideas about justice. People with this placement often search for the marriage made in heaven, and may dream of an ideal social order in which the individual is properly balanced with the collective and where legal forms arise from compassion instead of hierarchy.

Neptune in Libra emphasizes the spiritual oneness of man as a basis for relationship, and insists that individual relationship arises from a general sense of open-heartedness and compassion. And rightly so, up to a point. The spiritual oneness of mankind *is* probably the ultimate basis for all relationship. Neptune wants to dissolve boundaries; Libra wants to engage in relationship. Hence, the search for relationship without boundary.

All relationship is based, to a greater or lesser extent, on dropping boundaries and relinquishing territory. If we're not willing to drop our boundaries and recall the sentries from the passes, we'll have no relationship at all. So Neptune in Libra presents us with a valuable principle: relationships must be based on a willingness to drop those walls of fear and insistence through which we so often define ourselves in relation to others.

However, while we can't deny that relationships require openness, we have all seen Neptune-in-Libra marriages founder on the rocks of apparently incompatible personal differences—or because people did not live at ease within the personal boundaries necessary to satisfying relationships.

We tread, here, on the grounds of relationship disfunction. There's much discussion these days of the need for limits, for sponsibility and boundaries in relationship. Many have discovered that without self-definition there *is* no relationship. Relationship becomes possible only when people can be themselves and still be in relationship. The emphasis on boundary and separation may therefore be interpreted as an antidote to Neptune-in-Libra: though we might say that ultimately all people are one, on a relative level each person is alone, in a noble solitude from which communication is possible.

Much of this concern with boundaries has arisen as Neptune is transiting Capricorn, the sign of limits and structure. Both Libra and Capricorn deal with form, but in different ways. Libra emphasizes aesthetic form which encourages human participation; Capricorn emphasizes forms which either transcend or ignore human input. Neptune-in-Capricorn therefore idealizes limit and structure, and brings disillusion with patterns of relationship that don't sufficiently define personal boundaries. The problem seems to be not only that Neptune-in-Capricorn undervalues Neptune-in-Libra's overly idealistic relationships, but that it over-idealizes boundaries.

The idealization of boundaries is a collective issue, however, and we should be wary of blindly accepting collective feeling-patterns as our own. Neptune's transiting sign-position points to the collective current of feeling impinging on us, but it also tells us what must be dissolved and seen from a less egocentric point of view. Though they appear as obstructions, Capricorn's walls and boundaries are really part of Neptune-in-Libra's path toward complete relationships. Problems with tenuous boundaries indicate that boundaries need to be made part of the search for the alchemical sacred marriage:

> . . . the combination of what has been separated, by means of which the individual is raised to a higher state, that of wholeness of selfhood. The outward process . . . becomes the sym-

bolic expression of an inward state, and even more: of a *mysterium* that encompasses the dimensions of both inner and outer and provides a hint of the *unus mundus*, the reality of a unified world.*

The "unified world" suggests the larger social issues of Capricorn, ruled by Saturn, the builder of walls and promulgator of separateness. The relationship alchemy of Neptune-in-Libra must therefore be united with the socialized alchemy of Neptune-in-Capricorn. In Capricorn's world, political and economic barriers are dissolving—with the expected chaos. Yet we applaud in the external world what we mistrust in the internal one, probably because the dissolving personal boundaries threaten our cherished autonomy.

The collective situation provides metaphors for personal growth. The chaos in relationship is reflected in the dissolving of some authority structures (e.g. the Soviet Union) and in the deceptive maintenance of others (e.g. Central American "democracies"). This chaos signals a confusion of values (Libra) reflected in local—and household—economies: Libra is related to money because money provides for commerce what Rudhyar called a socially accepted standard weight, and it is the confusion of values which is undermining the established order both internationally and interpersonally. That Neptune is the "higher vibration" of Venus reiterates the connection to values. The old order must dissolve, and we should not block the needed chaos with the regimen of attachment. To shield ourselves from the disillusionment integral to midlife only courts further uncertainty. We should expect, however, that the dissolving of old structures, which were built as guards against chaos, *can* release long-hidden tensions. This brings us to Pluto.

---

* Gustave Wehr, *Jung: A Biography* (Boston: Shambhala, 1988).

Pluto Square Pluto: The Midlife Crisis of Consciousness

Today we can no longer get along unless we give our best attention to the ways of the psyche.

Modern Man in Search of a Soul, Carl Jung*

The midlife Pluto transit doesn't usually coincide with the other two.† That it occurs so early for those born in the 1940s and 1950s is due to specific astronomical factors which tell us much about the astrological material involved.

In accordance with Kepler's Second Law, Pluto moves more quickly when closer to the Sun. This tells us that issues related to Pluto will develop more quickly and come closer to each person's center. Because transiting Pluto is also in Scorpio, there will be a powerful dredging effect, and with Pluto inside of Neptune's orbit this dredging must now precede or prepare the ground for our yearning. The path to idealism has been temporarily re-routed through the psychic underworld. To discover our inherent unity with the world we must first suffer the rage and powerlessness of isolation. Being isolated, we long for Pluto's often-problematic fusion, the second twist in disfunction's narrow spiral.

Neptune dissolves the boundaries and makes fusion possible. Pluto exposes us to the actual process of emotional fusion. This could not take place with boundaries still in place, but Neptune's hope that openness will lead to bliss is often disappointed. Licenses for sacred marriages are now issued only in the underworld.

Pluto always confronts us with elemental forces, and with him so close to the Sun we must confront these forces on a very personal level (as distinguished from the collective level where Pluto has so commonly appeared). The need to "take Pluto per-

---

* Jung, op. cit., p. 209.

† The midlife transits can arrive in any order, so it's not possible to say which one will occur first in anyone's life. The following examples show how variable the order can be:

Those born in January, 1900 have Pluto at 15–18 Gemini, Neptune at 25–29 Gemini and Uranus at 10–12 Sagittarius. Their midlife Neptune square occurred 1939–1942 and the Uranus opposition 1944–1946. The Pluto square did not take place until 1964–1966.

Those born in January, 1930 have Pluto at 15–18 Cancer, Neptune at 26 Leo–1 Virgo, and Uranus at 0–7 Aries. They received the Uranus opposition 1968–1970, the Neptune square 1968–1971, and the Pluto square 1977–1979.

Those born January 1, 1950 have Pluto at 18–20 Leo, Neptune 15–19 Libra and Uranus at 1–9 Cancer. Their Uranus opposition occurs first, between 1989 and 1990. Pluto followed soon thereafter, between 1990 and 1991, while the Neptune square occurs 1991–1993.

sonally" is reiterated by the fact that though the mentioned astronomical factors recur once during every 242-year Pluto orbit, this is the first time they've occurred since Pluto's discovery in 1930. The discovery of a planet indicates that the energy symbolized by that planet must now be honored with more conscious attention by individuals and humanity at large.

So, what is this energy? Pluto is said to be a symbol of power, but this power is really *the unity of mind and phenomena*. We are best able to use this power when we begin to view our lives from a non-dualistic standpoint. While Neptune dissolves boundaries, Pluto releases into the collective the power of the mind-phenomena fusion. Jung spoke of the psychological issues involved, saying that if a man

> . . . turns away from the terrifying prospect of a blind world in which building and destroying successively tip the scale, and . . . turns his gaze inward upon the recesses of his own mind, he will discover a chaos and a darkness there which he would gladly ignore.*

Pluto is generally associated with raw emotion, so it may seem strange to see him connected to mind, or to the apparently esoteric union of mind and phenomena. However, collective developments at the time of a planet's discovery tell us much about that planet's nature, and the events following Pluto's discovery definitely point to this particular union. The early 1930s saw several important quantum physicists receiving Nobel Prizes† and Carl Jung writing *Modern Man in Search of a Soul*. Both announced the same principle, though in different terms: that which we call "reality" can not be distinguished from mind.

The quantum theorists said there was no such thing as an objective experiment; Jung wrote that "[the] upheaval in our world and the upheaval in consciousness is one and the same." Hitler's rise to power, so often cited in connection with Pluto's discovery, shows us the same principle, for Hitler was a manifestation of the power of unconscious complexes, a projection demonstrating mankind's collective refusal to claim its birthright.

---

* Jung, op. cit, p. 205.

† e.g. Werner Heisenberg in 1932, Paul Dirac and Edwin Schrodinger in 1933, Enrico Fermi in 1934.

Pluto's discovery told us in no uncertain terms that we could no longer afford to ignore psychic reality.

The midlife Pluto square therefore demands that we create life-structures which enable us to deal with the unity of mind and phenomena. Whereas Neptune demands structures to discipline the spiritual instinct, Pluto demands structures to discipline the resultant power. Through these structures, we not only become more conscious, but we take our personal power back from the world. Because the square lends itself to overstatement, we may find ourselves trying to gain power over others. At the same time, Pluto brings to the surface rather unpleasant psychic qualities like rage, bitterness, jealousy, and the desire for control.

What Pluto exhumes usually seems negative because it's been buried—rejected from consciousness—for so long. We therefore must cultivate non-judgmental ruthlessness: seeing what's there, acknowledging it personally, but remaining dispassionate. That Neptune is usually closer to the Sun than Pluto suggests that compassion yields power; the reversed position tells us that we can not uncover compassion until we probe the personal and collective underworld. Pluto's "negativity" must be transmuted: rage, for example, may become rage against delusion.

If we reject this demand, *we force Pluto to appear through phenomena.* The collective result is what Mephistopheles referred to when Faustus asked him why he was not in hell: "This is hell, Faustus," he said. "Nor am I out of it." On an individual level, therefore, we may find ourselves struggling against powerful forces—people rejecting our efforts to take power for ourselves, demonstrating that Pluto's power turns against us in direct proportion to our selfishness (though the results are not always immediate). On the other hand, people may urge us to change in some fundamental way. We may resist this transformation, either because the unconscious knows we're not ready, having not yet built the inner and outer structures to control it, or because ego is attempting to co-opt Pluto's power and control our experience.

Pluto is often associated with the money of others, and the midlife square may ask us to restructure various financial relations. This also means revaluing others, seeing how the inherent value of other people works in our lives. To value fully someone else may mean dying to some element of self-importance, an issue which always surfaces in another of Pluto's favorite dancing grounds, sexual intercourse (or fusion). In sexual union, one's own value is fused with the value of another, and the two may be hard to separate. So Pluto's search for re-valuation often takes place through relationship.

Again we see the union of Neptune and Pluto, because whether Neptune is in Libra or not, he always dissolves boundaries, opening the way to Pluto's powerful fusion. (We shouldn't reject this level of experience. In Tibetan Buddhist art, the union of wisdom [skt. *prajna*, analogous to Neptune] and skillful means [skt. *upaya*, analogous to Pluto] is said to be enlightenment.)

On a practical level, many of the activities recommended for Neptune are also appropriate for Pluto, but for different reasons. The arts, for example, may express our yearnings and ideals (Neptune), but they can also allow and empower the expression of the taboo. This is art-as-catharsis, and the artist becomes the vehicle through which others experience and transmute unacceptable aspects of themselves. Arts with a strong physical component are recommended for Pluto, whose needs are not often met by dreaming or philosophizing. Those needs are visceral, arising when mind is divorced from body; so we must try to re-unite mind and body into a powerful unity, releasing our deepest impulses by exploding the tension that kept them separate (and which came from their separation). Expressing these impulses seems, with Pluto closer to us than Neptune, the only path to artistic vision at this time.

Meditation is also recommended, as it unifies mind and body, and allows unconscious complexes to come to consciousness, be seen dispassionately, and then released. Counseling can be of some help too, as long as we realize that Pluto's power cannot be dealt with on an intellectual level alone. Erich Neumann's comments are applicable here:

> If . . . transpersonal contents are reduced to the data of a purely personalistic psychology, the result is not only an appalling impoverishment of individual life—that might remain merely a private concern—but also a congestion of the collective unconscious which has disastrous consequences for humanity at large.*

---

* Erich Neumann, *The Origins and History of Consciousness* (Princeton: Princeton University Press,1954), xxiv.

The midlife Pluto square squarely asks us to restructure our lives so we can exert appropriate power. Seeing where power or consciousness is blocked, dying to old blockage or old self-conceptions makes room for and fertilizes the next cycle of growth. The deaths may be graphic, our lives filled with breakdowns as various things come to the end of their cycle. External and psychological infrastructures decay. The process will be painful, even ruthless, because these external situations are rooted in unconscious complexes. But the Sage sometimes needs to be ruthless, and the midlife square asks us to recognize him in the breakdowns surrounding us.

Finally, though we should be wary of ambition (it's another of Pluto's favorite dancing-grounds), we should not reject the desire to change the world. This transit asks us to unite personal evolution and re-empowerment with that of the external world. We will naturally turn outward, into phenomena, and if we can work there for the higher good, there's no need to reject activity. However, if we seek *personal* power, Pluto will confront us with *greater* power, reminding us that his main transformations are altogether rooted in our relationship to mind. Power in the world comes from power over ourselves, and power over ourselves comes from complete self-acceptance—which some call self-knowledge.

Those born with Pluto in Leo (the late 1930s through the late 1950s) have the midlife square from Scorpio. Leo symbolizes the regality of the Self; Pluto there suggests that this generation must explore the sewer beneath the throne room. If the Self (cf. Jung) comprises all the conscious or unconscious elements in a person's life, then Leo's task here is to admit all those elements into consciousness. However, Pluto brings up taboo or "shameful" elements, taking off the emperor's clothes to show that there's nothing of which to be ashamed. Leo, however, doesn't usually take it that way. His pride may be offended, but monarchs offended by the hidden elements of life often become tyrants.

The Pluto-in-Leo generation must therefore explore all hidden areas of the psyche, flinching at nothing, realizing that one's shining kingdom also includes many hidden realms. People with Pluto in Leo often speak obsessively about personal consciousness-development, but they must realize that such development is impersonal. People must drop their personal stake in the process. Pluto, after all, is the power of change inherent in the world, and doesn't care a fig about individuals.

Finally, Pluto-in-Leo automatically implicates Aquarius. The self-obsession of this generation seeks confirmation and balance in the socializing values of Aquarius. People with this placement may fuse personal development with many New Age ideas. This is presently an uncomfortable union, as Pluto's transit through Scorpio brings to the surface the unpleasant detritus of the old age. Pluto, of course, is the ruler of drains, as well as of everything sent down them and everything which comes back up. This material is fertile, but offensive. The task of this generation, during their midlife square, seems to be to transmute these things (or energies) into a new growth of consciousness.

Both Leo and Aquarius tend to avoid unpleasant smells (though in different ways). If we avoid the unpleasant message of Pluto-in-Scorpio, however, the coming Age of Aquarius-Leo may turn out to be one of ecological barrenness, dry and hot (Leo), with electronic wires or impulses traversing burnt-out expanses. Isolated men may find that they can't live on information-bits alone.

The current period is therefore crucial. Mankind must confront the excrescences of Pluto-in-Scorpio. The Pluto-in-Leo generation, turned toward that material in a very personal way, therefore must come to center stage and act powerfully by becoming more conscious of themselves. Even unpleasant characteristics come into the limelight.

Pluto moved into Virgo in the late 1950s and remained there until the early 1970s. The square will happen from Sagittarius between 1995 and 2008. Because Virgo and Sagittarius are mutable signs, Pluto's issues may be more avoidable. People may not confront issues of power and personal control head-on. Virgo suggests work, health and daily ritual; Sagittarius suggests philosophical or abstract knowledge. There will surely be challenges between people's daily rituals and their philosophical views; people will no doubt find themselves *involved in jobs that do violence to their sense of truth.* Health problems may arise if this imbalance is not righted.

All of this seems a bit more impersonal—or avoidable—than the experience of Leo-Scorpio. The strain may seem less evident, embedded in situations instead of in the psyche. However, because the situation may seem more fluid, less rooted in personal phobias and attachments, people might not confront Pluto as directly. On the other hand, Pluto-in-Sagittarius may bring a change of view which, quite in keeping with the nature of Pluto described above, then brings about a change in the sustenance-systems (Virgo) of society. The socializing emphasis, built upon the personal changes of the previous Pluto-generation, may be quite powerful. Sagittarius also brings great concern for ethics; Pluto is the personal underworld and the social charnel ground: people may see the relationship between socio-cultural ethics and the natural hierarchies of earth (Virgo).

Sample Horoscopes

The first example (chart on page 241) is a man with Neptune in Libra in the 12th House, 6 degrees from his Libra Ascendant. Pluto is in the 18th degree of Leo in the 10th House, while Uranus is in the 3rd degree of Cancer in the 9th. Mercury in the 4th House in Aquarius is in conjunction with the Nadir and quincunx Uranus. The Moon rules the Midheaven from the 8th House (in the cusp area of the 9th), closely square Saturn.

In the years before the midlife transits, he married, purchased a house, and became a computer technician (Mercury in Aquarius quincunx Uranus), an occupation for which he has much aptitude but little inclination. The 8th House Moon suggests that he develops security through adherence to or acceptance of the values or valuation of others; its square to Saturn suggests that those values are often interwoven with an acceptance of possibly burdensome responsibility or external demand, tendencies reiterated by his Capricorn Sun. Saturn aspects are also notorious for urging us to take the views of others as more significant than our own. This had been his tendency, and as the midlife transits began he found himself with an unsatisfactory marriage, great financial responsibility, and a job which provided only the external stability which reflected his wife's values (8th House; the second House of the 7th).

Uranus came first, squaring his Mars as it opposed its own position. Seeing his overall life path (9th) as unsatisfactory (Uranus' restlessness), he rebelled—suddenly, as befits one with a natal Mars-Uranus square. He had always wanted to make his living as an actor, a field in which he had had considerable part-time success. So he decided to quit his job to pursue that career.

(Acting is also related to the 8th House Moon squaring Saturn because it forces one to work seriously with the values or evaluations of others.)

Transiting Uranus combined with the natal Mars-Uranus square to form a T-square to Mars in the 12th. The "empty leg" was in the 6th House of work. He changed jobs, seeing acting as a new way to make a living. But people with Mars in the 12th tend to undercut their own efforts: his need for adventure and daring (Mars-Uranus) undercut (12th) his world. Things fell flat.

Neptune was conjoining his natal Sun in the 3rd, increasing both his confusion and his yearning for "things Neptunian," the world of the actor. Finally, Saturn was moving toward his Nadir, so he was at the low ebb of his professional tide. Acting jobs didn't come. He was left in an unstable world characterized by transiting Uranus and Neptune in the 3rd: driving around, reading, talking at coffee-shops, seeking advice, jotting down endless notes on acting, teaching, and consciousness, and finally, seeking another job (Neptune rules 6th). His curiosity (Gemini Moon, among other factors) remained undiminished, but his world had none of the stability desired by his Capricorn Sun.

Meanwhile, Pluto was moving toward its midlife square, making a station in the 18th degree of Scorpio in February 1991. He was without a job, feeling powerless, seeking a way to restructure his world in order to make his dream more realizable (i.e., preparation for the midlife Neptune square, which would take place in 1992). The final phase of the Pluto square was in September 1991: after several months searching he landed another electronics position, with a firm that seems congenial to his "other life." He then found a new place to live (with a room for his daughter), a new base of operations, a place of self-discovery (natal Pluto in the 10th opposing Aquarius planets in the 4th). From this base, he is again seeking ways to make acting work for him as a vocation: seeking the structure demanded by the midlife Neptune square.

The process is clear: first, new insight, not particularly grounded, but in touch with his inner nature and his "individual genius." Then, confusion brought about by two Neptunian influences: a 12th House Mars and Neptune's transit over his Sun. Dissolving, then (with Pluto) death of the dream. Finally, new power, emerging through structure (Pluto square Pluto, and sextile Saturn). The Neptune square may bring new yearnings, and he will need to be wary, avoiding the quicksand of self-deception as he seeks a new foundation on which to build his acting dream. The Uranus-Neptune conjunction is about to take place at 17–18 Capricorn, forming a yod with his Moon-Pluto sextile, so something may come to him which enables or forces him to transform the basis of his security into something more empowering.

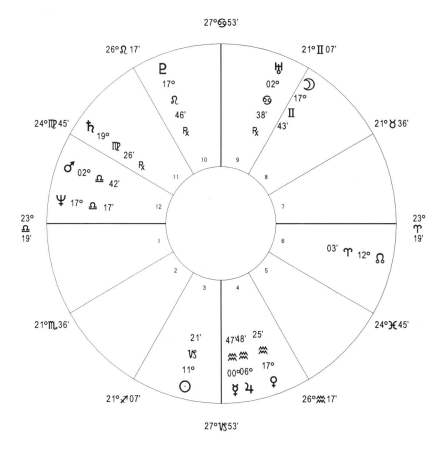

Example #1 – Male

The second example is a man with Uranus conjoining his Gemini Sun, Neptune retrograde on his Libra Ascendant and Pluto in the 11th House conjunct Saturn in Leo. The transiting Uranus opposition brought the birth of his first child (Uranus rules the 5th) as avenues opened up enabling him to make his living through acupuncture. This is an Uranian profession because it deals with electrical currents in the body, and reflects his Gemini Sun because it is a "hands on" technique. The natal Sun-Uranus conjunction is in the 9th House, and transiting Uranus conjoined Jupiter as it opposed its own position, both reflecting the foreign origin of his practice.

Sun-Uranus people are usually great individualists, and though this person had been a member of a rather hierarchical Buddhist meditation organization, adherence to that hierarchy had never been easy. He rebelled when his principles (strong Jupiter and 9th House) were violated by what he saw as the group-leader's sexual misconduct. This occurred during his midlife Neptune square.* Because Neptune rules his 6th House of teacher-student relationships, his disillusionment was with his teacher; because natal Neptune squares his Midheaven (and because transiting Neptune was in Capricorn), his disillusionment was with what was, in his view, the organization's paternalistic hierarchy. However, because transiting Neptune was at the Nadir, his reactions were not based only in intellect, but in deeply-felt convictions.

His midlife Pluto square demanded personal re-empowerment through a death of old relationships to hierarchy. This re-empowerment emerged from his rejection of group (11th) paternalism, reiterating some of the Neptune material. But Pluto is skillful means and he spoke out powerfully for people in the group (natal Pluto in 11th) to recognize and act on their own intelligence, integrity and personal value (transiting Pluto in the 2nd and ruling that House).

He still retains his connection to many people in the group, and to the meditative principles behind it; but his connection is

---

* Transiting Neptune in Capricorn brought disillusion with hierarchy to many members of spiritual groups, and many of these people experienced the midlife Neptune square partially through these issues. Disillusion often arose from the sexual activities and deceptions of spiritual leaders. The disillusion and deception are Neptunian; relationships implicate Libra, while hierarchies reflect Capricorn.

Because many of these people had the midlife Pluto square at about the same time, sexual issues came to the surface along with a demand for personal re-empowerment. These aspects do not tell us how to judge (or not judge) these events. They tell us, rather, that those events, in a paradoxical way perhaps to be expected with the outer planets, reflected a collective spiritual need.